Externalism

Externalism

Putting Mind and World Back Together Again

Mark Rowlands

McGill-Queen's University Press
Montreal & Kingston • Ithaca

ISBN 0-7735-2649-8   (bound)
ISBN 0-7735-2650-1   (paper)

Published simultaneously outside North America
by Acumen Publishing Limited

McGill-Queen's University Press acknowledges the financial support of
the Government of Canada through the Book Publishing Development
Program (BPIDP) for its activities.

National Library of Canada Cataloguing in Publication Data

Rowlands, Mark, 1962-
  Externalism : putting mind and world back together again / Mark
Rowlands.

Includes index.
Includes bibliographical references.
ISBN 0-7735-2649-8 (bound).—ISBN 0-7735-2650-1 (pbk.)

  1. Externalism (Philosophy of mind) I. Title.

BD418.3.R68 2003   128'.2   C2003-901385-5

Designed and typeset by Kate Williams, Abergavenny.
Printed and bound by Biddles Ltd., Guildford and King's Lynn.

To Emma, cariad annwyl

Contents

Preface and acknowledgements

I've been thinking about the idea of externalism for so long now it seems almost like an old friend. Our affiliation began, I suppose, back in about 1986 when I went up to Oxford to do my D.Phil., and has continued, in more or less an uninterrupted form, ever since. The concept of externalism has evolved considerably over that time and some versions now seem, at least to the uninitiated, to bear little relation to the exciting, but still essentially nascent, doctrines pertaining to semantic content associated with Hilary Putnam and Tyler Burge. And I suppose that I, for better or for worse, played some small role in that evolution.

The intellectual debts I have incurred on this journey have been many and varied. Colin McGinn was my thesis supervisor at Oxford and was working on his important externalist book *Mental Content* at that time. So I could scarcely have wished for a better induction. The work of Andy Clark has had an enormous influence on me for the past 15 years or so. More recently, so too has his friendship. The recent work of, and correspondence with, Alva Noë, has also helped shape my thinking on the scope of vehicle externalism. Less recently, but equally importantly, before his untimely death, the work of and correspondence with Ed Reed played an important role in shaping my thinking on matters externalist.

I would like to thank an anonymous reviewer for Acumen, whose extraordinarily perceptive comments helped shape this work into a more coherent whole than it would otherwise have been.

My thanks also to Marku Oksanen at the University of Turku, Finland, for organizing my extremely enjoyable visit there in June 2002 when, in addition to drinking copious amounts of truly outstanding Finnish beer, I was able to deliver a seminar series that was, in essence, a dry (obviously, no pun intended) run for this book. Thanks also to the students and staff who attended that series.

More generally, this book, in various places and to various degrees, has benefited from discussions with Elisa Aaltola, Paul Coates, Dan Hutto, Julian Kiverstein, Bill Lyons, Richard Menary, Marina Rakova, David Spurrett, Susan Stuart, John Sutton, Julia Tanney, Alan Thomas, Amie Thomasson, Steven Torrance and Mike Wheeler.

Thanks to Gail Ferguson and Kate Williams for copy-editing and Liz Murray for proofreading.

Matthew Ratcliffe, Tony O'Connor and Garrett Barden have been good friends and colleagues over the years. So too has Max Hocutt. And my thanks, as ever, to Emma for helping keep me sane in the less than sane times.

Mark Rowlands

CHAPTER 1

Introduction:
internalism and externalism

In the 1966 film *Fantastic Voyage*, starring Raquel Welch, humans are shrunk down to the size of body cells and injected into another (full-size) human being. Actually, it was a little spaceship of sorts that was injected, but Raquel was inside it. I can't remember precisely what the reason for this injection was, but, as I recall, some sort of errand of mercy was involved. So, let us engage in what philosophers call a *thought-experiment*. You are Raquel Welch aboard your little spaceship. But this ship has been modified. Instead of having to be injected into the blood supply, it now has a boring or tunnelling device, and you can bore directly into the person's body. The whole errand of mercy scenario would no doubt have to be changed given this technological innovation – we now seem to have a sort of inverse *Alien* scenario, and our film should now be directed by Ridley Scott – but we needn't worry about that. Our concern is not ethics but philosophy of mind.

Your preferred port of entry, let us suppose, is the skull. So, bore away you do. First you make your way through the skin: the boundary between your experimental subject/victim and the outer world. That's easy. The next layer, the skull, however, proves a lot more difficult, and you spend quite some time boring your way through that. Eventually you break through into the grey, gooey mess that is the brain. Actually, at your new cellular size, it may not appear grey and gooey at all. Electrical storms may very well surround you, your ship a ghostly galleon tossed on cloudy, chemical seas. Pretty nasty stuff.

Eventually, however, after many years of exploration, you manage to chart your new world. You map out how small parts of this world are arranged into larger parts, how the electrical storms you witness are ordered according to, and can to some extent be rendered predictable by reference to, the arrangements of these parts and so on. In short, you succeed in identifying the gross structural and functional components of

1

your subject's/victim's brain. Then you return to the surface, are restored to normal size and sign up for your next film, *One Million Years BC.*

In your quieter moments, you might reflect on what it is you achieved on your fantastic voyage. And if you are at all typical, the following sort of conflation may seem overwhelmingly tempting to you. In burrowing in through the skull to the brain, you are burrowing into the mind, for the mind is the brain. And in identifying the gross structural and functional areas of the brain, and mapping out the patterns of electrical and chemical activity, what you are doing, in effect, is mapping out the mind. In identifying patterns in the chemical eddies, and stabilities in the electrical fields, you are identifying mental events, states and processes – for it is precisely this sort of thing in which mental events, states and processes consist.

If you find this sort of temptation overwhelming, then, whether you realize it or not, you hold what is known as an *internalist* view of the mind. Internalism is, very roughly, the view that all mental things are located inside the head of the person or creature that has these things. *Externalism*, on the other hand, is the view that not all mental things are exclusively located inside the head of the person or creature that has these things.

It doesn't have to be the head, actually. There might be some logically possible creatures that have minds but no identifiable heads. More accurately, internalism is the view that all mental events, states and processes – mental phenomena, broadly construed – are located inside the *skins* of the creatures that have them. Externalism is the view that denies this. Of course, some creatures might not have identifiable skins, as such. What is crucial, however, is not heads or skins but the notion of an identifiable physical boundary between the organism that possesses the mental phenomena in question and its wider environment. I'll usually refer to this boundary as the *skin*, but the above qualifications should be borne in mind.

Perhaps, however, you don't find the assimilation of the mind to the brain very tempting at all. Perhaps, for example, the assimilation is unacceptably materialist for your tastes. You might, that is, hold a *dualist* view of the mind: the mind is a non-physical object, and mental phenomena consist in modifications or alterations in the properties of this object. Perhaps, on your fantastic voyage, you even think that you found this non-physical region of the person – the *seat of the soul*, if you will. No matter, you are still an internalist if you believe this seat of the soul to be located inside the skin of the person or creature whose soul it is. Internalism cuts across the distinction between dualism and materialism, and most versions of both views are internalist ones.

Chapter 2 introduces the concept of internalism, and traces its logical–historical development to the work of Descartes. I argue that this *Cartesian* (and I shall use the terms "Cartesian" and "internalist" interchangeably) conception of the mind – the conception bequeathed us by Descartes – is made up of three broad strands: *ontological*, *epistemological* and *axiological*. The ontological component of Cartesianism is composed of what I call the *Location Claim*, according to which mental particulars are spatially located inside the skins of mental subjects, and the *Possession Claim*, according to which the possession of mental properties by a subject is logically independent of anything external to that subject. Most views of the mind, at least until fairly recently, are forms of Cartesian internalism in that they are committed to both the Location Claim and the Possession Claim, and this is true whether these views are dualist or materialist in character.

The epistemological component of Cartesianism, I argue, consists in what I call the thesis of *epistemic internalism*: we know the contents of our own minds *first* and *best*. This provides us with an additional way – an essentially epistemic one – of understanding mental phenomena as internal: the limits of the mental coincide with the limits of what we know first and best.

The axiological strand of Cartesianism consists in the framework for thinking about value bequeathed us by the ontological and epistemological strands. If we adopt the Cartesian view of the mind as an interiority, then this gives us a fairly stark and unforgiving framework for thinking about the nature of value. Value must be something either objectively existing in the world or something subjectively constituted by the activities of the mind.

Future chapters will be primarily concerned with internalism and externalism as ontological doctrines. However, two chapters are reserved for discussion of the epistemological and axiological aspects of the competing views. Chapter 8 examines the epistemological ramifications of externalism and Chapter 11 examines its axiological consequences.

Suppose we wish to endorse the internalist view of the mind as an interiority. Then we are immediately presented with a problem that has played an important role in the development of modern philosophy. We can call it the *matching problem*. If the mind is something located inside the head (skin, boundary) of a creature that has it, how does the mind, so to speak, get a hold on the world in such a way that the creature might know, or even have any reason for believing, anything about that world? If mind and world are separated, in the manner prescribed by internalism, then how do we get the two back together again in the way they presumably need to be together in order for a creature to know or even think anything about the world?

3

The matching problem has played a pivotal role in the development of modern philosophy since it is what underpins Immanuel Kant's "Copernican revolution" in philosophy and his resulting endorsement of the position known as *transcendental idealism*. According to Kant, the world of our everyday experience is a world constructed by the activities of the mind, specifically through the activities of what he called *sensibility* and *understanding*. How does the mind latch on to the world in the way required for the possibility of thought and knowledge about that world? Kant's answer is that the world, or at least that portion of the world we can know and think about, is a world constructed by the activities of the mind. This idealist trend of seeing the world as, in one or another way, a construction of the mind is thus a direct response to the matching problem. And the matching problem is predicated on the separation of mind and world bound up with internalism. Idealism, then, is a natural development of – in the sense of a response to – internalism. Or, at least, so I shall argue in Chapter 3.

Moreover, it is a response that has proved enormously influential. More recent imitators of Kant have replaced the operations of the faculties of sensibility and understanding with *language*, *discourse*, *theory*, or, more generally, *structure*. But in any event, the core idea remains the same: the world, at least the world of which we can meaningfully speak, is a world that is constituted by human mental activity, either directly or via the products of that activity. This idea, I think it is fair to say, was virtually definitive of much twentieth-century thought. The idea that idealism can be understood as a response to internalism, and the enormous influence of this idealist response, is defended and discussed in Chapter 3.

One influential twentieth-century version of internalism, and ensuing idealism, is to be found in the work of the father of modern phenomenology, Edmund Husserl. However, in followers of Husserl we find the beginnings of a reaction to this internalism–idealism complex that takes an identifiably externalist form. Jean-Paul Sartre famously defends a view of consciousness as nothing but a directedness towards objects. In this, Sartre is developing the notion of intentionality that is central to Husserl's phenomenology. However, Sartre insists on the claim that these objects of consciousness are *transcendent* with respect to that consciousness. That is, these objects are not conscious or mental items; they are irredeemably external to consciousness and all things mental. On the basis of this, I argue in Chapter 4 that Sartre presents us with a form of externalism that turns on the rejection of both the Location Claim and the Possession Claim that constituted Cartesian internalism. Sartre is one of the first genuine externalists.

This development of an externalist alternative is, I argue in Chapter 5, carried on in the work of Wittgenstein. Wittgenstein's externalism is based centrally on a rejection of the Possession Claim (partly) definitive of internalism. At least some types of mental phenomena depend, for their possession by a subject, on structures that are external to – outside the skin of – that subject. Thus, according to Wittgenstein, to mean, intend or understand something by a sign is not to be the subject of an inner state or process. Rather, it is to possess a capacity: the capacity to adjust one's use of the sign to bring it into line with *custom* or *practice*. And this connects meaning, intending and understanding with structures that are external to the subject of this meaning, intending and understanding. The precise nature of these external structures depends on how we understand Wittgenstein's idea of a custom. But whatever understanding of this idea we adopt, Wittgenstein clearly emerges as someone who is committed to rejecting the Possession Claim (and probably also the Location Claim), and so as an externalist. Wittgenstein's externalism is the subject of Chapter 5.

Chapter 6 discusses what I call *content externalism*. This position is, in fact, what most people have in mind when they use or hear the word "externalism". Content externalism is the idea that the semantic content of mental states that have it is often dependent on factors – objects, properties, events and so on – that are external to the subject of that content. It is not possible, to use a classic example of Hilary Putnam's, to entertain the content that water is wet if you inhabit a world where there is no water. If you inhabited a world where there was no water but only, for example, something that was superficially indistinguishable from it, whatever content you entertained would not be the content that water is wet but, rather, that this superficially indistinguishable substance is wet. The content one is capable of entertaining depends on the nature of the world one inhabits.

However, many mental states are identified by way of their content. So, if content cannot be entertained in the absence of certain environmental items, neither can these mental states be possessed or instantiated in the absence of these items. Thus, we have a rejection of the Possession Claim, and this rejection is the cornerstone of the position known as content externalism. These issues will be discussed in Chapter 6. In Chapter 7, however, I go on to argue that content externalism is extremely restricted, both in scope and force. In particular, attempts to show that the arguments for content externalism also entail rejection of the Location Claim typically fail.

The attempt to strengthen externalism – to refashion it into a doctrine that entails rejection of the Location Claim as well as the Possession Claim – is taken up again in Chapter 9. The result is a position that goes by a variety of names: vehicle externalism, active externalism, architecturalism, environmentalism and so on. To regard these labels as all picking out a single position is, perhaps, overly simplistic. It is more likely that they designate several closely related positions. However, one common thread running through each of them is that the structures and mechanisms that allow a creature to possess or undergo various mental states and processes are often structures and mechanisms that extend beyond the skin of that creature. These *vehicles* of mental processes are extended, or distributed, out into the world and so too, we have every reason for supposing, are the mental processes themselves.

This form of externalism, therefore, is more radical than content externalism with regard to both its *force* and *scope*. Its *force* is greater than that of its content-based cousin because it rejects not only the Possession Claim but also the Location Claim. Not only is the possession of certain types of mental phenomena dependent on what is instantiated in the world of the creature that possesses such phenomena, but also such phenomena are often located, at least in part, out in that world. The *scope* of vehicle externalism is also greater in that content externalism is restricted to states that possess semantic content and, indeed, that do so essentially. If the arguments of Chapter 7 are correct, the restrictions on content external-ism are even greater than this: it is confined to a relatively small subset of mental states that possess their content essentially. The application of vehicle externalism is, I argue, much wider. Indeed, in Chapter 10 an attempt is made to apply vehicle externalism to the sorts of states typically thought of as being beyond the purview of externalism: conscious experiences.

Externalism is a striking and provocative view of the nature of mental phenomena, a view whose acceptance has important philosophical, and ultimately practical, consequences. What is at stake is nothing less than our ontic place in the world and our epistemic grip on that world. Mental phenomena, according to externalism, are not confined to what is going on inside the skins of mental subjects. Rather, such phenomena are, in one way or another, and to one degree or another, extended out into the world, distributed upon that world. In the eyes of many, externalism is a counter-intuitive view. The aim of this book is to make it less so.

CHAPTER 2

Cartesianism

There is a view of the mind that seems overwhelmingly natural to us. No one really knows why this is. Maybe the view simply is a natural one. Maybe it only seems that way for some other reason – cultural or whatever. No one really knows. However it came to be that way, it now pretty much passes as common sense. The view is pervasive and tenacious, not only as an explicit doctrine but, perhaps even more significantly, in the clandestine influence it has on explicit doctrines of the mind. In effect, it has the status of what Wittgenstein would call a *picture*, a pre-theoretical picture, and it holds in its grip our thinking about the mind and things mental. The most famous philosophical exposition and defence of this picture is to be found in the writing of the seventeenth-century French philosopher René Descartes, and its association with him is sufficiently robust for it to be called the *Cartesian conception*.

Even to speak of *the* Cartesian conception of the mind, however, is to suggest an underlying simplicity that is not really there. The Cartesian conception is not just a single view of the mind; it is an array of interwoven views, like the strands of a rope, each lending support to the others, and each being supported by the others. The strength of the Cartesian picture lies not merely in the strength of the individual theses that make it up but also, and perhaps even more importantly, in the way these strands bind together to yield a sweeping and comprehensive vision of the nature of human beings. And the strength of the individual components of this vision derives, in an important sense, from the strength of the vision as a whole.

What are the conceptual strands of the Cartesian conception? Broadly speaking, there are three: ontological, epistemological and axiological. "Ontological" means, roughly, "pertaining to the existence or nature of something". An ontological question about X, therefore, is a question about the existence or nature of X. And an ontological claim about X is a claim about the existence or nature of X. "Epistemological" means, roughly, "pertaining to our knowledge of something". An epistemological question about X, therefore, is a question about our knowledge of X – for example, how we come to have this knowledge, whether it is possible to know anything about X, and so on. An epistemological claim concerning X would, in effect, be an answer to this sort of question. That is, it would be a claim concerning our knowledge of X, the possibility of such knowledge, and so on. "Axiological" means, roughly, "pertaining to the value of something". An axiological question about X might be, for example, whether X has value, and if so what type of value this might be and from what source it might derive. And an axiological claim concerning X would be, in effect, an answer to these sorts of question.

Cartesian ontology: dualism

When we talk about Cartesian ontology, we are talking about Descartes's ontological claims concerning the mind. These claims can, broadly speaking, be divided into *Cartesian dualism* and *Cartesian internalism*.

Cartesian dualism

According to the Cartesian conception, minds are to be assimilated to the category of substance. Descartes uses the term "substance" in a scholastic (i.e. medieval) sense, one that ultimately derived from Aristotle, according to which a substance is, roughly, an object. A mind, for Descartes, is an object that possesses properties: mental properties. Indeed, for Descartes minds can, to some extent, be conceived of as relevantly similar to other objects found inside the body: body organs. Just as the heart circulates blood, the liver regulates metabolism, and the kidneys process waste products, the mind thinks. However, for Descartes, the fact that minds think means that the mind must also be radically different from these other organs.

> I recognize only two ultimate classes of things: first, intellectual or thinking things, i.e. those which pertain to mind or thinking substance; and secondly, material things, i.e. those which pertain to extended substance or body.[1]

According to Descartes, to say that something is physical is to say that it has what he calls extension. Roughly, this means that it takes up room. A physical thing is essentially something that occupies space, something that excludes other bodies from its spatiotemporal location. This, according to Descartes, is the essential feature of physical things. Minds, however, are quite different. The essential feature of minds, according to Descartes, is thought. Minds are essentially thinking things. However, according to Descartes, this means that minds and bodies must be fundamentally different sorts of things. This stems from a difference in the way thinking things and extended things work:

> Reason is a universal instrument which can be used in all sorts of situations . . . hence it is for all practical purposes impossible for a machine . . . to act in all the contingencies of life in the way in which our reasons makes us act.[2]

Thinking substance obeys, or is governed by, principles of reason; extended substance, however, obeys, or is governed by, mechanical principles. For Descartes the former cannot be reduced to, or be explained in terms of, the latter.

Therefore, according to official Cartesian doctrine, the major difference between the mind and bodily organs such as the heart, liver, kidneys – and brain – is that the mind is a *non-physical* substance. The mind and brain are, thus, distinct entities, and while the mind may receive input from the brain and, in turn, send information back to the brain, the two are nonetheless distinct. The brain is a physical organ operating exclusively on mechanical principles; the mind is a non-physical organ operating according to principles of reason. Each one of us, then, is an amalgam of thinking and extended substance. This view is known as *Cartesian dualism*.

Problems with Cartesian dualism

Cartesian dualism has been famously ridiculed as the myth of the *ghost in the machine*.[3] And it was Descartes's decision to make the mind ghostly (i.e. non-physical) that has drawn the principal fire from dissenters. The view of the mind as a non-physical thing does, indeed, suffer from profound problems. Most of the problems can be organized around a single theme. Once you make the mind so fundamentally different from the rest of the physical world, you are always going to have major problems trying to reincorporate this mind into the world.

Dualism is a response to the fact that each one of us seems to possess two sets of properties, ones that, on the face of it, seem quite disparate.

The first set includes features of us such as rationality, thought, consciousness, subjectivity, infallible first-person knowledge, freedom, meaning and self-awareness. The second set includes such mundane physical properties as height, weight, size, shape and spatiotemporal location. The reason there is a mind–body problem in the first place is because each one of us is a bearer of properties of both sets. I, in my intricate image (and presumably you in yours), stride on two levels, as Dylan Thomas put it. The problem is that we cannot quite understand how the same thing could have properties of both kinds, and we cannot see how one set of properties could simply reduce to, or be explained in terms of, the other. Hence, we have a problem.

Dualism is a fairly natural response to the pressures that motivate this problem. We cannot understand how one thing could possess properties so fundamentally disparate precisely because one thing does not possess properties so fundamentally disparate. Each one of us is essentially hybrid; we are composed of a physical, extended part and a non-physical, thinking part. It is the former part of us that possesses mundane physical properties such as size, mass and spatiotemporal location. But it is the latter part that possesses properties such as rationality, consciousness and freedom.

However, the invocation of a non-physical mind as the bearer of properties such as these is problematic for the simple reason that the part of us that possesses properties such as rationality, consciousness and freedom is inextricably bound up with the part of us that possesses properties such as size, shape and mass. And if each part of us is as different as Descartes seemed to believe, we are going to have a hard time accounting for this fact.

Therefore, since the time of Descartes, the *problem of interaction* has always loomed large over the Cartesian project. Descartes, like most other dualists, wanted to maintain that mind and body affect each other; he is, that is, what is known as an *interactionist* dualist. He had very good reasons for wanting to maintain this: it's obvious. What we think can affect what we do and what happens to us can affect what we think. That is, events occurring in the mind and the body can affect each other in a variety of ways. The problem for Descartes's dualism is explaining how this interaction between mental and physical takes place. The general problem is that Descartes makes the mental and the physical so different that they don't seem to share the necessary properties to make this sort of interaction intelligible. One class of properties that the mind seems to lack, for example, consists in a certain subset of spatiotemporal properties. Minds may or may not have spatial *location* on a Cartesian view – the textual evidence is indecisive – but it is clear that they do not have spatial *extension*: they take up no room. But it seems quite plausible to suppose that our ordinary concept of causation is bound up with the notion of spatial extension. Hume's famous analysis of causation, for example, identifies *contiguity* – convergence or contact in space and time – as one of the conceptual constituents of our ordinary concept of causation. This is why we are, even now, reluctant to accept the idea of action at a distance and try to explain such apparent action in terms of fields of force and the like. But how is it possible to be contiguous in space with something that takes up no room? We have a clear difficulty in explaining how the concept of causation can legitimately be applied to non-physical things such as minds. And if we retreat to the claim that the mode of interaction between mental and physical is non-causal, it seems, in the absence of a theory of this peculiar mode of interaction, that we are trying to save our theory by an unprincipled retreat into the obscure.

Other well-known objections to Descartes's dualism continue this general theme of relating non-physical minds to the physical world. Thus, it is often argued that any interaction between the physical and the mental – as defined by Descartes – would require a violation of the first law of thermodynamics: the principle of conservation of energy. Moreover, dualism has difficult questions to answer with regard to what we do know about the brain. Why, for example, is there a systematic correlation between the types of injury a brain can undergo and the impairment in mental functioning that will result? For example, why is injury to a certain clearly identifiable part of the brain correlated with a loss of the ability to recognize faces, even though other visual abilities are unimpaired? Why is injury to another clearly identifiable part of the brain correlated with the loss of the ability to understand speech, although no other auditory dysfunction results?

Perhaps the most damning objection to dualism, however, is that it does not explain what it was supposed to explain, indeed, what it was introduced to explain. It is, we might say, *explanatorily vacuous*. According to Descartes, one of the most important reasons for believing that we possess non-physical minds is that we can do things that, as he saw it, no purely physical thing could do. In particular, we can *reason* and we can *speak*.

> If any machines bore a resemblance to our bodies and imitated our actions as closely as possible for all practical purposes, we should still have two very certain means of recognizing that they were not real men. The first is that they could never use words, or put together signs, as we do in order to declare our thoughts to others . . . Secondly, even though such machines might do some things as well as we do them, or perhaps even better, they would inevitably

fail in others, which would reveal that they were acting not through understanding but only from the disposition of their organs.[4]

It is not surprising that Descartes should include the capacities to reason and to produce (meaningful) speech together. It is commonly thought that they rely on essentially similar principles of operations (specifically, symbol structures whose interaction is governed by formal rules of some sort). However, what we have to ask ourselves is does the postulation of a non-physical mind in any way help matters? That is, does it in any way explain how we are capable of reasoning and using language? And, I think, a moment's reflection should convince us that it does not. For it to be of any help in this explanatory project, we would have to be told about the nature of this non-physical mind, about its structure and about how this structure allows it to embody the formal rules of operation that allow us to reason and to use and produce language. Postulating a non-physical something, by itself, will not do any of this work. And one consistent failing of dualism since Descartes's time is its utter failure to tell us any of these sorts of thing. It is a common mistake, in philosophy as everywhere else, to confuse two very different things. On the one hand there is an explanation of a given phenomenon. On the other, there is an admission that you have no idea what the explanation is. The latter does not add up to the former. And dualism almost certainly falls into the latter category. That is, dualism is not really a theory about the nature of the mind at all; rather, it is a theoretical hole or vacuum, waiting for a theory to be put in its place.

Not many philosophers or psychologists would now regard themselves as Cartesians in the dualist sense. If the Cartesian conception is the dogma of the ghost in the machine, then the ghost has – at least officially – been exorcised from contemporary philosophical and psychological theorizing (although, as with all ghosts, its echoes can reverberate in a variety of ways – we'll encounter some of them later).

Cartesian ontology: internalism

Ryle's slur, the dogma of the *ghost in the machine*, has another facet. Not only is Descartes's mind a ghost, but it is one *in* a machine. It was this latter aspect that was, in fact, the principal object of Ryle's derision. But whereas the revolt against ghostly views of the mind has been almost entirely successful, criticism of the second aspect of Descartes's view has, until recently, been comparatively muted. Most theorizing about the mind is predicated on the assumption that the mind is physical; that is, that some sort of materialism, however attenuated, is true. However, such theorizing has been, and largely still is, predicated on the assumption that some form of what we can call *Cartesian internalism* is true. Cartesian dualism may have been expunged but its internalist cousin has not.

Cartesian internalism can be regarded as the combination of two, closely connected, theses: one concerning the location of mental phenomena, the other concerning the possession of such phenomena by a subject.

Cartesian internalism
The Location Claim: any mental phenomenon is spatially located inside the boundaries of the subject, S, that has or undergoes it.
The Possession Claim: the possession of any mental phenomenon by a subject S does not depend on any feature that is external to the boundaries of S.

The claims are, in fact, quite distinct. The first claim concerns the location of mental phenomena and applies most naturally to mental *particulars*: concrete, non-repeatable, event-, state- and process-*tokens*. The second claim concerns the possession of mental phenomena and applies most naturally to mental *properties*, which, for the purposes of this book, we can treat as abstract, multiply-exemplifiable, event-, state- and process-*types*. A claim about the *location* of a mental particular is logically quite distinct from a claim about the *possession* of a mental property. And this point applies quite generally, whether or not the phenomenon in question is mental. It is plausible to suppose, for example, that the property of being a heart is an essentially relational property. Whether or not a structure, S, counts as a heart, that is, instantiates the property of being a heart, depends on whether or not it stands in an identifiable functional–historical relation to structures contained in the ancestors of the individual that now possesses S. Roughly: (i) S, possessed by individual X, must pump blood; (ii) the ancestors of X must have possessed structures that pumped blood; and (iii) the reason X has S is because those ancestors of X possessed structures that pumped blood.[5] If this is correct, and something like it almost certainly is, then possession of the property of being a heart is an essentially relational matter, involving complex relations both to blood and one's ancestors. One cannot possess this property unless one stands in appropriate relations to ancestors, blood and the like. However, this does not mean that an individual heart, a concrete, particular, heart-token, is located where the blood that it pumps and the ancestors that produced it are located. Quite the contrary, a particular heart is located at a specific and clearly identifiable region within the body.

Questions about the location of heart-tokens (i.e. individual hearts) are logically independent of questions about the possession of heart-types (i.e. the property of being a heart). We should, I think, expect precisely the same for mental phenomena. The Location Claim is, accordingly, directed at mental particulars, and the Possession Claim at mental properties. The two claims are, therefore, non-equivalent although, as we shall see shortly, importantly related.

The Location Claim

Whether Descartes actually adhered to the Location Claim is, in fact, not as clear-cut as it may seem, because Descartes's official position is that minds lack extension. This makes their relationship to space ambiguous. Nonetheless, as subsequent Cartesians have pointed out, lack of spatial occupation is perfectly compatible with the possession of spatial location. And while Descartes was less than clear on exactly where inside the skin minds were supposed to be located, somewhere in the vicinity of the pineal gland, which he regarded as the seat of interaction between the body and mind, seemed to be his preferred option. In any event, whether or not the Location Claim can be attributed to Descartes, it is certainly a cornerstone of the Cartesian tradition that derives from him.

One way of formulating the Location Claim is as a thesis that involves the notion of identity, specifically token-identity.

1. Mental particulars are identical with particulars that are located inside the skin of the subject of those particulars.

There exist, however, certain rather thorny issues concerning the mereological part–whole relation, specifically of whether a whole is identical to the sum of its parts. Some have argued that a mereological whole should not be identified with the sum of its parts on the grounds that the former possess certain properties – specifically modal and (perhaps) counter-factual properties – that the latter lacks. If one is impressed by these sorts of arguments, then one might want to reformulate claim 1 as the thesis:

2. Mental particulars are exclusively composed of particulars that are located inside the skin of the subject of those particulars.

The Location Claim is a claim about particulars not properties. However, it is also in fact possible to formulate it in terms of properties rather than particulars. The key to understanding how this is possible lies in two concepts: intrinsicality and supervenience. We can define the notion of an *intrinsic* property as follows:

> Property P is *intrinsic* to subject S if and only if, necessarily, if p_n is an instance of P, then p_n is spatially located within the boundaries of S.[6]

I shall leave open what is involved in being an instance of a property. On most views, instances of properties are concrete particulars; property-instances are simply the concrete particular things that exemplify them. On the view that I (think I)[7] favour, however, property-instances are understood as abstract particulars or tropes. While this difference may be crucial in other contexts, nothing much turns on it in the present one.

Following Kim, we can define the relevant notion of *supervenience* as follows. Suppose family of properties A supervenes on family of properties B. Then:

> A supervenes on B just in case, necessarily, for each x and each property F in A, if x has F then there is a property G in B such that x has G and, necessarily, if any y has G it has F.[8]

Supervenience is essentially a one-way relation of dependence or determination. If F supervenes on G, then any two things (objects, events, states, processes, etc.) that are identical with respect to G must also be identical with respect to F. Equivalently (roughly), it is impossible for a thing to change with respect to F unless it also changes with respect to G. In each case, the relation of dependence is one way only. Supervenience of F on G does not entail that any two objects that are identical with respect to F must also be identical with respect to G. Nor does it entail that an object cannot change with respect to G unless it also changes with respect to F.

Supervenience is a relation that holds, in the first instance, between properties. This is fairly obvious. It makes little sense to speak of objects being identical with respect to particulars; by definition, distinct objects are composed of distinct particulars. Nevertheless, the notion of supervenience can be used to provide a formulation of the location claim. Suppose, again following Kim, we understand particulars as exemplifications of properties. An event, e, will have a structure that can be represented as: $[x, P, t]$. That is, an event, e, is the exemplifying by object x of property P at time t. Using this property-exemplification account, and armed with the concepts of supervenience and intrinsicality, we can formulate the Location Claim in a third way:

3. Any mental event, occurring in subject S, is either (i) an instance of a property that is intrinsic to S or (ii) an instance of a property that supervenes on a property that is intrinsic to S.[9]

The Possession Claim

The core of the Possession Claim is the idea that the possession of any mental property by a subject S does not depend on factors that are in any way external to S. Mental properties are, in this rough, but reasonably intuitive, sense *non-relational*. What counts as external to S, of course, depends on your view of what sort of thing S, essentially, is. If, like some versions of Cartesianism, you are tempted to view mental subjects as essentially non-physical substances, only contingently related to physical, extended substances such as the body, then the body will count as external to S, and the Possession Claim amounts to the claim that the possession of any mental property is exhaustively determined by what is occurring within this non-physical substance. This is what seems to underlie the sort of program of methodological doubt associated with Descartes. Both the body of an individual, and the physical world in which that body is located, are, for Descartes, external to the mental substance that, at least in part, constitutes an individual. And so the Possession Claim, thus understood, has the following implication: change the body of a subject, and the external world in which that body is located, all you want, and the mental properties possessed by that subject can, nevertheless, remain essentially unchanged. Indeed, even if the body and external physical world were destroyed, the mental features of a subject need not, necessarily, be altered one bit. Thus, the possession of any given mental property by a subject S does not logically depend on anything external to S, where, in this instance, S is understood as an unextended, non-physical substance.

The same idea can easily be amended to suit the purposes of the materialist form of internalism. In this case, S is identical with the physical body. Only things outside the skin of this body thereby count as external to S. Then, the Possession Claim amounts to the claim that the possession of any mental property by a subject S is exhaustively determined by what is occurring inside this physical body. It would, in principle, be possible to change radically the nature of the physical environment surrounding the bodily subject S, and even to destroy this environment entirely, and not change the mental properties exemplified by S. If some method were found of preserving S in such a way that he is kept in ignorance of what is happening in his environment, then he need not change mentally at all.

The 1999 Wachowski brothers' film, *The Matrix*, provides a good illustration of this idea. In a future dystopia, human beings are raised in egg-like containers by machines that use them as batteries: as providers of electrical energy to power the machines. However, by way of a complex computer-generated reality known as "the matrix", the machines fool the human beings into believing they are living relatively pleasant lives in a late-twentieth-century metropolis, rather than in a pod being fed the liquefied remains of other human beings. In this sort of situation, the internalist would allow that it is perfectly possible for one of the human beings being raised in a pod to have precisely the same mental properties they would have if they were living in the real world. If the computer-generated illusion causes you to believe you are eating steak, for example, then you might have precisely the same belief – namely, the belief you are eating steak – as you would have if you were actually eating steak in the real world.[10]

According to the Possession Claim, then, the possession of any given mental property by a subject *S* does not depend on factors that are external to – spatially outside the boundaries of – *S*. This may seem obviously false. It is a truism that what we think and feel can depend on what is going on in our environment. Therefore, mental properties are clearly implicated in causal relations between what is internal and what is external to a subject. The Possession Claim, however, need not deny this. Its claim that the possession of any given mental property is not dependent on factors external to *S* is not a claim about *causation* but, rather, one about *individuation*. You believe you are eating steak. This might be because you are actually eating steak, and your senses – sight, touch and so on – are working normally. However, it might be because you are in a pod, the victim of a computer-generated illusion, and your belief has nothing to do with your perceptual senses. In both cases you can, according to the internalist, have the same belief. The reason is that the physical steak on your plate and the computer-generated facsimile cause, in you, the same states. If you are a materialist you will probably regard these states as some form of activation in a certain, appropriate, part of the brain. If you are a dualist you will regard these states as occurring in a non-physical substance. Nonetheless, on both versions, these states are ones internal to their subjects. And it is the presence of these internal states, *however these states get to be caused*, that determines which mental properties a subject possesses or exemplifies. Although external items – objects, properties and the like – can be implicated in a causal story of how a given mental property, in a given situation, comes to be acquired, the individuation of any mental property depends only on what is occurring inside the subject of that property.

We can give this notion of individuation a somewhat more sophisticated rendering. According to the Possession Claim, mental properties are *individuation independent* of any items that are external to the subject of those properties. We can identify three components to a claim of individuation independence.

- *Epistemological*: it is possible to know which mental properties a subject, S, instantiates without knowing what items exist outside S.
- *Metaphysical*: it is possible for a mental property to exist in S independently of the existence of any item external to S.
- *Conceptual*: it is possible to possess the concept of any given mental property possessed by S without possessing the concept of any item external to S.[11]

You can know that a subject, whether this subject is you or someone else, believes that they are eating steak, whether or not you know whether their environment is the real world or a computer-generated illusion (the epistemological condition). It is possible for a subject – you or another – to have the belief that they are eating steak whether or not their world contains actual steak or a computer-generated facsimile (the metaphysical condition). And it is possible for a subject to possess the concept of the belief that they are eating steak whether they exist in the real, steak-containing, world or in a computer-generated alternative (the conceptual condition). The Possession Claim, if true, is true because any given mental property *M* is individuation independent of any item that is external to the subject *S*, of *M*.

Mechanism: the root of dualism and internalism

Descartes's dualism and his internalism have, arguably, the same root: the rise of mechanism associated with the scientific revolution. This revolution reintroduced the classical concept of the atom in somewhat new attire as an essentially mathematical entity whose primary qualities could be precisely quantified as modes or aspects of Euclidean space. Macroscopic bodies were composed of atoms and the generation and corruption of the former were explained in terms of the combination and recombination of the latter. Atomism is, then, mechanistic in the sense that it reduces all causal transactions to the translation, from point to point, of elementary particles, and regards the behaviour of any macroscopic body as explicable in terms of the atoms that comprise it.

It is widely recognized that Descartes's dualism stems, at least in part, from his acceptance of mechanism. The physical world, for Descartes, is governed by purely mechanical principles. He was, however, unable to conceive of how such principles could be extended to the thinking activities constitutive of the human mind. As we have seen, minds, for Descartes, are essentially thinking things and, as such, governed by principles of reason. But such principles, Descartes thought, are distinct from, and not reducible to, principles of mechanical combination and association. Rationality, for Descartes, cannot be mechanized. Each mind is thus a small corner of a foreign field, inherently non-mechanical, hence inherently non-physical. Descartes's dualism, in this way, stemmed quite directly from his mechanism.

Of equal significance, however, is the connection between mechanism and internalism. Mechanistic atomism is, we might say, methodologically individualist. A composite body is ontologically reducible to its simple constituents. And the behaviour of a composite body is reducible to the local motions of its constituents. Thus, if we want to explain the behaviour of a macroscopic body, we need focus only on local occurrences undergone by its parts. This methodological individualism would also have some purchase on the explanation of the behaviour of human beings since we are also, in part, physical. It is therefore no surprise that minds became analogously and derivatively conceived of by Descartes, and his dualist descendants, in atomistic terms. A mind, for Descartes, is essentially a psychic atom or *monad*.[12] And minds are self-contained in a way analogous to that in which atoms are self-contained. Each mind is a discrete substance insulated within an alien material cladding. Just like any other atom, the mind could interact with the physical atoms of the body. But crucially, and again just like any other atom, the essential nature of any mind was not in any way constituted or changed by this interaction. The rational nature of the mind is taken as an independent given and its interaction with other atoms is extrinsic to this nature. The legacy of this conception of the mind, and the mechanistic and individualistic conception of explanation that underwrites it, are very much with us today.

What emerges is the view of the mind as essentially an *interiority*. Minds are located inside individuals that have them, and the existence and essential nature of minds does not in any way depend on factors external to the individuals that have them. Henceforth, when I talk of the Cartesian conception of the mind, or when I describe a view as Cartesian, it is Cartesian internalism – the view of the mind as essentially an interiority – rather than the officially exorcized Cartesian dualism, that I shall have in mind. Cartesian internalism and Cartesian dualism are logically independent views in the sense that it is possible to be an internalist without being a dualist. Most present-day internalists are not dualists; they are materialists. We might call them Cartesian materialists.

Cartesian materialism

The Cartesian conception of the mind results from the combination of the Location Claim and the Possession Claim. It is possible to combine both these claims with a materialist view of the mind. The result is Cartesian materialism.

Mind–brain identity theories

The most obvious form of Cartesian materialism is what is known as the *mind–brain identity theory*. This, roughly, is the view that the mind is the brain. Slightly less roughly, it is the view that mental events, states and processes are identical with brain events, states and processes. Such a formulation, however, is itself ambiguous. There is a major division between forms of identity theory and to understand this division we must understand the distinction between *tokens* and *types*. We have already encountered this distinction: it is essentially that between a particular and a property. Tokens are dated, concrete, particular occurrences or instances. Types are the general properties that these occurrences exemplify or the kinds to which they belong. Pain, on this construal, should be understood as a type. The particular instance of pain suffered by a person at a particular time should be understood as a token of this type.

What is known as the mind–brain *type identity theory* claims that mental state or event-types are identical with neurophysiological state or event-types. "Pain is identical with C-fibre firing" is the philosopher's favourite example of this type of identity claim. A mind–brain *token identity theory*, on the other hand, would restrict its identity claims to tokens of these sorts of general types. For example, the sort of identity claim licensed by this latter theory might be something like: "The particular instance of pain suffered by Jones at 4pm on 5 May 2001 is identical with a particular instance of C-fibre firing occurring in Jones at that time." The differences between type and token versions of the identity theory are, in other contexts, extremely important. However, they need not concern us.

For our purposes what is important is that both are versions of Cartesian materialism. They are examples of what happens when Cartesian internalism is given a materialist interpretation. The token identity theory asserts an identity of mental particulars – event- or state-tokens – with physical particulars that satisfy the Location Claim. That is, according to this version of identity theory, mental particulars are identical with neurological particulars, and these are events, states or processes occurring in the brain (or wider nervous system), and hence inside the skin of the subject of these mental particulars. The type identity theory, on the other hand, asserts an identity of mental properties – event- or state-types – with physical properties that satisfy the Possession Claim. That is, according to this version of the identity theory, mental properties are identical with neurological properties, and these are ones that are individuation independent of anything occurring outside the skin of the subject of these mental properties. Both versions of the identity theory thereby qualify as materialistic forms of internalism.[13]

Psychophysical supervenience

Another common way of developing or explaining the idea of materialism is in terms of the concept of *supervenience*. Mental properties, it is often claimed, supervene on physical ones. This is thought by some to be a way of cashing out one's materialist commitments in a way that avoids some of the untoward reductionist consequences associated with the type identity theory. Indeed, one often finds a supervenience thesis concerning the relation between mental and physical properties combined with a token identity theory concerning the relation between mental and physical particulars. Even without the latter amalgamation, however, it is easy to see how a supervenience thesis can be shaped to serve the purposes of the Cartesian materialist. All that is required is that the physical properties that form the supervenience base of any given mental property are restricted to intrinsic properties of mental subjects; that is, properties that satisfy the Possession Claim. The most obvious candidates for such properties are, of course, neurophysiological properties. If this requirement is met, then (i) mental properties will be supervenient on properties that satisfy the Possession Claim and, hence, will also themselves satisfy the Possession Claim, and (ii) any mental event, occurring in subject S, is an instance of a property that supervenes on an intrinsic property of S. And this, as we have seen, is one way of satisfying the Location Claim. Therefore, it is not surprising that internalism is often formulated in terms of a supervenience thesis.

Functionalism

In recent decades, perhaps the most popular way of developing the idea of materialism is known as *functionalism*. According to functionalism, again very roughly, mental properties are individuated according to their *functional role*. Consider an analogy. A carburettor is a physical object located somewhere in the innards of a car (or older cars anyway – fuel injection systems have replaced them in most newer models). What is a carburettor? Or, more to the present point, what makes something a carburettor? The answer is that a carburettor is defined by what it does. Roughly, it is something that takes in fuel from the fuel inlet manifold, takes in air from the air inlet manifold, mixes the two in an appropriate ratio and sends the resulting mixture on to the combustion chamber. It is fulfilling this role that makes something a carburettor, and anything that fulfils this role in a car engine thereby counts as a carburettor. Most carburettors tend to look pretty similar. But this is at best a contingent fact, because it does not really matter what a carburettor looks like as long as it fills this role. The details of its physical implementation and structure are of secondary importance compared to the role it fills, for it is filling this role that makes something a carburettor and not details of its physical structure or implementation.

The functionalist takes a similar view of the nature of mental properties. That is, such properties are defined by what they do – by their functional role. What is it that mental properties do? Fundamentally, they relate to each other, to perception and to behaviour in various complex, but in principle analysable, ways. Consider an example. Take a belief, say the belief that it is raining. This is a belief that is typically caused by perception of certain environmental conditions, rain being the most obvious. Of course, perception of other environmental conditions might produce the belief, for example, someone, unbeknown to you, using a hosepipe outside your window. But rain is the most typical cause of the belief. The belief can in turn go on to bring about certain sorts of behaviour. In virtue of the belief, for example, you might carry an umbrella with you when you leave the house. However, the belief has ramifications for behaviour not in isolation but only in combination with other mental states. For example, you will carry the umbrella if you believe it is raining only if you desire to stay dry. So the desire is necessary for your behaviour too. And, this belief–desire combination will produce the behaviour only if you also believe that the umbrella will keep you dry, believe that the thing you have picked up to take with you is an umbrella and so on. What emerges is a complex network of mental states, perception and behaviour. According to functionalism, each mental state is defined by its place in this system: by the relations in which it stands to perception, to other mental states and, via those other mental states, to behaviour. To specify the place of a mental state in this network is, according to functionalism, to define that state. Of course, any such definition would be grotesquely long. Indeed, if one spent one's whole life attempting to give a functional definition of even one mental state, one might well not have time to finish the task. But this problem need not concern us. What does concern us is the general vision of mental properties supplied by functionalism. The vision is of mental properties forming a vast causal system – a system of interrelated causal connections – where each mental property is individuated by way of its place in this system: by way of its causal connections to other mental states, to perceptual stimuli and to behavioural responses.

Is functionalism, understood in this way, a form of internalism? Not necessarily, but it can easily be understood in that way, and it usually has been understood in that way. Functionalism becomes a form of internalism once we understand the functional roles that define mental properties as ones that begin and end at the skin. That is, the sort of perception and the sort of action that enter into the functional roles of mental states must be understood *narrowly*.

Consider perception. Part of the functional role of the belief that it is raining, for example, is that the belief is typically caused by the perception of rain on one's window. However, it can also be caused by the perception of water on one's window caused by a garden sprinkler. Are these the same perception? There is a way of understanding perception according to which they are. In each case, the same pattern of light energy is distributed across one's retina. Indeed, in principle, the same pattern on one's retina could be produced not by water on one's window at all, but by, say, mud splashes. If we think of perception as beginning at the retina – with a pattern of energy distribution – then we are thinking of perception as beginning at the skin of the perceiving organism. We are, that is, thinking of perception narrowly.

There is an analogous way of thinking about behaviour. I believe that it is raining, desire to stay dry and so on. So I pick up my umbrella and head off to work. However, suppose I inadvertently pick up my fiancée's red umbrella, instead of my manly black one. Is this the same action? On one way of understanding behaviour, it is not. The former action is one of picking up my umbrella, and the latter is one of picking up my partner's umbrella. However, on another way of understanding action, it clearly is the same action. It is umbrella-picking-up action, as we might say. Suppose, now, that instead of picking up an umbrella at all, I inadvertently pick up a walking stick instead. Is this the same action? Again, on one interpretation no, and on another yes. On the latter interpretation, the common thread that unites these actions is the picking up of something that I (correctly or incorrectly) believe will keep me dry. Suppose, now, however, that I am hallucinating. Under the influence of some serious hallucinogens, let us suppose, I pick up nothing at all. But I go through the same bodily motions, lean over to the rack, reach out for the umbrella, put the imagined umbrella under my arm and so on. It is just that in this case, I never pick anything up. There is a way of understanding behaviour according to which this counts as the same behaviour. And, it seems, it calls out for the same psychological explanation: I believe that it is raining, want to stay dry, believe that the umbrella will help me in this regard and so on. What sense of behaviour is involved here? Basically, bodily motion. Action, or behaviour, understood *narrowly*, amounts to bodily movement. More precisely, it amounts to bodily movement that is caused in an appropriate way – by beliefs, desires, intentions and so on.

If we understand both perception and behaviour narrowly, then we understand both as beginning and ending at the skins of organisms. This yields a narrow conception of functional role: the functional role associated with any given mental state begins and ends at the skin of the subject of that state. This has been far and away the most popular way of understanding functionalism, and this understanding is unremittingly internalist. Mental states are constituted by functional roles that are instantiated inside – or certainly not outside – the skin of the individuals that have them.

Functionalism is almost always understood materialistically as well as internalistically. To understand functionalism materialistically is simply to make a claim about what *fills* the functional roles that are definitive of mental states. Just as the carburettor role is filled by something, a physical object of some sort, so too, according to materialist functionalism, the causal roles definitive of mental states are filled by brain states of some sort. Indeed, on some versions of this view, the mental states can then, legitimately, be *identified* with these brain states.[14] Others identify the mental state with the functional role itself but allow that the mental state is realized by the brain state that realizes it. According to the first view, functionalism entails a form of mind–brain type identity theory. According to the latter, it entails a form of mental–physical supervenience thesis. Either way, functionalism is an unremittingly materialist view.

Functionalism is, therefore, almost invariably understood as being an expression of both materialism and internalism. So it is another version of Cartesian materialism.

Mind–brain identity theories, psychophysical supervenience and functionalism are not incompatible views of the nature of mental phenomena. They can be combined in various ways. For example, one can combine a token identity theory of mental events, states and processes with a supervenience-based understanding of the nature of mental properties and their relation to neurophysiological properties, and then use functionalism to provide an explanation of why this supervenience should hold. But compatible or otherwise, what unites all these views is that they all admit an internalist interpretation, according to which mental phenomena are constituted by factors that are internal to the individuals that have them. Indeed, not only do these views all admit an internalist interpretation, but such interpretations have, by a considerable extent, been the most popular ways of understanding them. When understood in this way, then, mind–brain identity theories, psychophysical supervenience theses and functionalist accounts are all forms of Cartesian materialism. They are materialist forms of internalism – materialist expressions of the Cartesian idea of the mind as interiority.

Cartesian epistemology

Within the Cartesian conception of the mind, ontological theses are inextricably entangled with epistemological counterparts, each giving support and succour to the other. It is genuinely unclear if any particular thesis precedes any of the others. It is, perhaps, more realistic to suppose that ontological and epistemological aspects of Cartesianism evolved together.

As we have seen, the core idea underpinning the Cartesian conception of the mind is the idea that the mental phenomena are contained *within* the subject that has them. At the level of tokens, this can be understood in terms of the Location Claim: mental state- and event-tokens are located inside the boundaries of subjects that possess them. At the level of types, this can be understood in terms of the Possession Claim: the possession of any given mental property by a subject is independent of anything existing outside the boundaries of that subject. And this idea can be further explained in terms of the notion of the individuation independence of mental properties of anything external to the subject of those properties. These are all ways of expressing the idea that, *ontologically*, any given mental phenomenon is contained within the subject that has it.

There is, however, another sense of *containment within* a subject, one that is not ontological but fundamentally *epistemic*. In many ways, this corresponds more closely to Descartes sense understanding of the idea.[15] To understand the epistemic or epistemological sense of *containment within a subject*, consider one of Descartes's more famous arguments for dualism. This is often called the *argument from certainty* (or, sometimes, the *argument from doubt*). It goes something like this.

P1. I cannot be certain that my body exists.
P2. I can be certain that I exist as a thinking thing.

C. Therefore I, as a thinking thing, am distinct from my body.

Since minds are essentially thinking things, to talk of myself as a thinking thing is equivalent, in Cartesian parlance, to talking of my mind. If the argument works, therefore, it will show that my mind is not the same thing as my body or any part of my body (since the doubt expressed in P1 applies both to my body as a whole and any part of that body). Does the argument work?

Descartes made graphic his support of P1 by way of two scenarios: the *dream conjecture* and the *evil demon* conjecture. Can you be sure you are, at this moment, not dreaming? Can you be *certain* of it? It may seem to you as if you are awake and reading this book, but how do you know you are not just dreaming that you are reading it? A pretty uninspiring dream to be sure, but could it be a dream nonetheless? It is true, after you wake up from a dream, that you are pretty sure that what you just had was a dream. Usually anyway. But that is not the point. The point is this. Can you always be certain from *within* a dream that you are dreaming? Are there, for example, any features of dreams that give it away, so to speak? Well, often, dreams do not hang together in the way waking life does. Weird things happen. You have a different body; dogs can talk. Dreams are typically more disjointed, less vivid, less coherent than what we call waking life. But how do you know that what you are presently experiencing is not just an exceptionally vivid and coherent dream (assuming, that is, the general coherency of the present book)? It is not likely that you are now dreaming, but that is not the point. The point is that it is not possible to be absolutely certain that you are not dreaming. And that is all we need to get Descartes's argument going. But, then, if you cannot be certain that you are not now dreaming, neither can you be certain about how long this dream, if you are having one, has been going on. It is possible, barely possible, that the whole of what you call your life has been a dream. If you cannot tell whether you are dreaming at any particular time, then you cannot tell whether you are dreaming the whole time. Therefore, you cannot be *certain* that you are not dreaming the whole of your life. And if you cannot be certain that your life has not been a dream, then you cannot be certain that you have a body. And this gives us Descartes's first premise.

There is another famous line of reasoning that Descartes used to defend P1: the so-called *evil demon conjecture*. Many people think that the universe is ruled by a God who is good, but suppose they are wrong and the universe is in fact ruled by an evil deity who gets kicks from fooling people into believing things that are not true. So this demon tricks you into believing that you have a body when in fact you do not. Now, again, this is not simply a paranoid fantasy. Descartes was not insane. He does not think the universe is ruled by this evil demon, nor does he think such a scenario is probable. He thinks it is possible, barely possible, infinitesimally possible: a possibility so small that it is not really worth worrying about, but a possibility nonetheless.

And if it is a possibility, however marginal, this shows that you cannot be certain that you have a body. Therefore, you cannot know, in Descartes's sense, that you have a body. Again, we have P1.

What about P2? If Descartes is right, and we cannot be certain even about the existence of our own bodies, then how can we possibly be certain about the existence of ourselves as thinking things? Well, look at it like this. Suppose you become convinced that Descartes is right about our knowledge, or rather lack of knowledge, of the body, and this makes you worry about whether you exist at all. Then *who* is it that is worried about not existing? To worry about not existing, or to doubt that you exist, involves thinking that perhaps you do not exist. But in order to think this, you must exist, otherwise there would not be anyone there to do the thinking. So every time you think you do not exist, you do exist. To think that you don't exist proves that you do exist! Descartes encapsulated this idea in his famous phrase *cogito ergo sum*: I think, therefore I am.

It is generally accepted that Descartes's argument from certainty does not work as an argument for dualism. Nonetheless, there is embodied in the argument a principle that has a powerful intuitive appeal, and this principle strongly supports internalism. We can call this the *principle of epistemic internalism*.

> *Epistemic internalism*: each person knows his or her mind *first* and *best*.

According to the argument from certainty, it is possible to be deluded about the existence of the physical world in its entirety, including the existence of one's physical body. Nonetheless, it is still not possible to be deluded about the existence of one's mind as a thinking thing. And while it is possible to be mistaken in all of one's thoughts about the physical world, still one cannot be deluded about *that* one is thinking, and *what* one is thinking. That is, one can know *that* and *what* one is thinking about the external world, even if one cannot know whether what one is thinking is true. This is, roughly, what it means to know one's mind *best*: you know the contents of your own mind better than you know the contents of the physical world. You have, that is, a special kind of *authority* over the contents of your own mind, an authority that you do not have with respect to the contents of the external world.

This idea of special authority, or *first-person authority* as it is commonly known, can be interpreted in several ways, some more plausible than others. On one interpretation, first-person authority consists in the *infallibility* of your knowledge about your own thoughts and other mental states. If you claim sincerely to be thinking that grass is green, then you cannot be wrong – not over whether grass is green, but over whether you are thinking that thought. This was probably Descartes's view. A little less extreme is the idea that first-person authority consists in the fact that your knowledge of your own mental states is *incorrigible*. This does not mean that you are infallible but means that you are not subject to correction by others. You may not be an infallible authority but you are nonetheless the *highest* authority over the contents of your own mind. An alternative is to understand first-person authority in terms of the idea that the contents of your own mind are transparently available to you, or *self-intimating*: if you are, in fact, thinking that grass is green, then you know you are thinking this. And this does not require that you are either infallible or incorrigible about the contents of your mind.

Each way of understanding the notion of first-person authority provides an interpretation of the idea that we know the contents of our own minds best – that is, better than we know the contents of the world. And the idea that we know our own minds best, however this is interpreted, can be used to explain one of the central features of Cartesian internalism: the idea that mental phenomena are contained within the subjects that have them. This idea can be understood epistemically as well as ontologically. That is, the limits of the mind – of mental phenomena broadly construed – can be drawn precisely in terms of those things over which we have first-person authority. The mental incorporates those things, and only those things, over which we have this sort of authority. And, therefore, everything over which we have first-person authority lies inside the mental subject, and everything over which we do not lies outside. This provides us with an epistemic, rather than spatial, understanding of the notion of *containment within a subject* of mental phenomena.

Once we have this idea of knowing the contents of our own minds *best*, we can use it to make sense of the idea that we know the contents of our own minds *first*. Each one of us has first-person authority over the contents of our own minds. Our knowledge of the contents of the world – or even if there is a world – is, in comparison, a poor relation. Thus, the idea that the boundaries of the mental subject are, in part, epistemic ones leads very quickly to a downgrading of our knowledge of the external physical world and, consequently, to the spectre of scepticism. And it is precisely this sort of scepticism, of course, that Descartes exploited in the argument from certainty.

The relatively underprivileged nature of our information of the external world – and it is not clear that we can even call this information "knowledge" – leads rapidly to the following idea. To the extent that we can have reliable information, perhaps even knowledge, about the external physical world, this information must be built up from information that is reliable. Our beliefs about the external world can be made legitimate only if they can be justified in terms of the contents of our own minds, contents over which we have authority. And it is this idea that I have been getting at in terms of the claim that we know our own minds *first*. Knowing the contents of our own minds first amounts to the following claim about the direction of epistemic justification. We are authoritative about the contents of our own minds, and to the extent that we can be authoritative about the contents of the world, our judgements about these latter contents must be justifiable in terms of our judgements of the contents of our own minds.

This idea of the direction of justification, embodied in the claim that we know our own minds first, leads to a certain type of well-known project in epistemology, indeed, one that has dominated epistemological concerns for centuries. The central idea underpinning this project is that the difference between true belief and knowledge consists in some form of justification and, crucially, that justification consists in factors that are internal to the subject of the belief. The relevant notion of internality, however, is fundamentally epistemic. The activities of my heart, liver and kidneys are activities internal to me but these are clearly not candidates for transformers of true belief into knowledge. What transforms true belief into knowledge, it is commonly thought, is something of which the believing subject can be aware, something to which the subject has epistemic access. I can, however, be aware of many things including whether or not it is presently raining and the week's activity on the New York stock exchange. But this, it is thought, is not access of the relevant sort. Rather, justification must consist in a special sort of access. According to Descartes, the special access consists in a special type of authority: the thinking subject can determine with certainty whether a belief has justification and consequently whether it qualifies as knowledge. And according to Chisholm, a recent epistemic internalist descendant of Descartes, whether a belief has justification is something that can be determined by reflection alone.[16] The central idea of this sort of approach to epistemology is that the factors that make a true belief justified and, consequently, transform a true belief into knowledge are properties over which the believer has a special sort of access, that is, first-person authority. And this idea is simply an (influential) expression of what I have called epistemic internalism: the idea that we know our own minds first and best.

Cartesian axiology

An axiological theory is a theory of value: moral value, aesthetic value and so on. Descartes did not propound a theory of value but there is, implicit in Cartesian internalism, a stark framework for thinking about the sort of thing value must be.

Suppose we accept the idea of the mind as an ontic and epistemic interiority, contained within the subject of mental phenomena. Then everything that does not lie within the boundaries of this subject – the external world broadly understood – is outside the mind. This external world, however, is a locus, or apparent locus, of *value*. Some of the things that happen in it are good, some bad, some right, some wrong, and some none of these things. If we enquire into the source of this value, however, the Cartesian conception of the mind gives us a simple choice. Either this value properly belongs to the world outside the mind or it belongs to the mind. That is, either the value that appears to reside in the world exists there objectively, independently of the activities of the mind or it is in some way constituted by those activities and then projected on to the world.

Hume's meta-ethical theory is a classic example of the latter sort of account. Suppose, to use one of Hume's examples, we come across the scene of a murder. Through sensory experience of the scene, and reasoning based on this experience, we might be able to work out various things: the identity of the murdered person, the time of death, the murder weapon employed and so on. We might even be able to work out things such as the identity of the murderer, the motive for the murder and so on. But, according to Hume, one of the things we will never be able to work out from sensory experience and reasoning based on such experience is that the murder is wrong. The wrongness of the murder is not something contained in the world: not a property of the murder considered in itself. Rather, according to Hume, witnessing the murder scene evokes in us various feelings of what we might broadly term "disapproval": feelings of shock, horror, revulsion, outrage and so on. We then *project* these feelings, and our resultant judgement that the murder was wrong, on to the world, and end up with the idea that the murder is somehow wrong in itself. But, according to Hume, this idea is incorrect. The wrongness of the murder consists solely in the fact that it evokes various appropriate feelings in us, combined with our projection of these feelings on to the world. A property – wrongness – that appears to be in the world is really in us. A property that appears to reside outside the mind has its true location inside. This sort of view is usually called *subjectivism*.

The alternative is to hold that value – goodness and badness broadly construed – exists in the world independently of the valuing activities of the mind. This view is known as *objectivism* and, like subjectivism, it has a long history. Plato, for example, regarded the ultimate location of value as the world of *forms*: part of the external world, albeit a non-physical part. Plato begins a long tradition of meta-ethical theory that sees value as external to and independent of the mind but not part of the physical or natural world as such. This view received influential twentieth-century exposition in the hands of G. E. Moore. We might refer to it as *non-naturalistic objectivism*. Other forms of objectivism – naturalistic forms – attempt to identify value with some natural feature of the world, increase in utility providing a prominent example. According to all forms of objectivism, values exist outside the mind and independently of the mind.

Historically, in meta-ethical theory, the choice has always been between regarding value as an objectively existing feature of the world outside the mind or a feature subjectively constituted by the activities of the mind. The true locus of value is either in the world or in the mind. However, this choice seems to be predicated on a more basic division of reality into self-contained minds and worlds external to those minds. If reality turns out not to be this way, then the axiological choice between inside and outside may turn out to be a false choice. If so, meta-ethical theories of the nature of value may have to be seriously revised or even abandoned.

Conclusion

The Cartesian conception of the mind is made up of three broad strands: ontological, epistemological and axiological. The ontological component of Cartesianism is composed of the Location Claim, according to which mental particulars are spatially located inside the skins of mental subjects, and the Possession Claim, according to which the possession of mental properties by a subject is logically independent of anything external to that subject. The epistemological component of Cartesianism consists in the thesis of epistemic internalism: we know the contents of our own minds first and best. The axiological strand of Cartesianism consists in the framework for thinking about value bequeathed us by the ontological and epistemological strands. Value must be something either objectively existing in the world or something subjectively constituted by the activities of the mind. Cartesian views of the mind can exist in both dualist and materialist forms.

CHAPTER 3

Idealism

Suppose we separate mind and world in the manner prescribed by Cartesian internalism. A mind is an interiority: mental phenomena are located exclusively inside the skin of any organism that possesses them, and possession of such phenomena by a creature is logically independent of whatever exists or occurs in the world outside that skin. Then we are immediately presented with a problem, one that has been and continues to be enormously influential. It is sometimes called the *matching problem*. The matching problem, then, is a direct result of the sort of separation of mind and world essential to Cartesian internalism. And this result of internalism leads to a response: the *transcendental idealism* of Kant and a succession of imitators. Idealism – the view that reality is in one or another way, and to a greater or lesser degree, mental – is, therefore, a direct result of internalism. This matters – because idealism has provided the dominant intellectual *Weltanschauung* of the twentieth century, and not only in philosophy. And there is, I think, little current evidence of its decline.

The transition from Cartesian internalism to neo-Kantian idealism and the debilitating excesses of recent versions of this idealism are the subject of this chapter. These excesses are precisely the sort of mess one can get oneself into through an uncritical acceptance of the dichotomizing of mind and world along Cartesian internalist lines.

The matching problem

Kant's monumental *Critique of Pure Reason* is, justifiably, one of the most influential books in the history of philosophy.[1] It is, in effect, dominated by a single question, a *transcendental* question concerning the possibility of knowledge. A transcendental question, in Kant's sense, is one that deals with the possibility of a given sort of phenomenon. With respect to knowledge, then, it has the form: "How is knowledge possible?" Or, more accurately, "What must be the case if knowledge is to be possible?" Or, alternatively, "What does the existence, or at least the possibility, of knowledge entail about the nature of reality?"

Consider, for example, our knowledge of the world around us. It is natural to suppose that there is such a thing as a real world. It is equally natural to suppose that we are, at least in principle, capable of finding out about this real world, of obtaining knowledge about it. If this is true, then this entails that the world is the sort of thing that can become an object for us, the sort of thing that can become an object of investigation and examination for those of our faculties – broadly, rational and experiential – in virtue of which we find out about the world. But how is this possible?

The natural temptation is to suppose that our knowledge of the world is grounded in the fact that the world simply impresses itself on us by way of some sort of causal relation. Things in the world causally affect us by way of our senses and this is, ultimately, what grounds our knowledge of such things. However, this in itself will not solve the transcendental question. If our minds were not suitably receptive to the influence of the world, the causal impression the world makes upon us could not result in knowledge of that world. High-pitched frequencies causally impinge upon us since they are just a certain type of short-wavelength compression wave in the air around us. But, they are undetectable by us and, thus, this causal impingement does not by itself yield knowledge of them.

We gain knowledge of the world by way of what we can call, trivially, *knowledge-acquiring faculties*, of which reason and experience are the most obvious examples. But that these knowledge-acquiring faculties are capable of yielding knowledge of the world is not a necessary truth. We might, conceivably, possess faculties that were simply hopeless at this sort of task. Of course, if they were, then we presumably would not have survived for very long. But that the human race survived and flourished is not a necessary truth and, therefore, neither is the claim that our knowledge-acquiring faculties are suitable or appropriate for yielding knowledge about the world.

If our knowledge-acquiring faculties are capable of yielding knowledge of the world, then this must be, Kant thought, because these faculties must, in some way, *match up* to the world. There must be some sort of *fit* or *match* between the nature of our knowledge-acquiring faculties and the nature of the world. A high-pitched sound is inaudible to us but not to dogs because their auditory apparatus somehow fits the short-wavelength compression wave in the air in a way that ours does not. Similarly, Kant argues, if knowledge of the world is to be possible at all, there must be some sort of generalized fit between our knowledge-acquiring faculties and the world. The two must cohere, mesh or match up in an appropriate way. The transcendental question of how knowledge of the world is possible, then, translates into the question of how this fit or matching occurs.

Transcendental idealism

Kant's answer to this question is one of the most controversial, yet one of the most influential, in the history of thought. Our knowledge-acquiring faculties mesh with the world in the requisite way because the latter is, in an important sense, a *product* of the former. This view is known as *transcendental idealism*.

Transcendental idealism is the view that things in space and time – the items we encounter in our everyday experience of the world – are only appearances or *phenomena*. And to say that an item is a phenomenon is to say, very roughly, that it exists only as the content of some actual or possible representation. The world that we experience, and the objects we encounter in it, are a logical construction out of experience. Thus:

> If the subject, or even only the subjective constitution of the senses in general, be removed, the whole constitution and all the relations of objects in space and time, nay space and time themselves, would vanish. As appearances, they cannot exist in themselves but only in us.[2]

What distinguishes transcendental idealism from straightforward idealism of, say, the sort attributable to Berkeley is that Kant allowed, indeed sometimes insisted, that there must be some things that do not depend for their existence on being represented or cognized. He called these things *noumena*, or *things-in-themselves*, and distinguished them from *phenomena* whose existence were not thus independent of experience.

In broad outline, and glossing over some of the well-known difficulties of interpretation, the Kantian picture looks something like this. Objects affect us, impress themselves upon us, providing what Kant calls *sensible intuitions*. Our faculty of *sensibility*, in virtue of which we can have such intuitions, is constituted in such a way that it can receive intuitions only as relations ordered in space and time. That is, our minds are structured in such a way that our sensible intuitions are necessarily spatial and temporal in character. Space and time are what Kant calls *forms of intuition*: they determine the character of our sensible intuitions as spatial and temporal. As such, they are conditions of the possibility of experience, and not part of the content of experience.

It is possible to express Kant's point in terms of the distinction between the *form* and the *content* of experience. Experiences are essentially structured entities. If not, they would simply be, as William James put it, a "blooming, buzzing confusion". This shows that experiences have more than simply content; they also have form. The content of an experience, Kant accepts, derives from sensation. However, form cannot be similarly derived: what gives form or structure to sensations cannot itself be derived from sensations because it is a precondition, or condition of possibility, of sensations. Therefore, what gives form to sensations must, Kant argues, be a priori: an aspect of intuition that is prior to experience (understood as a manifold of sensations). This he calls *pure intuition*. Space and time are not features of the noumenal world, but forms of intuition whereby the world that we do experience, the phenomenal world, is given to us. As such, they are not part of the content of experience, but part of its form – not part of *what* we experience, but a *condition of the possibility* of our experiencing what we do.

According to Kant, sensible intuition, by itself, is not sufficient for experience. For experience to occur, what is presented to us through sensible intuition must be supplemented by the faculty of *understanding*. This faculty is responsible for the *synthesis* of sensible intuitions. That is, the understanding structures or synthesizes the deliverances of sensibility in such a way that a unified experience is made possible. This synthesis proceeds according to certain rules. The faculty of understanding, in virtue of its nature, is necessarily constrained to synthesize sensible intuitions by way of what Kant calls *categories*, the most important of which are *substance* and *cause and effect*. Thus, in virtue of the character of our faculty of understanding, we are necessarily constrained to see all changes, for example, as modifications of some or other substance and as subject to laws of cause and effect.

Phenomena, according to this Kantian view are, therefore, items constructed according to the demands of the faculty of sensibility and the faculty of understanding. They are items whose existence and identity derive from the structuring activities of the mind. What of noumena? In any positive sense of understanding, the best we could do, according to Kant, is in terms of the idea that a noumenon is an "object of a non-sensible intuition".[3] Kant thought that we cannot comprehend the real possibility of such an intuition. So we must think of a noumenon in a purely negative sense, that is "so far as it is not an object of our sensible intuition".[4] And, according to Kant, we can have no knowledge of items that are not objects of sensible intuition.

Therefore, we arrive at the idea of reality as essentially bifurcated: divided into the phenomenal and the noumenal. Of the latter, we can have no knowledge. And, hence, a metaphysics of the latter – a transcendent metaphysics in the traditional sense of the term – is impossible. We can, however, have knowledge of the phenomenal. And we can have such knowledge for the simple reason that the denizens of the phenomenal world are items, in part, constructed by the activities of our minds. They are, therefore, items whose very nature is conducive to being known by our minds. The transcendental possibility of knowledge of the external world is grounded in the fact that this world is one constituted by us.

Imposition versus restriction

There are many obscurities in Kant's discussion of the relation between the mind (or its faculties) and the a priori necessary features of empirical (i.e. phenomenal) objects. One of these obscurities is, for our purposes, particularly important. Does the mind *impose* space and time and categories, such as substance and cause and effect, on empirical objects? Or is it merely that our mind *restricts* our cognition to features of noumenal objects, such as spatiotemporal features, and those features identified by way of categories such as substance and cause and effect. If the former view, then space and time, substance, cause and effect are not elements of noumenal reality at all. They are, literally, constituted by the activities of the mind. On the latter view, however, this does not follow. Space and time, substance, cause and effect would all be part of noumenal reality. It is just that, in virtue of the character of our minds, these are the only features of noumenal reality we can access, or of which we can have knowledge, since these are the only features of that reality for which there is the requisite fit with our knowledge-acquiring faculties.

General consensus favours the imposition view. This yields the standard interpretation of Kant according to which empirical objects can be reduced to the deliverances of representations structured a priori in ways determined by the forms of intuition and categories of understanding. This interpretation of Kant's view, which seems to be licensed by the bulk of his writing, leads to radical scepticism regarding our knowledge of noumena. It also leads to profound internal difficulties for Kant's view. For example, how do we characterize the relation between noumena and phenomena? We cannot, consistently, claim that noumena *cause* phenomena, for causation is one of the categories of the understanding and hence applies only to relations between phenomena themselves. To claim that the relation between noumena and phenomena is a causal one is, in effect, a claim of the transcendent metaphysics that Kant has disavowed. Moreover, even if we could circumvent this problem, what reason do we have for thinking that there is any resemblance or correspondence at all between phenomena and the noumena that produce them? The consistent Kantian position must surely be that there cannot be any such resemblance or correspondence since phenomena are identified by way of properties (spatial, temporal, substantial, causal, etc.) that noumena cannot, by definition, possess. It was this aspect of Kant's view that was taken up by Fichte, and which led most directly to German idealism's denial of the noumenal thing-in-itself.[5] Kant's transcendental idealism, then, appears to be an inherently unstable position and collapse into outright idealism is always just around the corner.

If we adopt the restriction, rather than imposition, interpretation we end up with a very different, and I think far more sensible, doctrine – one adopted in broad outline by at least one Kantian realist, the appropriately named Alois Riehl.[6] On this view, not only do phenomena – empirical objects – have an existence in themselves, but we can also actually know these independently existing things via a subset of their properties, those properties that our faculties of sensibility and understanding allow us to experience and subsequently know. Phenomenal features are features of noumenal reality, but they are the only features of that reality that requisitely match up with our sensibility and understanding, hence the only features of which we can have any sort of knowledge. It is arguable that this is Kant's position in the B edition "Refutation of Idealism", where Kant's idealism seems to be at its most attenuated.

The problem with this sensible view, however, is that it contradicts most of Kant's formulations (including, notably, the A edition "Refutation of Idealism"). It is also probably not compatible with Kant's appeal to transcendental idealism to resolve the first two antinomies, since these seem to require treating empirical objects as nothing more than actual or possible representations.[7] Most obviously, it is incompatible with Kant's clear assertion that space and time have no existence in themselves.[8] If sensible intuition and understanding simply restrict our experience to a subset of properties, rather than construct such properties by way of intuition and understanding, then such properties would exist independently of intuition and understanding.

The restriction view is clearly not Kant's view. Why then do I bother bringing it up? Two reasons. First, to show how easy it is, how marginal the tinkering that is required, to turn an outrageous view into a rather sensible one. Secondly, because the distinction between imposition and restriction is systematically misunderstood, overlooked or ignored by modern-day descendants of Kant. Kantianism, in its most straightforwardly impositional or idealistic form, exerts a stranglehold on many, almost certainly most, of the "softer" disciplines studied at universities today. The sort of idealism to be found in Kant can also be found, in one form or another, and to varying degrees, in most of the social sciences and humanities including, alas, philosophy. Indeed, its influence on the "hard" natural sciences is very far from negligible, particularly in the more theoretical branches of natural science. But, in all cases, the Kantian-idealist strand in these disciplines has its basis in arguments that are very bad indeed.[9] Most of the arguments involve, quite centrally, a confusion of imposition with restriction. It is to a consideration of the modern-day descendants of Kant that we now turn.

The Sapir–Whorf hypothesis

An influential version of contemporary neo-Kantian idealism can be found in the writings of the anthropologists Edward Sapir and Benjamin Whorf.[10] What is usually referred to as the Sapir–Whorf hypothesis is this: the language we speak structures the world we are in. Speakers of radically different languages, therefore, live in radically different worlds. What does this mean? And how do we get to this seemingly counter-intuitive conclusion? We begin, in fact, with the solidly Kantian premise:

1. Thought (broadly construed to encompass operations of the faculty of understanding and that of sensibility) structures reality. The world we live in is, at least in part, one constructed by the activities of the mind (e.g. its forms of intuition and categories of understanding).

We then add another premise characteristic of twentieth-century neo-Kantianism, one dealing with the relation between thought and language.

2. The structure of language determines the structure of thought.

And reach the conclusion:

3. The structure of language determines the structure of reality.

The so-called "Kantian turn" in philosophy consisted in the idea that the world of our experience – the empirical or phenomenal world – is one, in part, constructed by the forms of sensibility and categories of under-standing peculiar to our minds. Twentieth-century mutations of this idea are typically forms of linguistic Kantianism: the world of our experience is one, in part, constructed by the structures, forms and categories of the language we speak. If the former was the Kantian turn, we can with some justification speak of the latter as the *linguistic turn*.

One important difference between the Kantian turn and the linguistic turn is that the latter allows for a more thoroughgoing relativism than the former. Kant was not a relativist. He thought that the forms of sensibility and the categories of understanding were common to all human beings. Reality is, therefore, relative *to* human beings, but not *between* human beings. However, the shift of emphasis to language introduces the possibility of a far more radically relativistic conception of reality. If language structures reality, then, to the extent that people speak different languages they also occupy different realities. And unlike, for example, Chomsky, Sapir and Whorf are both impressed by the divergence between different languages. The most important differences between languages are, they argue, *syntactic* differences.

Whorf's central arguments, for example, turn on the differences between the syntax of "Standard Average European" (SAE) languages like English and languages of Native Americans such as Hopi. His suggestions of what these differences consist in are, however, largely brief and obscure. His main suggestion seems to concern *time*. Whorf argues that SAE languages compel us to adopt a certain conception of time. Because of the type of language we speak, he alleges, we see time as a:

> smooth flowing continuum in which everything in the universe proceeds at an equal rate, out of a future, into a past; or, in which, to reverse the picture, the observer is being carried in the stream of duration continuously away from a past and into a future.[11]

How does our language do this? The key, according to Whorf, is that SAE languages make us see time as an objective quantifiable entity. Thus, we employ a tense system that is structured by way of the tripartite distinction past/present/future. This distinction, Whorf argues, is easily *spatialized*. We can, for example, imagine it as akin to left/centre/right or bottom/middle/top. And this causes us to think of time in essentially metaphorical terms, as analogous to space, and hence to employ essentially kindred terms in our description of temporal occurrences as in our description of spatial entities.

> All languages need to express durations, intensities, and tendencies. It is characteristic of SAE ... to express them metaphorically. The metaphors are those of spatial extension, i.e.

of size, number (plurality), position, shape, and motion. We express duration by "long, short, great, much, quick, slow," etc; intensity by "large, great, much, heavy, light, high, low, sharp, faint," etc: tendency by "more, increase, grow . . ."; and so on through an almost inexhaustible list of metaphors that we hardly recognize as such, since they are virtually the only linguistic media available.

It is clear how this condition "fits in". It is part of our whole scheme of OBJECTIFYING – imaginatively spatializing qualities and potentials that are quite non-spatial.[12]

According to Whorf, this spatializing tendency is characteristic of SAE languages, but not Native American languages such as Hopi. The Hopi tense system does not map, at least not neatly, onto our past/present/future trichotomy. Hence, metaphors for duration, intensity and tendency are not spatial. For example, one aspect of the Hopi tense system indicates *expectation*. But this can be used to describe both future occurrences and occurrences that are contemporaneous but spatially distant from the utterer. Another is what Whorf refers to as a *nomic* form, which corresponds, roughly, to our tenseless use of "is". The other form is *direct report* and encompasses both what we would call past and present.

Details aside, Whorf's view seems to be that our SAE language compels us to adopt one view of time, whereas the Hopi's language compels them to a quite distinct view. Assume, for the sake of argument, that this is correct.[13] How do these arguments, even if correct, tell us anything whatsoever about the nature of reality? That is, let us accept, for the sake of argument, that the structure of language determines the structure of thought (although I personally do not believe a general claim of this sort for a second). How do we move from this to the claim that language structures reality? The answer is, I think, that we cannot. Underlying Whorf's argument in this regard is a simple, but apparently pervasive and tenacious, confusion: a confusion of, on the one hand, concepts and experience and, on the other, what our concepts and experience are about.

We can accept that language plays a role in shaping both our experience and the nature of thought. The concepts we possess certainly play a role in structuring and organizing our experience of, and our thinking about, the world. That is, we can accept, more or less, Whorf's claim that a language structures our experience: "the world is presented in a kaleidoscopic flux of impressions which has to be organized by our minds – and this means largely by the linguistic system in our minds".[14] But this claim has nothing whatsoever to do with the world. This is a claim about how we organize or structure *experience* of the world, not how we organize or structure the *world*. We must be careful to distinguish the imposition of order on *experience* by way of language from the imposition of order on *the world* by way of language. In particular, we must not say things like: "different languages differently 'segment' the same situation or experience".[15] This is a risible conflation. A situation is not an experience; at most, a situation is something an experience may be of.

It is plausible to claim that our language plays a central role in organizing and structuring experience although I think it would be easy to overplay the role of language here. It would also, therefore, be plausible to claim that language plays a central role in the construction of the theories we develop about the world. But neither of these claims comes anywhere near to entailing that language plays a central role in organizing or structuring the world, or that it plays a pivotal role in the construction of the world. The world does not consist of experience and theories. Therefore, to structure or even construct experience or theories is not to structure or construct the world.

We can express the same point in terms of the distinction between imposition and restriction introduced in the previous section. Language may play an important role in *imposing* a certain organization or structure on experience. And, in virtue of its structure or organization, experience might selectively filter out or neglect certain features of the world. That is, experience, in virtue of its structure or organization, might *restrict* which properties of the world we can experience (or even think about). That is, *imposition* of language upon experience might yield some *restriction* on the experienced or represented properties of the world (note *experienced properties* of the world, not *properties* of the world). Or, in more Kantian mode, imposition of language on experience might yield some restriction on which real properties of the world can count as phenomenal. But imposition of language upon experience is not equivalent to, and does not in any way entail, imposition of language on the world.

The point can be developed in terms of a concept closely related to that of restriction: *revelation*. When certain properties or features of the world are excluded from experience by the very structure or *form* of that experience (whether this is imposed by language, as Whorf would have it, or by faculties of intuition and understanding, as in the classical Kantian version), then this means that the world is revealed in one way rather than another. It is revealed in terms of those of its features that are not excluded by the structure of experience. Therefore, restriction of the experienced properties of the world, a restriction brought about by the structure or form of experience, is simultaneously a revelation of the world as being one way rather than another. If experience had a different structure, so the thought goes, then the world might be revealed in a quite distinct way.

41

However, *revealing* the world in one way rather than another is very different from *constructing* the world in one way rather than another. Revelation consists in the uncovering of features that are antecedently there, independently of the act of revelation. Construction consists in the creation of features that are, precisely, *not* there independently of the act of construction.

Therefore, the failure of the Sapir–Whorf hypothesis results, ultimately, from a simple confusion of *construction* and *revelation*. Our language may play a role in structuring – and so, in a loose sense, constructing – our experience. At least, it can be said to play such a role so long as we are careful to remember that construction in this context amounts to nothing more than structuring or organizing and *not* the sense of providing the raw materials. And in virtue of the role language plays in constructing our experience, it may also play a role in revealing the world to be one way rather than another. But construction of experience is not construction of the world; at most it is revelation of the world. To reveal a portion of the world, say an object, as being one way rather than another is simply to represent it by way of various properties that it has independently of the structuring activities of mind or language. In short, language may indeed, to an extent, structure our experience and so help bring about a certain way of revealing the world. But it is only if we make the inane mistake of confusing structuring of experience with structuring of the world that we end up with any sort of idealist conclusion. Unfortunately, some inane mistakes can be extremely pervasive and influential.

Structuralism and post-structuralism

Another extremely influential form of neo-Kantian linguistic idealism can be found in the work of structuralists and post-structuralists. Structuralism derives from the linguistics of Ferdinand Saussure and central to his linguistics is the idea that language is constituted by its *internal relations*.

Any language can be analysed or described at several different levels: phonetic, morphological, syntactic and semantic. Consider the phonetic level. Sound types, for example, the hard "t" in "hut" and "tag", are called *phonemes*. This particular phoneme would commonly be represented by way of the notation /t/. It is natural to suppose that sound types are divided into phonemes by way of their *acoustic* properties: the physical properties of the compression wave that produces them. But Saussure argues, convincingly, that this is not correct. Crucially, the phonetic environment of a sound affects the way it is pronounced and hence its acoustic properties. For example, /t/ pronounced at the end of a word is acoustically quite distinct from /t/ pronounced in the middle of a word.

The acoustic properties of a given phoneme can vary, within certain limits, depending on the phonemic context in which it occurs. One of the central claims of Saussure's linguistics is that the limits of allowable variation are determined by nothing other than the linguistic system itself. Consider one example. In English, some consonants are *voiced*. This means that their pronunciation involves the rapid expulsion of air past the vocal chords and, consequently, rapid vibration of the vocal chords. In English, the phoneme /d/ is voiced, but /t/ is not. Thus, in English /d/ and /t/ are considered distinct phonemes. That is, the difference between /d/ and /t/ is said to be *marked*. However, not every language marks the same distinctions and there can also be significant dialectal variation. The distinction between /d/ and /t/, for example, is far less noticeable in many North American dialects of English. And many Asian languages do not mark the distinction between /l/ and /r/. Therefore, in order for differences between acoustic properties of phoneme tokens to amount to a difference in the type to which those phonemes belong, these differences must be marked. And, according to Saussure, whether or not an acoustic difference is marked is determined by the linguistic system itself. The type to which a phoneme token belongs is determined by the linguistic system in which that phoneme token occurs.

This idea underpins what is known as *binary feature analysis*. Any given phoneme can be analysed as a cluster of articulatory features. These will include: voice – whether or not the pronunciation involves vibrating or non-vibrating vocal chords; nasality – whether or not the phoneme is uttered with open or closed nasal passage; tongue position – whether the utterance involves the tongue being placed at front or back of mouth, and upper or lower mouth; lip orientation – whether the utterance involves round or non-round lips; and so on. These features are binary in that they are either present or they are not. The significance of a given binary feature, present or not present in an utterance, is determined, according to Saussure, by the linguistic system itself. It is this system that determines which features are to be emphasized and which are to be ignored. Thus, at the level of dialect, round versus non-round lips is a difference that is marked in standard English but not in a number of North American dialects.[16] Therefore, according to Saussure, it is the linguistic system itself that determines which articulatory features are relevant to the identity of phonemes.

Structuralism extends this idea to *all* linguistic categories: phonetic, morphological, syntactic and semantic. The contribution each item makes to the larger linguistic structures in which it figures is determined by its differences from other items in the linguistic system. Or, as Saussure puts it, "each linguistic term derives its value from its opposition to all other terms".[17] Any linguistic item is defined not by what it is in itself but by the relation it bears to a structure.

Consider, for example, the semantic level. A central claim (some might say dogma) of structuralism is that the meaning of a lexical item, such as a word, is constituted by the totality of what Saussure calls its *syntagmatic* and *paradigmatic* relations. A syntagmatic relation is one that a word bears to another where the former can be combined with the latter to form a syntactically correct sentence or sentence part. The relation between "Jesus" and "wept" is, thus, syntagmatic, since the two words can be combined to form a grammatically correct string of words, known as a syntagm. Paradigmatic relations, on the other hand, are those that a lexical item bears to another that could be substituted for it in a syntagm. So, "Jesus" and "Peter" stand in a paradigmatic relation to each other, since the latter could be substituted for the former to yield a distinct syntagm (i.e. "Peter wept").

According to structuralism, the meaning of any given lexical item is determined by *all* of that item's syntagmatic and paradigmatic relations. Indeed, not only does the totality of these relations constitute the meaning of a word, but they also *exhaust* the meaning of that word. There is nothing more to the meaning of a word than the syntagmatic and paradigmatic relations it enters into with other words. This is, in effect, a radically holistic view of language. The meaning of any term in a language is defined by its place in the entire structure of syntagmatic and paradigmatic relations into which it enters. Moreover, since lexical items such as words are typically individuated according to their semantic properties (a method of individuation, for example, according to which "bank" in the sense of "place where you put your money" is a distinct lexical item from "bank" in the sense of "place beside a river"), this means that the identity of any given word also depends on its place in this structure. If we change the structure of syntagmatic and paradigmatic relations surrounding a lexical item, even marginally, we not only change the meaning of that item, but also change the identity of the item. Not only does the term have a distinct meaning, but it is not even the same term.

A corollary of this syntactic and semantic holism is the claim that language can be understood, even at the semantic level, independently of its relation to the world. There is an analogy used by Saussure, and eagerly seized upon by many followers, that provides a graphic illustration of this claim. The analogy is with chess. Saussure writes:

> In chess, what is external can be separated relatively easily from what is internal . . . everything having to do with its system and rules is internal.[18]

> But just as the game of chess is entirely in the combination of the different chesspieces, language is characterized as a system based entirely on the opposition of its concrete units.[19]

Chess is defined by its internal relations, and is, in this sense, autonomous of the world outside it. The ways in which each piece can move, for example, are arbitrary and determined by, and only by, the internal rules of the game. And the various game-defining and game-deciding situations such as check and checkmate are defined only within the rules of the game. Structuralism is committed to an essentially similar view of the functioning of language at all its levels. The identity of any property of a linguistic system – phonetic, morphological, syntactic, and even semantic – is constituted within the system itself. Its identity does not, in any way, depend on anything external to that system.

Structuralism is not a marginal or recherché doctrine, but dominated much twentieth-century intellectual enquiry and, to a considerable extent, continues to do so today. The structuralist approach was adopted in linguistics and linguistic anthropology (indeed, Sapir and Whorf are commonly regarded as structuralists), social theory, psychology, psycho-analysis, literary criticism, philosophy, the history of ideas and much else besides. This structuralizing of, essentially, *everything* involved such key figures as Claude Lévi-Strauss, Louis Althusser, Jacques Lacan, Roland Barthes and many more. In each of its applications the guiding idea was the same. The meaning and identity of an item – word, cultural practice, psychoanalytical symbol and so on – is constituted by its internal relations: by its relations to other items of the same sort. The meaning and identity of a cultural practice, for example, is to be explained only by appeal to its place in a system of other practices, and not in terms of relations to anything external (such as the world at large).

Indeed, as structuralism developed, and gradually mutated into what is known as post-structuralism, the very idea of there being something outside the system of internal relations, something outside a meaning-giving, identity-constituting structure, was increasingly thrown into question. "There is nothing outside the text," Jacques Derrida, probably the most influential post-structuralist, tells us. Everything is text, everything is defined by its internal relations, even items belonging to what we naively think of as the world at large.

What is common to both structuralism and post-structuralism is what we might call a certain *forgetting of the world*. Consider again Saussure's analogy with chess. This, I think, is a stunningly bad analogy for understanding the nature of language. Why? Because it simply overlooks the fact that words, at least some of them, can gain their meaning through referring to things outside them. That is, the meanings of words are constituted, at least in part, by their *external relations*. Perhaps "overlooks" is a little harsh. Structuralists are quite aware of the idea that meaning is constituted by external relations; they simply reject this idea. Thus, in an influential textbook on structuralism, we are told: "The word 'dog' exists and functions within the structure of the English Language, without reference to any four-legged barking creature's real existence."[20] So the question is whether structuralists have ever given us good reason to believe this somewhat counter-intuitive view. And proponents of structuralism are, to say the least, not very explicit on the matter. Usually, however, the idea of the *arbitrariness of the sign* is wheeled out at this juncture. Thus, in another influential book on structuralism, we are told that structuralism:

> strikes down ... the apprehension of language as names and naming. There can no longer be any question of such an intrinsic relationship once the utterly arbitrary character of language has been made clear.[21]

And the way in which structuralists typically move directly from arbitrariness to their internal relational view is exhibited in another influential introduction to Saussure.

> The fact that the sign is arbitrary ... means that [it] require[s] ahistorical analysis ... Since the sign has no necessary core which must persist, it must be defined as a relational entity, in its relation to other signs.[22]

The thought that should immediately cry out to one here is this: how can the arbitrariness of the sign possibly have anything to do with, let alone undermine, reference? Most signs, and certainly all *linguistic* signs, are, of course, arbitrary. No one denies this. But all this shows is that, for any particular sign, S, another sign *could* have been used to refer to the object S in fact refers to. So the connection between "dog" and dogs is arbitrary in this sense. We could have used the syntactic form "cat" to refer to dogs. But this in no way shows that we in fact do not use the word "dog" to refer to dogs, or that the meaning of the word "dog" does not, in fact, derive from its relation to dogs. That we could have used another sign to do the work of "dog" in no way shows that the word does not do the (referential) work we take it to do. The logical confusion – a confusion of "could" and "does" – exhibited here is, to say the least, staggering.

So, once again, what does arbitrariness have to do with reference? A passage from Hawkes is, I think, particularly revealing.

> The overall characteristic of this relationship is ... arbitrary. There exists no necessary 'fitness' in the link between the sound image, or signifier "tree", the concept, or signified that it involves, and the actual physical tree growing in the earth. The word "tree", in short, has no 'natural' or 'tree-like' qualities.[23]

Perhaps the scales begin to fall from our eyes. Hawkes seems to be presupposing some kind of picture theory of reference, at least this is what his somewhat coded use of "fitness", "natural" and "tree-like" – complete with scare quotes – seem to indicate. But, as everyone who has even the slightest acquaintance with philosophy will realize, no one believes a picture theory of reference, and no one has for a very, very, very long time. In short, the structuralists' rejection of reference rests either on arguments that are stunningly inept or on an ignorance that is inexplicably profound.

With the rejection of reference, however, comes a *forgetting of the world*. Thus, Hawkes tells us, "Language ... allows no single, unitary appeals to a 'reality' beyond itself. In the end, it constitutes its own reality"[24] and "Writing ... can be seen to *cause a new reality to come into being*."[25] Taken literally – and Hawkes gives us no reason for thinking he is writing metaphorically – this claim is absurd. To the extent that structuralists have any arguments in support of this seemingly ridiculous claim, they involve the same tired slide between constitution of experience and constitution of the world that we saw in the Sapir–Whorf hypothesis. Thus, Hawkes tells us:

> Since [language] ... constitutes our characteristic means of encountering and of coping with the world beyond ourselves, then perhaps we can say that it constitutes the characteristic human structure. From there, it is only a small step to the argument that perhaps it constitutes the characteristic structure of human reality.[26]

A small step for Hawkes, perhaps, but a giant leap for anyone on even nodding terms with principles of rational inference. It is one thing to constitute (i.e. organize and/or structure) experience of the world; it is quite another to constitute the world itself. Indeed, it is at this point that the structuralists' intellectual debt to Kant is most evident. Structuralism is, despite its pretensions to originality, nothing more than a form of neo-Kantian idealism. The world we know is one created, constructed and so on by our language. This is essentially Kant's phenomenal world but the job of construction has been taken over by language instead of forms of sensibility and categories of understanding. Some structuralists even make room for something akin to Kant's noumenal world. Thus, Jameson writes:

> All the structuralists; Levi-Strauss with his idea of nature, Barthes with his feeling for social and ideological materials, Althusser with his sense of history, *do* tend to presuppose, beyond the sign-system itself, some kind of ultimate reality which, unknowable or not, serves as its most distant object of reference.[27]

The end result is that this real world becomes something that cannot even be talked about, any passing references to it necessarily accompanied by scare quotes. Or, as Jameson puts it, "a formless chaos of which one cannot even speak in the first place".[28] This is the same tired old neo-Kantianism we found in Sapir and Whorf's anthropology. This is the *forgetting of the world* characteristic of twentieth-century thought.

Neo-Kantian philosophy of science

Some of the most influential twentieth-century philosophy of science carries on the same neo-Kantian themes. In the work of so-called *radical* philosophers of science such as Thomas Kuhn and Paul Feyerabend, we find arguments paralleling those that inform Sapir–Whorf anthropology and structuralist linguistics.[29] That is, here too we find a semantic thesis – a thesis about how the theoretical terms of the natural sciences gain their meaning – gradually, through various bad arguments and other forms of logical slippage, becoming transformed into a metaphysical thesis about the nature of the world.

To see how this process of logical slippage unfolds, we can begin with what was, at least prior to Kuhn and Feyerabend, a fairly orthodox conception of how science works. Science is, first and foremost, an empirical study of the world and so theories stand or fall on how well they are able to accommodate the data provided by observation. On some versions, accommodating the data is an essentially accumulationist enterprise: observational data are steadily accumulated, resulting, given the presence of sufficient data, in the formation of theories that can explain gathered data and/or predict further, as yet unobserved, data. This essentially placid process is punctuated only by the occasional episode of theoretical reorganization as theories become more general and/or more precise. Others, influenced by the work of Karl Popper, dispute this accumulationist story, choosing instead to focus on the role of observational data in refuting or falsifying proposed theories. Theory change, on this latter view, is not an elaboration of existing theory but, rather, a replacement of a falsified theory by way of an, as yet, unfalsified alternative.

Nevertheless, both models of science are predicated on the assumption that theory change, whether elaboration or falsification, is made possible by the possession of a *common observation language* in terms of which theoretical rivals can be assessed and evaluated. Observation thus provides the common coin in terms of which theoretical alternatives must, ultimately, be cashed out. It is this assumption that provides the port of entry for the radical philosophers of science.

Kuhn and Feyerabend deny that observation can provide the common coin in terms of which theoretical alternatives can be evaluated. First, they point out that it is not observation *per se* that allows us to adjudicate between theories, but observation only under one or another *description*. That is, when adjudicating between theories we must compare and contrast statements of what the theories predict will happen in the world in given circumstances with statements about what actually does happen in the world in those circumstances. On the traditional view, these observation statements are *epistemically* prior to theories in that they can be used to judge, and even settle the fate of, theories, and *semantically* prior to the statements of theory in that the latter can, in principle, be defined in terms of observation statements.

Kuhn and Feyerabend deny that observation language can be epistemically and semantically prior to theory in this way. Competing theories do not share a neutral observation language. Rather, statements of observation implicitly presuppose various background theoretical structures and assumptions, ones that they garner from the very theories they are, on the traditional conception of science, supposed to adjudicate. Thus, in many of the most important episodes in the history of science, we have a clash between two comprehensive theories, neither of which possesses a neutral observation language. In such situations, according to Kuhn and Feyerabend, the competitors cannot even be compared. The theories are, as Kuhn put it, *incommensurable*.

This would be a striking conclusion if it were proved correct. However, it seems to rest on a series of bad arguments. In particular, it seems to rest on a misguided view of how the terms within a theory acquire their meaning. We have, in fact, encountered this view already; it is essentially the structuralist view applied to the semantics of lexical items within a scientific theory. According to Kuhn, each theory is a complex intellectual and practical structure, a structure that, in effect, creates its own language.

The meaning of a theoretical term is defined by its place in this structure. Consider, for example, the term "electron". In classical (i.e. pre-quantum) mechanics, electrons were regarded as point particles of negative charge, circling an atomic nucleus made of (typically) positively charged protons and neutral neutrons. In classical mechanics, these sorts of descriptions, Kuhn argues, collectively determine the meaning of the term "electron". Quantum mechanics, however, gives us a very different account of electrons. Sometimes they act as waves, sometimes as particles, sometimes they seem to disobey laws (e.g. first law of thermodynamics) that classical electrons were constrained to obey. But, according to Kuhn, within quantum theory these sorts of descriptions collectively determine the meaning of the term "electron". Therefore, the meaning of the term "electron" varies across these theories.

Because of this variation in meaning from one theory to another, Kuhn, Feyerabend and their followers think that comprehensive theories cannot be compared in ways presupposed by the orthodox conception of science. Each theoretical term is defined by its place in a structure: a theoretical–practical complex or paradigm. The meaning of theoretical terms, that is, is determined only *within* a theory. Because there are no meanings or concepts that exist *across* competing theories, there can be no logical relations, including relations of entailment, consistency and inconsistency, between these theories. Therefore, one theory cannot be reduced to another, for reduction requires that statements of one theory entail those of the other. Nor can one theory refute another, since this would require, at minimum, that the two theories be inconsistent. Nor can the theories be adjudicated by way of a neutral observation language, for the observation statements employed in such adjudication would have to employ terms that acquired their meanings independently of the theories in which they are, according to Kuhn, embedded.

The first point to note about this argument is that it rests on an essentially structuralist rendering of the semantics of theoretical terms. They are defined by way of their place in a theoretical–practical system or structure. In this vein, Kuhn and Feyerabend adopt a *description theory of reference*. The term "electron" refers to whatever satisfies the descriptions associated with electrons. Since these descriptions vary across classical and quantum dynamics, so too must the reference of the term vary between these theories. And presumably reference failure occurs in at least one of these cases. Thus, the meaning of the term "electron" derives from the descriptions that, within a given theory, are associated with it. It does not derive from any extra-theoretical item to which the term, allegedly, refers. Thus, like Saussure, Kuhn and Feyerabend would deny that the meaning of a theoretical term such as "electron" has, in the final analysis, anything to

50

do with the fact that it refers to something outside the theory. The meaning of the term is constituted by its *internal relations*.

The serious inadequacies of description-based accounts of theoretical terms have been detailed elsewhere.[30] But, for the sake of argument, let us grant Kuhn and Feyerabend their semantic thesis. Does anything follow from this about the nature of reality? Kuhn, at many points, seems to suggest that it does. Consider the following passage from Kuhn's *The Structure of Scientific Revolutions*.

> At the very least, as a result of discovering oxygen, Lavoisier saw nature differently. And in the absence of some recourse to that hypothetical fixed nature that he "saw differently", the principle of economy will urge us to say that after discovering oxygen Lavoisier worked in a different world.[31]

Here Kuhn acknowledges the distinction between claiming that we see and understand the world differently as a result of theory change and claiming that the world is, in fact, different as a result of such change. But, then, *he still goes on to claim that the world is different*![32] This is the same mistake as that made by Sapir and Whorf and by the structuralists: a slide from the claim that different theories (languages) impose different structures or organizations on our experience – causing us to see the world differently – to the claim that they impose different structures on the world – causing the world to actually be different. But this slide is unsupported by anything Kuhn and his followers have ever said.

What seems to underlie Kuhn's claim here is the idea expressed in the phrase "And in the absence of some recourse to that hypothetical fixed nature". That is, the argument seems to be something like this. Our theories impose a certain structure or organization on our experience. We can never get outside this structure and get at the world as it is "in itself". Therefore, we should not talk about or even consider this world. Therefore, a change of theory brings about, via the change in the structure of experience it imposes on us, a change in the nature of the world.

If this is a correct reconstruction of Kuhn's "argument", then it is clear that it follows the same tired neo-Kantian line. The experience-imposing activities of Kant's forms of intuition and categories of understanding are taken over by Kuhnian *paradigms*. But the underlying theme is the same. The role played by paradigms in structuring our experience leads to scepticism about the world that exists independently of our experience. This leads Kuhn to slide, quite consciously and explicitly, from change in theory to change in world. This, once again, is the *forgetting of the world* instigated by Kant, a forgetting that came to dominate twentieth-century thought.

Philosophy of language

A hard-nosed Anglo-American philosopher might be tempted to suppose that neo-Kantian idealism might afflict only our deluded continental cousins, and philosophers of science unhealthily influenced by them. But, in fact, variants of neo-Kantian idealism have also come to dominate much Anglo-American philosophy. For most of the twentieth century the central philosophical discipline was thought to be philosophy of language. The switch of focus on to linguistic rather than traditional metaphysical disputes, a switch that occurred around the beginning of the twentieth century, was so pronounced that it acquired a name: the *linguistic turn*. Many non-philosophers wonder, quite legitimately, why philosophy became apparently obsessed with language to the extent that it did. But the linguistic turn was no aberration. It was clearly motivated and the roots of this motivation again lie in Kant. Underpinning the linguistic turn is what we might call a certain approach to understanding philosophical problems, an approach that we might call *methodologico-linguistic idealism*.

Methodologico-linguistic idealism consists in the idea that traditional philosophical problems can usefully be reformulated as problems concerning the truth-conditions of sentences. There exists, for example, a traditional dispute concerning the existence of the external world. Traditional metaphysical theses about the status of this world can, broadly speaking, be divided into two camps: *realist* and *idealist*. According to realism, the world exists independently of its being known or represented by subjects. Idealism, on the other hand, denies this, asserting that the world is, to one degree or another, a mind-dependent entity. The *modus operandi* of twentieth-century philosophy of language was to transform a metaphysical dispute of this sort into a dispute about language; specifically a dispute about how we should understand the truth-conditions of sentences that make claims about the external world. Generally, realism/idealism disputes are to be reduced to disputes about how to understand the truth-conditions of a relevant set of sentences.

Michael Dummett, who has done as much to champion this sort of approach as anyone, points out that sentences with realist truth-conditions behave logically quite differently to those with idealist truth-conditions.[33] Significantly, Dummett argues, statements with realist truth-conditions do, whereas statements with idealist truth-conditions do not, obey the principle of *bivalence*: the principle that a proposition be either determinately true or false. And with the rejection of bivalence, statements of idealist truth-conditions are also not subject to the Law of Excluded Middle ($P \vee \sim P$). Adjudicating between realism and idealism about the external world, then, is a matter of adjudicating between the types of truth-conditions appropriate to statements that make claims about the world. And adjudicating between these alternative truth-conditions is a matter of identifying which sets of logical properties (acceptance or rejection of bivalence, etc.) best characterize these sorts of statements.

One glaring question immediately arises: *why think this will help?* In particular, on the face of it, it seems that precisely analogous issues and disputes will arise over the interpretation of truth-conditions for a given group of sentences as initially arose in the form of traditional metaphysical issues and disputes. Dummett's rationale is essentially Kantian.

First of all, Dummett reiterates the Kantian mistrust of *transcendent* metaphysics, where "transcendent" in this case refers to that which, allegedly, transcends, or lies outside of, language. In this vein, Dummett reminds us of the failures of the traditional metaphysical approach to solving philosophical disputes.[34] In 2500 years (and counting) of metaphysical trying, no real progress has been secured. The "moves and counter-moves are already familiar, having been made repeatedly by philosophers on either side throughout the centuries".[35] This, Dummett argues, is evidence of some fundamental shortcoming in the approach itself and suggests the need for a methodologico-linguistic alternative.

Dummett also traces this lack of progress in the metaphysical approach to the status of metaphysical statements. A metaphysical statement such as "The external world exists independently of us" is, in itself, only a metaphor or "a picture which has in itself no substance otherwise than as a representation of a given conception of meaning".[36] Why is this? Dummett's answer is that the statement lacks any empirical content because there are no possible empirical observations that could adjudicate between it and the idealist alternative. No observation of ordinary physical objects will tell us whether they exist independently of our observation of them.[37] Thus, Dummett argues, the statement is only a metaphor, one that must be cashed out by way of a theory of meaning. In the absence of such a theory, we have a metaphysical dispute where no knockout blow can be delivered; a dispute that must be won on points, but where we do not know how to award points.[38]

Therefore, Dummett advocates a form of methodologico-linguistic idealism in general: we solve metaphysical problems by way of solving linguistic problems. Metaphysical disputes are to be solved by linguistic idealism. The motivation for this again lies, ultimately, in Kant. Suppose we accept the general underpinning for the *Kantian turn* in philosophy. That is:

1. Thought – broadly construed to include the operations of the faculties of sensibility and understanding – determines the character of the phenomenal world.

If we accept this claim, then we can study the phenomenal world – as opposed to the unknowable noumenal world – by way of an analysis and dissection of the operations of thought. This, in essence, is the Kantian project. However, we need add only one further premise to get from this to the *linguistic turn*. It is a premise that Dummett explicitly endorses, and that provides the ultimate rationale for the linguistic approach:

2. The structure of language mirrors the structure of thought.[39]

Thus, Dummett tells us that "an analysis of the logical structure of sentences can be converted into a parallel analysis of the structure of thought".[40] Therefore, if we can, as Kant tells us, study the phenomenal world through analysis of thought, broadly construed, then we can accomplish the same thing through the analysis of language. This essentially Kant rationale is what underpins the linguistic turn of the early-twentieth century and the methodology of linguistic idealism upon which it is based.

Conclusion

In a passage entitled "How the 'Real World' at last became a Myth", Friedrich Nietzsche describes a discernible trend towards increasing idealism running through the history of Western philosophy.[41] According to Nietzsche, the roots of this idealism were present as long ago as Plato. Plato equated reality with what can be known to a suitably educated (i.e. educated by him) rational subject and thus established the connection between knowledge and reality that, Nietzsche thought, had come to dominate philosophy. The connection was strengthened by Descartes, who, according to Nietzsche, made being known with certainty by a subject a *criterion* of reality. But, as Nietzsche points out, it was undoubtedly in the hands of Immanuel Kant that this trend towards idealism received its most significant expression.

According to Kant, the world of our everyday experience is a world constructed through the activities of sensibility and understanding: thought, broadly construed. More recent imitators of Kant have replaced the operations of the faculties of sensibility and understanding with *language*, *discourse*, *theory* or, more generally, *structure*. The world, at least the world of which we can meaningfully speak, the world that does not have to be put into "scare quotes" when we attempt to talk about it, is a world that is constituted by human beings, either directly or via their structural products.

We live in an age of Kantian and neo-Kantian idealism. The *forgetting of the world* characteristic of neo-Kantian idealism constituted, in many ways, the intellectual *Zeitgeist* of the twentieth century. The Kantian turn, in various forms, has come to dominate philosophy, philosophy of science, linguistics, psychology, psychoanalysis, anthropology, sociology and literary theory, to name but a few. Its hegemony transcends national, cultural and ideological boundaries. And it is all predicated upon, and made possible by, the view of the mind as an interiority that is characteristic of Cartesian internalism. It is because, and only because, we dichotomize mind and world in the manner prescribed by internalism that we get a matching problem. And without the problem there is no need of a solution, idealist or otherwise. One only has to look at the excesses of recent neo-Kantian idealism to realize that internalism is a position with blood on its hands.

CHAPTER 4

The "radical reversal" of idealism

An influential combination of Cartesianism and idealism is to be found in the phenomenology of Edmund Husserl. However, in the work of followers of Husserl we find the roots of what Jean-Paul Sartre, one of those followers, dubs a "radical reversal" of idealism. This radical reversal provides the basis of a very different view of the mind: anti-Cartesian and anti-idealist. Indeed, in this radical reversal of idealism we find what is, in effect, an important source of externalism. This chapter is concerned with Husserlian phenomenology and the radical reversal engendered by it.

The focus for the chapter is provided by Sartre's reinterpretation of Husserlian phenomenology. Readers familiar with the work of Martin Heidegger might think it somewhat strange that I have chosen to ignore his work when it contains so many ideas – particularly the core idea of *dasein* as essentially *being-in-the-world* – that are so obviously amenable to externalist machinations. Sartre, on the other hand, is often taken to be much closer to Husserl, and/or as being far more Cartesian than Heidegger, and thus less suitable to such machinations. Actually, I do not think either of these latter claims is true, and certainly attempts to interpret Sartre as some form of reconstructed Cartesian rest on profound misunderstandings. But I focus on Sartre for a slightly different reason. I am interested not only in the way in which Husserlian phenomenology – essentially a form of transcendental idealism – might spawn a radical version of externalism, but also in the conceptual mechanisms, the sorts of changes required in the central premises of Husserlian phenomenology, that allow this sort of transformation. These issues can, I think, be identified much more clearly and easily in the relation between Husserl and Sartre than in the relation between Husserl and Heidegger.

The "transcendental clue"

Husserl's phenomenology begins with a basic empiricist premise: every item, regardless of its ontological category or kind, becomes accessible to us only through various *phenomena* in which it appears. That is, existing items – objects, events, properties and so on – appear to us in various ways, and our knowledge of such items is obtained by way of these appearances. We know objects, and other items, ultimately, because they appear to us. Suppose now that we understand appearances in a certain, very orthodox, way, as mental occurrences of some sort. Appearances are *experiences* of some sort. When an object, for example, appears to us, it does so by way of certain experiences that it causes us to have, and these experiences are identical with the way the object appears to us. If we combine the claim that objects are known to us only through their appearances, and that appearances are equivalent to experiences, then we quickly arrive at the claim that objects are known only through experiences we have of them. And this is a familiar empiricist idea, one that underwrites Husserlian phenomenology.

The experiences in virtue of which we become aware of an object are not chaotic but ordered. As we move around a physical object, a bottle for example, the visual experiences we have unfold in an ordered manner. Likewise, as we move our eyes up and down the bottle, the experiences change in a way consistent with the presence of a bottle. As our eyes move upwards, the foreground of our visual field narrows, consistent with the narrower neck of the bottle; as they move downwards, the foreground of our visual field expands, consistent with the presence of the wider base and so on. It is because, and only because, our experiences change in this ordered and predictable manner that we have any reason to believe in the presence of a bottle in our visual field.

The content of our visual experience, however, is constituted by more than these straightforward visual impressions. In addition, we have expectations or anticipations concerning how our experiences will change as we change the position or location of our body, as we move our eyes and so on. As we slide our eyes up the bottle, for example, we expect or anticipate the foreground of our visual experience to narrow in a way consistent with the narrower neck of a bottle, and we anticipate that it will expand as we slide our eyes back downwards. As we move around the bottle, we expect that the green label visually present to us now, will become gradually occluded, moving steadily, but predictably, out of our field of view.

These anticipations or expectations are, for Husserl, an essential part of the visual experience of the bottle.[1] And this is true whether or not we know exactly what to anticipate. Suppose the object is a mysterious one, and our knowledge of it, accordingly, is unclear. This will be reflected in an indecisiveness or imprecision in our anticipations. Indeed, not only is our lack of knowledge reflected in such imprecision, but it is, according to Husserl, *constituted* by such imprecision. The content of our visual experience is, to this extent, vague. Nevertheless, despite this uncertainty or imprecision in our anticipations, we will, necessarily, have *some* anticipations. We would be able to anticipate at least the form of the experiences that would follow contingent upon our actions. If we look at an object from the front, for example, we may have no idea whatsoever what the back of that object looks like. What we will anticipate, however, is that it *has* a back: that if we move to the other side of the object we will see *something*, something that coheres, in one way or another, with the experiences we had while at the front of the object. These anticipations, no matter how vague or indeterminate, cannot be missing from the perception of an object. Indeed, such anticipations enter into the content of the perceptual experiences we have of that object.[2] Thus each appearance of the object – each experience in virtue of which the object is revealed to us – as Husserl puts it, *refers* to further appearances: to further experiences contingent on the performance of certain acts or on the occurrence of certain events.

Suppose, for example, we are looking at the front of what we take to be a house. This will, in Husserl's terms, refer us to further experiences. That is, we will have various expectations about the further experiences we will have if we do certain things. If we open the front door, for example, we expect that we will have a visual experience of a room of some sort. These expectations are, for Husserl, partly constitutive of the content of our visual experience of the house. However, suppose we open the front door, and our expectations are confounded. We find no room. What we thought was a house is, in fact, a house-façade. This is itself a new experience, and as such refers us to further experiences. We might now, for example, suspect that we have wandered into a film set, and thus expect, upon appropriate investigation, to discover (i.e. have experiences of) film-making paraphernalia of some sort.

Because one experience, E, necessarily refers us to others, the expectations bound up in such reference being partly constitutive of the content of E, experiences form a *structure* or *hierarchy*.[3] Each experience points to other experiences, ones whose occurrence will confirm the former, or whose failure to occur will disconfirm the former, where such failure directs us to a distinct experiential hierarchy. In this sense, experiences support each other. Accordingly, the experiences form a system that has a well-determined structure of its own and is regulated by a *principle of unity*. The idea of a unified object existing independently of experience emerges from this systematic network of mutually referring, hence supporting, experiences. That is, the unity of the object is, as Husserl puts it, a *correlate* of this unity of experience.

Beginning with the idea that an object can be known only through its appearances, and with the identification of appearances with experiences, we are led smoothly to the idea of the object as a *correlate of consciousness*. The unity of an object is reflected in the unity of the system of experiences of that object. Accordingly, the object is a "transcendental clue" to the character of consciousness.[4] That is, we study consciousness by studying the contribution it makes to the unity of objects since, beginning with the object, we have been led regressively to its equivalent in consciousness. That is, in connection with our experience of a unified object: (i) we study the particular experiences that belong to the experiential system in question; (ii) we make explicit whatever these experiences imply; (iii) we establish the connections between these experiences; (iv) we attempt to penetrate the nature and structure of the system they form; and (v) we attempt to identify the elements on which the unity of the object depends.[5] To engage in this sort of analysis is, as Husserl puts it, to *disclose the phenomenological constitution of the object for consciousness*. In such disclosure, we focus not so much on what the experience is in itself but, rather, in the role it plays in making the *synthetic unity* of the object possible. That is, the experiences should be viewed in terms of the places they occupy, hence the roles they play, in the experiential system that they form, because the role they play in the experiential system they form is, precisely, the contribution they make to the constitution of the object. To understand experiences in this way is to understand them not empirically – that is, as objects of inner sense or awareness – but *transcendentally*: as necessary conditions for the nature, unity and hence existence of the object that they collectively constitute.

Cartesianism and idealism in Husserl

In Husserl's phenomenology, we find a position that is clearly both Cartesian and idealist. As we shall see, it is difficult to divorce the idea that the world is a correlate of consciousness from either of these views. Attempts to distance Husserl from Cartesianism and/or idealism typically advert to the fact, in itself quite correct, that when Husserl talks of the constitution of the object by way of mental acts or experience, these should not be taken in their traditional senses. We can distinguish between *empirical* and *transcendental* senses of experience. Understood empirically, "experience" refers to those objects of inner sense that one might encounter when one introspects or, so to speak, "turns one's attention inwards". In introspection, one encounters a collection of conscious states that possess various properties. One might, for example, encounter a thought that has the property of being perplexing, a desire that has the property of being troubling and so on. Experiences, as empirical items, are objects of awareness. However, Husserl's interest lies in experiences in what we can call their *transcendental* role: that is, in the role they play in constituting the unity, hence existence, of objects. As such, experiences are not objects of awareness but items that *constitute* objects of awareness, or in virtue of which objects of awareness can exist. One might argue that traditional Cartesianism involves the idea that the mind is constituted by mental items understood empirically, and that traditional idealism involves the idea that the world consists in these sorts of empirical mental items. And this claim may, largely, be true.

Nevertheless, within the framework of Husserl's thought, it would be easy to make too much of this distinction. One of the central presuppositions of Husserlian phenomenology is that it is possible to become aware of experiences in their transcendental role. That is, it is possible to become aware of the various acts of consciousness that constitute the appearance of objects. And this means that, for Husserl, it is possible to make the transcendental role of experience into an empirical item – an object of empirical, specifically phenomenological, enquiry. The same experience, that is, can occur in both empirical and transcendental contexts. Without this assumption, Husserlian phenomenology would make little sense.

Bearing this complication in mind, the question is: to what extent is Husserl's position Cartesian and/or idealist? Husserl is, of course, quite clear that any object is a *correlate* of consciousness. But what, precisely, does this mean? In claiming that the world is a correlate of consciousness, Husserl is best interpreted as endorsing claims of what we can call *logical* and *methodological* idealism. Consider, for example, the idealism of Berkeley. Berkeley's idealism is usually interpreted as an assertion of *fact*. That is, Berkeley claimed that the external world is, in fact, composed of a collection of mental entities or *ideas*. This claim we might call an assertion of *factual* idealism: a claim about how the world, in fact, is.[6] Husserl, however, was not interested in any claim concerning what the world is, in fact, composed of. That is, whether or not the external world is, as a matter of fact, physical, is a question that is of little concern to Husserl. Questions such as this must, as he put it, be *bracketed*. However, he does believe that consciousness – experience in both empirical and transcendental roles – is *logically* prior to the physical world. Consequently, he also believes that an investigation of the structure of consciousness is *methodologically* prior to an investigation of the physical world.

Logical idealism, the view that consciousness is logically prior to the world, is best understood in terms of a claim of *asymmetric dependence*: the physical world is logically dependent for its existence and nature on consciousness but consciousness is not similarly logically dependent on the physical world. Husserl, in Cartesian fashion, cashes out the notion of logical dependence in terms of the notion of conceivability. It is impossible to conceive of the physical world existing without consciousness.

> It must be borne in mind that *whatever physical things are* – the only physical things about which we can make statements . . . *are as experienceable physical things* . . .
>
> As a consequence, one must not let oneself be deceived by speaking of the physical thing as transcending consciousness or as "existing in itself". The genuine concept of the transcendence of something physical . . . can itself be derived only from the proper essential contents of perception or from those concatenations of definite kinds which we call demonstrative experience.[7]

This, in effect, is Kantian transcendental idealism without noumena. Whereas for Kant, phenomena, experienceable things, are ultimately grounded in a noumenal reality, a reality of non-experienceable things, Husserl denies that phenomena require such grounding. There may or may not exist a transcendent, noumenal world, but if there is one we can neither know nor say anything at all about it. The physical world of which we can speak is not a transcendent world but one that must be understood in terms of actual and possible experiences. As such, it cannot exist independently of consciousness.

This is not to say that, for Husserl, a physical object is to be *identified* with a set of actual or possible experiences. An object transcends each individual experience of the set of experiences of which it is the correlate. This is so for the obvious reason that, as we have seen, the content of any one experience is intimately tangled up with anticipations and expectations of the way in which subsequent experience will unfold contingent upon certain occurrences, whether performed by the subject of consciousness or simply occurring to or around that subject. Thus, each experience is bound up with, or refers to, other experiences, and the existence and unity of the object is bound up with the unity of this structured set of experiences. On the other hand, Husserl argues that the object cannot be identified with the set or totality of experiences with which it is correlated, for these experiences comprise a multiplicity of distinct, if related, items and the object is a unified entity. A unity cannot be identical with a multiplicity.[8]

Nevertheless, while a physical object can, for Husserl, be identified neither with any individual experience nor with a structured set of such experiences, it is clear that Husserl regards physical objects as logical constructions out of such experiences. The reason for this is that, as the above passage makes clear, the distinction between appearance and reality is one that can be drawn only from *within* experience. Therefore, the only sense in which we can talk of a physical object existing "in itself" is a sense that is constituted by two different types of experience. As such, physical objects can be nothing other than logical constructions out of experience.

Husserl's distinction between appearance and reality is based on the idea that we can distinguish the subjective appearance of an object from the true reality of the object. However, this "true reality" is a further type of appearance: an appearance that takes the form of experiences with a certain structure. An individual appearance is, admittedly, subjective but it is also possible to integrate that experience into a structured whole: a hierarchically ordered set of further appearances. Such integration, or the possibility of such integration, reveals the individual appearance to be one-sided and partial, one that corresponds to a certain point of view or is obtained by way of a special orientation. As such, it is an experience subject to completion. And this, for Husserl, is the hallmark of subjective appearance as opposed to reality. When we talk of the reality of an object, we are, according to Husserl, adverting to the fact that the experience we have of the object can be slotted into a hierarchically structured set of further experiences (sensory, anticipatory, etc.), where this set is made up of a possibly infinite, or at least indefinite, number of experiences. In short, the distinction between appearance and reality is reduced to the distinction between a single experience and an indefinitely large, hierarchically ordered set of experiences. Thus, reality is constituted by a certain type of experience and the distinction between appearance and reality is, accordingly, drawn from within experience. Consequently, the existence of any object whatsoever is necessarily linked to the possibility of a subject's having quite determinate experiences under certain conditions (conditions that, perhaps, cannot be fulfilled). And, in this sense, objects are, for Husserl, logical constructions out of experiences. Therefore, objects are dependent upon consciousness for their existence.

Consciousness, however, is not similarly dependent upon physical objects for its existence. This claim is particularly evident in §49 of *Ideas*, where Husserl identifies "absolute consciousness as the residuum after the annihilation of the world". Suppose, as experiences unfold, we encounter vast numbers of contradictions, incoherencies, incompatibilities and the like.

We are unable to harmonize these and, as a result, no world of objects could be constituted. In such a situation, Husserl claims, "there might no longer be any world". Such circumstances, however, would not entail the end of consciousness but, at most, a modification of it. The existence of consciousness, Husserl claims, would be untouched by such an eventuality. Therefore, Husserl concludes, although the physical world *qua* constituted (and, as we have seen, we cannot talk of any other way it might be), may require the existence of an actual or possible consciousness, since its existence is only an existence for the consciousness constitutive of it, consciousness itself is not similarly dependent on the world for its existence. The existence of consciousness is an absolute, rather than relative, phenomenon.

> Immanental being is therefore indubitably absolute being in the sense that by essential necessity immanental being *nulla "re" indiget ad existendum*.
> In contradistinction, the world of transcendent "res" is entirely referred to consciousness and, more particularly, not to some logically conceived consciousness but to actual consciousness.[9]

In short, Husserl's position is a form of logical idealism, in the sense characterized above. The existence of consciousness, or "immanental being" is absolute. Consciousness does not depend on anything other than itself for its existence. The existence of the world, on the other hand, is relative rather than absolute. The world depends for its existence on the constituting activity of consciousness, that is, on consciousness in its transcendental role. Consciousness is, thus, primary, and the world is derivative.

Husserl's claim that consciousness is absolute also illustrates the extent to which his position is Cartesian. To claim that consciousness is absolute is to claim that it is capable of existence independently of anything else, in particular, independently of the world that it constitutes (and that is, therefore, a relative existence). While the constituted world may occasion certain "modifications" in consciousness, these are an entirely contingent matter and do not affect consciousness as it is in its essential nature. The claim that consciousness is logically independent of the world in this way is a straightforward statement of the Cartesian conception.

Sartre's radical reversal of idealism

Husserl's view is a working out of what he sees as the implications for the relation between consciousness and the world of what he takes to be the essential feature of consciousness: intentionality. Consciousness is intentional in that it is, in its essence, directed towards objects. Husserl takes the implication of this to be that these objects are ones essentially constituted by consciousness. Sartre points out, however, that this implication does not follow. Instead, there are two possibilities.

> All consciousness is consciousness *of* something. This definition ... can be taken in two very distinct senses: either we understand by this that consciousness is constitutive of the being of its object, or it means that consciousness in its inmost nature is a relation to a transcendent being. But the first interpretation destroys itself: to be conscious *of* something is to be confronted with a concrete and full presence which is *not* consciousness.[10]

Husserl takes the first option. Sartre, however, opts for the second. "Consciousness cannot construct the transcendent by objectivising elements borrowed from its subjectivity."[11] In this, we have the basis of what Sartre refers to as his "radical reversal of idealism".

The key to understanding Sartre's adoption of the second option – the claim that the intentional objects of consciousness are transcendent, or non-mental, entities – lies in his assertion that *consciousness has no content*.

> All consciousness, as Husserl has shown, is consciousness *of* something. This means that there is no consciousness which is not a *positing* of a transcendent object, or if you prefer, that consciousness has no "content". . . . All consciousness is positional in that it transcends itself in order to reach an object, and it exhausts itself in this same positing.[12]

However, while Husserl would accept this doctrine of intentionality, he has, according to Sartre, failed to appreciate its implications. For Sartre, an entailment of the doctrine of intentionality is that consciousness has no content. Husserl's transcendental method, however, is based on the presupposition that it does. On the one hand, Husserl is clear that the aim of phenomenological enquiry is to identify the features of consciousness in its *transcendental* role – that is, consciousness in its role as (as he sees it) constituter of the world. Thus, in Husserl's transcendental phenomenology, we begin with the object and work from this to the corresponding noetic structures in virtue of which the constitution of the object is disclosed for consciousness. The object, in this way, is a transcendental clue that reveals the object constituting features of consciousness. However, Husserl is also clear that these transcendental features of consciousness are features that, through the employment of the transcendental method, we can bring to awareness. That is, the transcendental method is what allows *transcendental* – object-constituting – features of experience to appear in *empirical* contexts. It allows them to appear as items of which we are aware in the having of an experience. As such, these transcendental features appear as *contents* of consciousness. And it is this possibility that Sartre would deny.

For Sartre, the most important implication of the intentionality of consciousness is that consciousness *has no content*. There are several things Sartre intends to deny by this claim. Most obviously, the intentional objects of consciousness are not, in any way, *in* consciousness. As we shall see, this entails that they are not in any way constituted by consciousness either. However, he means to deny much more than this. According to Sartre, there is *nothing* whatever in consciousness. Consciousness is, precisely, nothingness. Not only are the intentional objects of consciousness not in consciousness, but also there are no *representations* of these objects. For example, with regard to mental images, one of the traditionally popular construals of mental representations, Sartre writes:

> We [have assumed] that the image was *in* consciousness ... We pictured consciousness as a place peopled with small likenesses and these likenesses were the images ... This [I] shall call the *illusion of immanence* ... when I "have an image" of Peter ... [I have a] picture of Peter in my consciousness ... [this picture being] the object of my actual consciousness.[13]

There are, according to Sartre, no mental images in consciousness, nor are there ideas or representations of any sort. Rather, consciousness is pure emptiness: it exists only as directedness towards things that are other than itself. Consciousness exists as, and only as, directedness towards objects and these objects are, necessarily, not part of consciousness. Indeed, these objects are logically prior to consciousness: "Consciousness is born supported by a being which is not itself. This is what we call the ontological proof."[14]

In his early work, Sartre's arguments for this striking claim tend to focus on the implications of the denial of this claim for the *unity* of consciousness. For example, in *The Psychology of Imagination*, Sartre argues that the presence in consciousness of such items as representations would, in effect, shatter the unity of consciousness. He argues that it would be:

> Impossible to slip these material portraits into a conscious synthetic structure, without breaking the contacts, arresting the flow, breaking the continuity. Consciousness would cease being

transparent to itself; its unity would be broken in every direction by unassimilable, opaque screens.[15]

These remarks are, if you will forgive the pun, less than transparent. However, what Sartre seems to have in mind is the idea that if we suppose that consciousness is populated with representations, then we have awkward questions to answer about the effects of these representations on the unity of consciousness. For example, ordinary pictures occlude each other from view. Therefore, if the representations are pictorial would they similarly occlude each other? If so, then the transparency of consciousness is lost. And since Sartre thinks the unity of consciousness is bound up with its transparency, its unity would be lost too: it would dissolve into a diverse collection of pictures.

This argument may be thought less than convincing on a variety of counts. In particular, it seems to presuppose that the claim that representations are among the contents of consciousness entails that there is a representer to whom the representations are represented. Without this, issues of occlusion and so on would not arise. Most representational accounts of the mind would, now, deny this claim. While representational accounts may have been devised against an implicit background of the idea of the inner representer, it is not clear that they logically entail such a view.

By the time he wrote *Being and Nothingness*, however, Sartre was advocating a quite different defence of the claim that consciousness is devoid of content. Here, his argument begins with the claim that consciousness cannot be *identified* with its objects, even when those objects are conscious states.

> Thus consciousness (of) belief and belief are one and the same being, the characteristic of which is absolute immanence. But as soon as we wish to grasp this being, it slips between our fingers, and we find ourselves faced with a pattern of duality, with a game of reflections. For consciousness is a reflection (*reflet*), but *qua* reflection it is exactly the one reflecting (*réfléchissant*), and if we attempt to grasp it as reflecting, it vanishes and we fall back on the reflection.[16]

Consciousness cannot be objectified, made into an object, because whatever consciousness takes as its object, consciousness is also the *taking* of that object as its object. Consciousness is that in virtue of which an object is taken as an object of consciousness. Therefore, it cannot be identified with its object. We can, of course, typically take conscious states as objects of consciousness. We can focus on an experience we are having, for example, identifying its features, delineating its contours and so on. However, this sort of experiential item cannot be *identified* with consciousness because it cannot *exhaust* consciousness. Consciousness is also that in virtue of which this experiential item is taken as an object. Indeed, for some modes of consciousness – which he labels *being-for-others* and *impure reflection* – Sartre would go so far as to claim that consciousness cannot be made an object at all. Underlying this claim is his celebrated dictum that *consciousness is not what it is and is what it is not*. When we try to focus our attention on our consciousness, there is at least one aspect of that consciousness that necessarily evades our focusing – the focusing of attention itself. One aspect of consciousness, that is, always evades our conscious grasp. The result is that consciousness is a "decompression of being"; consciousness is characterized by an essential "fissure". Or, as Sartre more famously expresses it, consciousness is essentially infected with nothingness.

> Nothingness is always an elsewhere. It is the obligation for the for-itself never to exist except in the form of an elsewhere in relation to itself, to exist as a being which perpetually effects in itself a break in being. This break does not refer us elsewhere to another being; it is only a perpetual reference of self to self, of the reflection to the reflecting, of the reflecting to the reflection.[17]

To claim that consciousness cannot be identified with its objects because it cannot be exhausted by them is one thing. However, to claim that these objects are not a proper part of consciousness – not among the contents of consciousness – is quite another. When we focus on an experience, for example, and identify its principal features, Sartre's view is that this experience and its features are no longer even proper parts of consciousness. They are precisely what consciousness is *not*. But this is much stronger than the claim that consciousness is not *exhausted* by its objects. How do we establish the stronger thesis?

It is here that Sartre's acceptance of the intentionality of consciousness is crucial. Consciousness, in its essence, is essentially a directedness towards objects. However, objects of consciousness are not the sort of things that are essentially directed towards objects. And if there are any cases in which objects of consciousness do exhibit such intentionality, this intentionality is derivative; it derives from consciousness understood, as Sartre recommends, as an essential "fissure".

Most objects of consciousness are, of course, not representational. They are either environmental objects and properties or non-representational mental items such as pains, tickles and the like. Environmental objects and properties are, of course, not the sort of things that can have intentional objects. And it is still entirely orthodox to claim that pains, tickles – bodily sensations in general – are not representational, hence not intentional, states.

However, it might be thought that intentional states can be found among the objects of consciousness. Orthodoxy also has it that it is possible to make representational states – perceptual experiences and propositional attitudes – into objects of consciousness. However, Sartre's view is that, when this occurs, such states no longer have intrinsic intentionality or representationality. Suppose, for example, the representational state is pictorial in character. As Wittgenstein and others have pointed out, pictures, even mental ones, are logically merely symbols. That is, a picture can in principle represent, or mean, just about anything. A photograph of a dog, for example, can represent a dog or a mammal, a four-legged creature, a furry creature, a creature with a tail, a creature with a cold nose and so on. In order for the picture to represent or mean anything, it first has to be interpreted. And this is the case with all symbols. A symbol does not bear its meaning, so to speak, on its face. For it to mean something it must represent something, and for it to represent something it must be interpreted. And interpretation is, in the first instance, an act of consciousness.

Objects of consciousness, on Sartre's view, can be nothing more than *symbols*. Often they will not even be this but, at most, this is all they can be. When an item such as a perceptual experience or a thought is made into an object of consciousness, it is thereby made into a symbol, and its intentionality, necessarily, becomes derived intentionality. In order for it to mean or represent anything, it must first be interpreted. Interpretation, however, is an act of consciousness. Thus, the intentionality of *any* object of consciousness – whatever this object is – necessarily derives from the act of consciousness in virtue of which that object is an object of consciousness. A thought that the sky is blue, for example, when taken as an object of consciousness, can be thought of as continuing to represent the fact that the sky is blue, but it can do this only on the basis of a prior act of interpretation on the part of consciousness, understood as that structure of being whereby this experience or thought is taken as an object of consciousness. The intentionality of objects of consciousness is, thus, derived intentionality: intentionality that derives from the act of consciousness in virtue of which those objects are taken as objects of consciousness. Therefore, if intentionality – in an original and underived sense – is definitive of consciousness, as both Husserl and Sartre claim, then, Sartre argues, consciousness must be essentially that in virtue of which objects of various kinds are taken as objects of consciousness, and not those objects themselves. Objects of consciousness, being in themselves non-intentional, must be other than consciousness; they must be what consciousness is *not*. They must, that is, be *transcendent*.

The structure of consciousness that allows it to take items – including thoughts and experiences – as objects is, according to Sartre, *nothingness*. Consciousness is separated from its objects by nothingness, and it is this, and this alone, that allows these objects to become objects of consciousness.

> The structure at the basis of intentionality and of selfness is the negation, which is the internal relation of the For-itself to the thing. The For-itself constitutes itself outside in terms of the thing as the negation of that thing; thus its first-relation with Being-in-itself is negation.[18]

Objects of consciousness such as experiences and thoughts – objects that are standardly taken to be intentional items – have only derived intentionality. Their intentionality derives from an act of interpretation on the part of consciousness understood as an act or directing of awareness. However, a precondition of such interpretation is, phenomenologically speaking, a distance *within* consciousness, a distance between consciousness and its objects.

> We shall best account for the original phenomenon of perception by insisting on the fact that the relation of the quality to us is that of absolute proximity (it "is there," it haunts us) without either giving or refusing itself, but we must add that this proximity implies a distance. It is what is immediately out of reach, what by definition refers us to ourselves as to an emptiness.[19]

This phenomenological distance or gap is what Sartre calls nothingness.

Nothingness, in Sartre's system, is intimately connected with a certain type of self-consciousness that is implicit in consciousness itself. Crucial to Sartre's position are the closely related distinctions between *positional* (or *thetic*) consciousness versus *non-positional* (or *non-thetic*) consciousness, and *reflective* versus *pre-reflective* consciousness. It is sometimes supposed that these distinctions are equivalent. In fact, they cross-classify each other.

For Sartre, every act of consciousness has both a positional and non-positional aspect. Suppose I am looking at a seagull outside my study window. Then my consciousness of the seagull is positional consciousness: the seagull is "posited" as the object of my consciousness. Sartre, as we have seen, claims that consciousness is essentially intentional. Thus, all consciousness is necessarily positional consciousness. However, according to Sartre also, "every positional consciousness of an object is at the same time a non-positional consciousness of itself". [20] This can be explained in terms of the distinction between pre-reflective and reflective consciousness. My positional consciousness of the seagull is, ordinarily, pre-reflective consciousness, where this is understood as consciousness directed towards something other than itself. However, suppose I attempt to focus my attention on my consciousness of the seagull. In this case I have reflective, positional, consciousness of my consciousness of the seagull, and the consciousness that is doing the reflecting remains non-positionally conscious of itself.

Each positional act of consciousness is, therefore, non-positionally aware of itself. No reflection is involved in this mode of non-positional self-consciousness; it is a non-cognitive, non-intentional and crucially non-dyadic mode of self-awareness. Nonetheless, it is a necessary condition of positional consciousness.

> However, the necessary and sufficient condition for a knowing consciousness to be knowledge of its object, is that it be consciousness of itself as being that knowledge. This is a necessary condition, for if my consciousness were not consciousness of being consciousness of the table, it would then be consciousness of that table without consciousness of being so. In other words, it would be a consciousness ignorant of itself, an unconscious – which is absurd. This is a sufficient condition, for my being conscious of being conscious of that table suffices in fact for me to be conscious of it.[21]

The type of awareness yielded by non-positional consciousness, then, is awareness of itself as a specific act or mode of consciousness (e.g. a perception of a table). That is, pre-reflective consciousness is, as Sartre puts it, "consciousness conscious of itself as consciousness of an object".[22]

Non-positional consciousness is, for Sartre, not numerically distinct from the act of positional consciousness. This is a claim consistently asserted by Sartre in both *The Transcendence of the Ego* and *Being and Nothingness*. In the former we are told, for example, that "To be and to be aware of itself are one and the same thing for consciousness."[23] In the latter it is emphasized over and over again that the existence of pre-reflective consciousness does not break the unity of consciousness. Every positional consciousness of an object *just is* a non-positional consciousness of itself: "We understand now why the first consciousness of consciousness is not positional; it is because it is one with the consciousness of which it is consciousness."[24] Any attempt to reduce non-positional consciousness to positional consciousness yields an infinite regress.

> The reduction of consciousness to knowledge in fact involves our introducing into consciousness the subject–object dualism which is typical of knowledge. But if we accept the law of the knower–known dyad, then a third term will be necessary in order for the knower to become known in turn, and we will be faced with this dilemma: Either we stop at any one term of the series – the known, the knower known, the knower known by the knower, etc. In this case, the totality of the phenomenon falls into the unknown; that is we always bump up against a non-self-conscious reflection and a final term. Or else we affirm the necessity of an infinite regress . . . which is absurd.[25]

That is, if we conceive of the relation between the pre-reflective consciousness and the consciousness of which it is consciousness in terms of dyadic model we end up with either a regress or a final term in the series, a final term that is not consciousness and that, Sartre thinks, therefore cannot ground the consciousness of the terms in the series. To avoid this we need to accept that "there must be an immediate, non-cognitive relation of the self to itself".[26]

To emphasize the indivisibility of pre-reflective consciousness from positional consciousness, Sartre recommends a syntactic intervention.

> We understand now why the first consciousness of consciousness is not positional; it is because it is one with the consciousness of which it is consciousness. At one stroke it determines itself as consciousness of perception and as perception. The necessity of syntax has compelled us hitherto to speak of the "non-positional consciousness of self". But we can no longer use this expression in which the "of self" still evokes the idea of knowledge. (Henceforth we shall put the "of" inside parentheses to show that it merely satisfies a grammatical requirement).[27]

Non-positional consciousness is, therefore, a distinguishable but non-separable part of every positional conscious act. Sartre chooses to express the distinguishability but non-separability of non-positional consciousness from positionally conscious acts by way of the concept of nothingness. What is it that separates non-positional consciousness from the positionally conscious acts (of) which it is a non-positional consciousness? Nothing; nothing at all. However, this nothingness is vitally important in

71

that it is the precondition of positional consciousness. A precondition of any object being taken as an object of consciousness is that there is, at least phenomenologically, a distance between the consciousness and its object. This nothingness derives from the gap between positional acts of consciousness and the non-positional consciousness of those acts.

Sartre and externalism

In the work of Sartre, we find what is in essence a form of *externalism* about the consciousness. Like the later forms we shall examine in due course, Sartre's externalism derives from the intentionality of mental states. For the basis of comparison with the later forms, to be examined in subsequent chapters, it is worthwhile highlighting the principal contours of Sartre's version of externalism.

1. Consciousness is essentially a directedness towards objects. That is, consciousness is essentially intentional.

However, Sartre claims that this has an entailment that Husserl (and everyone else for that matter) failed to grasp.

2. Consciousness has no *content*. There is nothing *in* consciousness.

The contents of consciousness are those things of which we are aware when we introspect or turn our attention inwards. Trivially, perhaps, point 2 is true of ordinary physical objects. But Sartre also applies it to ideas, images and mental representations in general. To the extent that these are things of which we are aware, they are not proper parts of consciousness. As we have seen, Sartre argues that this is entailed by the thesis of intentionality. To the extent that something is an object of consciousness – as mental representations are classically taken to be – it is not essentially intentional, but derives whatever representational function it has from the prior act of consciousness in virtue of which it becomes an object of consciousness. Thus, anything that could be thought to be among the contents of consciousness cannot, in fact, be part of consciousness. This, in turn, has a further implication.

3. Appearances are transcendent entities, not mental ones.

An appearance is something of which we are aware in the having of an experience. Contrary to Husserl, Sartre has argued that appearances have to be regarded as transcendent entities rather than mental ones. This follows from point 2. Any object of consciousness – whether this is an ordinary environmental object or a mental idea, thought or representation – cannot be part of, a content of, consciousness but must be outside consciousness, or transcendent. Appearances as objects of consciousness, therefore, are transcendent entities. In this claim lies Sartre's radical reversal of idealism. Husserl had supposed that appearances were immanent, mental entities: experiences of some sort. Thus, the world, for Husserl, is a correlate of consciousness, something that is "referred entirely to", or is logically dependent on consciousness for its existence. Consequently, the distinction between appearance and reality can be drawn only from within experience. For Sartre, the relation of logical dependence between consciousness and the world is reversed: "Consciousness is born supported by a being which is not itself. This is what we call the ontological proof."[28] That is:

4. The existence of the world (the *in-itself*) is "absolute". The existence of consciousness (the *for-itself*), on the other hand, is relative to the world.

Consciousness logically depends on the world for its existence but the world does not similarly depend on consciousness; hence the reversal of Husserl's idealism. The existence of consciousness, or the for-itself, is relative to the transcendent world because consciousness is nothing but a relation to transcendent objects. Consciousness is a pure directedness towards transcendent objects. It has no contents that could bestow upon it any sort of absolute being – that is, being independent of those objects towards which it is directed. All it is, and all it can ever be, is a relation to those things that it is not. Thus:

5. Consciousness is nothing but a relation to the world.

Consciousness can be defined only as a relation to the world of transcendent things that it is not. Or, as Sartre puts it:

> for we affirm that there is *nothing* outside the in-itself except a reflection (reflet) of that nothing which is itself polarized and defined by the in-itself inasmuch as it is precisely the nothingness of this in-itself, the individualized nothing which is nothing only because it is not the in-itself. . . . The for-itself is outside itself in the in-itself since it causes itself to be defined by what it is not; the first bond between the in-itself and the for-itself is therefore a bond of being.[29]

There is nothing more to the mental than directedness towards the world. The mental is, thus, logically and metaphysically dependent on the world but the world is not similarly dependent. This, as we shall see, is an extremely strong form of the doctrine that has now become known as externalism. It is interesting, and I think instructive, to see how the transformation of Husserl's view – in which transcendental idealism without noumena is a polar opposite of this form of externalism – required the amending of only a single premise: the reconstrual of appearances as transcendent rather than immanent (i.e. mental) entities. This amendment, Sartre argued, is mandated by proper understanding of the notion of intentionality.

To see why Sartre's position qualifies as externalist, consider it in relation to the two claims that, I argued in Chapter 1, constituted internalism as an ontological doctrine.

> *The Location Claim*: any mental phenomenon is spatially located inside the boundaries of the subject, S, that has or undergoes it.
> *The Possession Claim*: the possession of any mental phenomenon by a subject S does not depend on any feature that is external to the boundaries of S.

Sartre is committed to denying both of these claims. He is committed to denying the Location Claim on the grounds that consciousness, on his view, is nothing at all other than a directedness towards transcendent objects. It exists only in this directing and cannot, itself, be an object directed upon. This means that no matter how hard you look around the world trying to find consciousness, you will not succeed; consciousness is not an item in the world but a directedness towards the world. So to the extent that consciousness *is*, for Sartre, it is nowhere; it is real, but nowhere at all. So consciousness does not conform to the Location Claim. If consciousness is nowhere at all, it can hardly be located inside the skin of its subject.

Sartre is also committed to denying the Possession Claim. Consciousness is essentially a directedness towards objects that are transcendent to it. It therefore cannot exist without such objects. This is the basis of Sartre's "ontological proof" described earlier. Therefore, it is not possible for a creature to be the subject of conscious states in the absence of the appropriate transcendent objects. And if we assume, as we surely must, that many of these transcendent objects will be ones that exist outside the skins of conscious creatures, the denial of the Possession Claim is unavoidable.

Conclusion

In Husserl's phenomenology, we find what is, in effect, a version of Kantian transcendental idealism, yet without the assertion of the existence of noumena. Husserl's position is a version of both Cartesianism and idealism. It is a version of Cartesianism because it regards consciousness as capable of existence logically independent of the world. That is, consciousness is an *absolute* existence. His position is idealist because it regards the world as "referred", or relative, to consciousness. Its existence is a *dependent* one.

In the work of Sartre, however, we find a radical reversal of this form of idealism. What is remarkable is that Sartre accepts almost all of the foundational principles of Husserlian phenomenology. His radical reversal of Husserl's idealism is occasioned by a single amendment to those principles: appearances are transcendent, rather than immanent, entities (an amendment he thinks is required by proper understanding of the concept of intentionality). With this one, apparently small, change, Sartre develops an extremely strong form of externalism, committed to the denial of both the Location Claim and the Possession Claim. Consciousness has no content and exists as nothing over and above directedness towards the world. It is, thus, logically dependent upon, and indeed metaphysically constituted by (in the mode of *not* being it), the transcendent world.

CHAPTER 5

The attack on the inner

Sartre's attack on the idea that consciousness has contents is, in effect, an attack on the idea that the mental possesses features that are hidden, inner and constituted or revealed by the individual's inwardly directed awareness. This attack is continued by the Austrian philosopher, Ludwig Wittgenstein.[1] Although developing wide-ranging arguments concerning mentality in general, the focus of Wittgenstein's concern is items such as meaning and understanding – meaning something by one's use of a sign and understanding something by way of someone else's (or indeed your) use of a sign. Accordingly, I shall focus, at least initially, on these.

Wittgenstein's discussion of meaning and understanding contains both positive and negative strands. In both cases he is concerned neither to attack a certain theory of meaning nor to put forward a positive theory of his own. Rather, his concern is with a pre-theoretical picture of how language must work, a picture that, as he puts it, holds us captive.

The inner process model

There is a pre-theoretical picture of the nature of meaning that is influential in all branches of philosophical enquiry. In the Anglo-American tradition, the idea is evident in the work of John Locke, and, with a few exceptions, can be traced forwards to the work of Bertrand Russell, J. L. Austin, Paul Grice and John Searle. In the Continental tradition, the idea is likely to be associated with Condillac and, again with a few exceptions, can be traced forwards to Gadamer and Ricoeur. The view can be traced back at least as far as Plato. This is the view. We have various thoughts, ideas and other conscious states. These have a definite content. When we speak or write, what we do is give outer expression to this inner content; we, so to speak, drape the inner meaning in outer garb. Thus, when we mean something by a sign (e.g. a word), the content of the inner state is externalized: transmitted to an outer expression. And when we understand something by a sign, the reverse takes place. The content of an outer expression is internalized: transmitted to an inner state of understanding. Thus, to mean or understand something by a sign is in both cases to be the subject of an inner state or process. This view we can call the *inner process model*.

This picture of meaning has become deeply entrenched in philosophical – and, indeed, everyday – consciousness. It is not a theory of meaning as such, but it does provide the pre-theoretical starting point for much theorizing about meaning. This assimilation of meaning and understanding to an inner process has a profound, pervasive and, in Wittgenstein's opinion, ultimately destructive influence over our thought. Consequently, he subjects the assimilation to sustained and wide-ranging analysis and criticism.

Two different versions of the inner process model can be distinguished, according to whether the inner items are viewed as conscious or unconscious in nature. Thus, Wittgenstein's attack on the inner process model can be divided into two claims.

IP1:   Meaning or understanding something by a word is not constituted by a conscious inner state or process.

IP2:   Meaning or understanding something by a word is not constituted by a non-conscious inner state or process.

Conscious inner processes are, typically, experiences of some sort. Thus, the assimilation of meaning or understanding to a conscious inner process is an assimilation of meaning or understanding to the experiential. Wittgenstein thinks that this assimilation exerts a much more powerful influence on us than the corresponding view of meaning or understanding as non-conscious inner processes. Therefore, exorcism of the former assimilation requires correspondingly more work. The idea that meaning consists in some sort of experiential state occurs time and time again in his writings, in different contexts and with different connections. The view that meaning consists in some sort of non-conscious inner state, however, is discussed only in relatively few passages. Nevertheless, the arguments that he uses to undermine both views are essentially the same.

Inner processes are not necessary for meaning/understanding

The presence of an inner state or process in a subject S is, Wittgenstein argues, not *necessary* for S to mean or understand something by a sign. To appreciate this, what we have to do is follow a piece of advice consistently offered by Wittgenstein: *look and see!* That is, we must look, imaginatively as much as figuratively, at the great diversity of cases in which it would be appropriate to say of someone that he meant or understood such and such by an utterance. For example, suppose your partner asks you where you put their sunglasses. We can imagine the following scenario.

In the first case, you form an image of the sunglasses in the top drawer in the kitchen. You say, "They are in the kitchen drawer", and thereby mean that the sunglasses are in the kitchen drawer. That is the way it *could* have happened. However, it could have happened in countless other ways. Suppose you are watching television and feel irritated by your partner's untimely interruption. You say, "In the kitchen drawer", and thereby mean that the sunglasses are in the kitchen drawer, but all the while you are concentrating on watching Buffy stake yet another vampire. Or suppose you are talking to your co-worker on the telephone, a co-worker with whom you are having an illicit affair. Perturbed by your partner's unexpected appearance you say, "They are in the kitchen drawer", and thereby mean that they are in the kitchen drawer, but all the while you are hoping that your partner doesn't ask who is on the telephone. Obviously, these sorts of examples could be multiplied indefinitely, and in many of these cases, you simply will not form conscious images of the kitchen drawer or the sunglasses. You could form conscious images of various sorts, often completely unconnected with the location of the sunglasses. Indeed, often you will form no conscious image at all. Thus, although in these cases it would be appropriate to say of you that in uttering "The sunglasses are in the kitchen drawer" you meant that the sunglasses are in the kitchen drawer, there is, nonetheless, no feature of your experience that invariably accompanies this utterance.

A great many images, feelings and the like may accompany one's meaning something by a sign. But no one experience is essential for meaning the sign in a particular way. It is true that your meaning something by a sign might have *typical experiential accompaniments*. When you utter "The sunglasses are in the kitchen drawer", you might *often*, or even *typically*, form an image of the sunglasses in the drawer. But we must take care not to mistake an experiential *accompaniment* of meaning for the meaning itself. Your image of the sunglasses in the kitchen drawer, although perhaps an experiential accompaniment, cannot *constitute* your meaning that the sunglasses are in the kitchen drawer because you are capable of meaning that even when you form no such image.

There can be any number of experiential accompaniments to meaning or understanding, but these cannot constitute that meaning or understanding. Failure to appreciate this point stems from concentrating upon the most common kinds of accompaniment and conflating *accompanying* with *constituting*. This error, in turn, arises from the deeply ingrained assumption that meaning or understanding must consist in a distinctive sort of experience. But, as Wittgenstein argues, introspection just does not bear out this theoretical assumption. If you *look and see*, you will find that there is no invariant experiential accompaniment to meaning something by a sign. Indeed, introspection cannot even be relied upon to produce *any* kind of experience when one means or understands something by a sign.

This argument also applies to IP2: the claim that meaning or understanding something by a sign consists in a non-conscious inner state or process. The usual form this latter claim takes is the idea that meaning consists in some sort of neurophysiological process of some sort, or perhaps some higher-order functional property of the brain. Wittgenstein's point, here, is that once we look and see – imaginatively survey all the contexts and situations in which we mean or understand something by a sign S – there is little plausibility in the claim that there must be some one neurophysiological (functional, or other sub-doxastic) state common to all these contexts and situations.

Inner processes are not sufficient for meaning/understanding

Even more important than the claim that inner processes are not necessary for meaning or understanding something by a sign, however, is the claim that they are not *sufficient* for meaning and understanding. Again, the most straightforward idea is that meaning or understanding something might consist in some conscious image that, so to speak, passes through one's mind. For example, meaning something by the word "dog" consists in forming a conscious mental image of a dog. More generally, meaning something by a sign consists in associating an image with that sign.

Wittgenstein argues that the presence of such an image is not sufficient for meaning or understanding. The reason for this is quite simple. It is the image that is supposed to give meaning to the sign. However, the image is itself merely another sign, with a logical status precisely the same as the spoken utterance or written inscription. The image of the dog could, in principle, represent an indefinite number of things: dog, mammal, furry thing, thing with tail, thing with cold nose and so on. If the image is to give meaning to the inscription "dog", then, the meaning of the image must first be determined. However, on the present suggestion, it is the presence of an image to one's conscious gaze that fixes the meaning of a sign. Therefore, the meaning of the first image would have to be determined by appeal to a second image. However, this second image would, itself, have the logical status of just another sign. It no more carries its meaning on its face than does the first image. Therefore, if it is to lend meaning to the first image, it too must have its meaning fixed. And clearly we have now started down the road to infinite regress.

Two things immediately follow from this. The first is metaphysical. Meaning something by a sign cannot, ultimately, be based on an act of *interpretation*.[2] Interpretation, for Wittgenstein, is a matter of substituting one sign for another, in this case a conscious one for a written or spoken one.[3] As we have seen, this merely postpones the problem. Any given sign, even a conscious or experiential one, is, logically, open to a variety of interpretations. Thus, substituting the conscious sign for the spoken or written one simply leads to the problem of the significance of the conscious sign. Wittgenstein's point is not that meaning can *never* involve interpretation. Rather, it is that it cannot *always* involve interpretation. The meaning of a sign cannot be constituted by interpretation alone for we would never be able to halt the regress of interpretations. Therefore, meaning must ultimately rest on something more than interpretation.

The second corollary is epistemological in character. It is not possible to discover the meaning of a spoken or written sign by *reflection*. Discovering the meaning of a spoken or written sign cannot be a matter of comparing that sign to an inner experiential sign. For, again, we would have the problem of ascertaining the meaning of the experiential sign, and would thus be unable to halt the regress of reflection. When I mean something by a spoken or written sign, I do not consult something inside me that tells me that a certain application of the word is correct. This would transfer the epistemological problem on to whatever it is that guides me in this way.[4] Therefore, meaning something by a sign does not rest on a foundation of conscious or experiential justifying reasons in the sort of way envisaged by certain classical foundationalist conceptions. Again, Wittgenstein's point is not that we can never discover the meaning of a sign by reflection. His point is that we cannot always do so. Grasping the meaning of a sign cannot require reflection alone because this would lead to infinite regress. Meaning must, ultimately, rest on more than reflection.

It is worth noting that essentially the same arguments that establish that conscious inner processes are not sufficient for meaning or understanding also establish that *unconscious* inner processes are insufficient for meaning or understanding. The inner process, or interpretational, model entails that whenever meaning something by a sign occurs, this must rest on an infinitely nested set of acts of interpretation; one sign being interpreted by way of another, which is itself in turn interpreted by way of another and so on. Thus, any act of meaning must be accompanied by an infinite number of additional acts of interpretation. Given that any act of interpretation, whether conscious or unconscious, takes a finite amount of time, this entails that any act of meaning or understanding something by a sign would take an infinite amount of time, which is clearly an unacceptable entailment. Therefore, the unconscious version of the inner process model must be rejected also.

Rules for the use of a sign

It may be thought that the case against the inner process model of meaning and understanding rests on a simplistic and implausible conception of the sorts of inner processes involved. In particular, it might be thought, images provide a poor template for the inner items responsible for meaning and understanding. A far better template might be provided by the idea of a *mental rule*: a rule for the *use* of a word.

To see this, consider why the presence in your mind of a conscious image of a dog is insufficient for your meaning something by the word "dog". According to Wittgenstein, the key to the failure of the image to determine meaning is that it fails to determine the *use* of the word "dog": "What is essential is to see that the same thing can come before our minds when we hear the word and the application still be different. Has it the *same* meaning both times? I think we shall say not."[5] Images, pretty clearly, fail to determine the use of the signs with which they are associated, hence to which they are supposed to impart meaning. Nevertheless, it might be thought, there is a much better candidate for a type of mental item that determines the use of its associated sign than an image: a mental rule. A mental rule – whether conscious or unconscious – might determine the use of the sign it interprets even if an image does not. Therefore, perhaps, the presence in one's mind of mental rules of some sort might be sufficient for meaning or understanding something by a sign. Wittgenstein's argument against this claim is prolonged, profound and cogent.

Suppose someone begins a mathematical sequence as follows: 2, 4, 6, 8, 10, 12, 14, . . ., 996, 998, 1000, ... However, when they get to 1000, they continue as follows: 1004, 1008, 1012, 1016, ... It is overwhelmingly natural to suppose that, upon reaching 1000, they made a mistake. The natural response is that they were following a certain rule: the "$n + 2$" rule. Their behaviour after reaching 1000 is a contravention of this rule since they now, apparently, started to follow an "$n + 4$" rule. Simple. However, the sheen of simplicity is only apparent.

Perhaps, for example, they were, all along, following not the "$n + 2$" rule but the more complex rule: "$n + 2$ iff $n < 1000$, if not $n + 4$". So the question is: what constitutes the person following the "$n + 2$" rule (and subsequently making a mistake) and the "$n + 2$ iff $n < 1000$, if not $n + 4$" rule (and subsequently carrying on correctly)?

One response we cannot make, of course, is that subsequent to 1000 they made a mistake because they were supposed to go on doing *the same thing*. This is because, what counts as the same thing can only be defined relative to the rule they adopted. If they adopted the more complex rule then, after reaching 1000, they did in fact go on doing the same thing, for this is precisely what the rule they were following all along told them they should do when they reached 1000.

Perhaps, then, when a person understands how to follow a mathematical rule, the rule must somehow pass through their mind. But how would this occur? Is it that the picture of the rule "$n + 2$" appears in their mind's eye? If so, we have the problem already encountered. The picture is, logically, just another symbol. So for it to determine how we continue the mathematical progression, we would first have to interpret the formula "$n + 2$". Perhaps, for example, "$+$" is used in a way such that it means "$+ x$ iff $n < 1000$, $+ 2x$ otherwise", in which case, when the person reaches 1000, they, in fact, continue to follow the rule correctly. The presence of a mathematical formula before one's conscious gaze cannot provide an interpretation of what one is supposed to do, for it is itself subject to a variety of interpretations.

To say that the person following the "$n + 2$" rule consciously thinks to themselves, "when I reach 1000, I will continue adding 2 and not 4" would be ridiculous. It would entail that whenever a person correctly followed a mathematical rule, they must simultaneously be thinking an infinite number of thoughts. There are an infinite number of numbers, and the "change" might not occur at 1000, but at 998, or 1002 and so on. So the person would have to be thinking an infinite number of thoughts of the form "when I reach 2, I will continue adding 2 and not 4", "when I reach 4, I will continue adding 2 and not 4" and so on, for all the potential numbers in the sequence! Similarly, since the person might start adding a number other than 4 – say 3, 5, 6, 7, . . ., ∞ – at any point in the sequence, they would also have to have thoughts specifying that they add 2 and not any of the potential infinity of other numbers. Mathematics may sometimes be difficult, but it is not *that* difficult. Retreating to the idea that perhaps these thoughts are unconscious rather than conscious does not help matters. No brain is capable of entertaining an infinite number of thoughts, and this is true whether those thoughts are conscious *or* unconscious.

It is difficult, then, to find any mental fact about an individual at a given time that determines that they are following one rule rather than another. Perhaps, then, there is a non-mental fact of the individual. A behavioural fact, perhaps. On the face of it, however, this suggestion seems unpromising. A person's behaviour at any given time is compatible with their following an indefinite number of rules. A person continuing a sequence 2, 4, 6, 8, 10, 12, ... is compatible with their following an infinite number of algebraic formulae ("$n + 2$ iff $n < 16$, if not $n + 4$", etc.). Indeed, since there is an infinity of numbers, the person's behaviour will, necessarily, always be compatible with their following an infinite number of algebraic formulae. On the face of it, therefore, it is difficult to see how a person's behaviour can determine that they are following one rule rather than another. We shall, however, return to this issue later.

The sceptical paradox

There does not seem to be any fact – whether mental or behavioural – about an individual person at a given time that determines that they are following one rule rather than another. We are tempted into supposing that in following a mathematical rule we understand the rule we are following, and in one sense this is undeniably true. There is a huge difference between correctly following a mathematical rule and incorrectly following one, or writing down a sequence of numbers at random. The question we are having difficulty in answering, however, is: in what does this understanding of a rule consist? It does not seem possible to identify any feature of the individual person at any given time that would allow us to answer this question. Thus, we have arrived at what Wittgenstein refers to as a *paradox*, a sceptical paradox about meaning and understanding.

> This was our paradox: no course of action could be determined by a rule, because every course of action can be made out to accord with the rule. The answer was: if everything can be made out to accord with the rule, then it can also be made out to conflict with it. And so there would be neither accord nor conflict here.[6]

This paradox is not primarily an epistemological problem. The central problem is not how we can know, or find out, what rule someone is following. The core problem is metaphysical: what *constitutes* a person's following one rule rather than another? There is, it seems, no fact of the matter that constitutes a person's following the "$n + 2$" rule, rather than the "$n + 2$ iff $n < 1000$, otherwise $n + 4$" rule. That is, when a person, say, gets to 1000 and then continues the series 1004, 1008, ..., there is nothing that constitutes the difference between them following the "$n + 2$ iff $n < 1000$, if not $n + 4$" rule or the "$n + 2$" rule. In the former case they are continuing to follow the rule correctly, and in the latter case they have made a mistake. Since there is nothing that constitutes their following one rule rather than another, there is also nothing that constitutes the difference between their following a rule correctly and their making a mistake. The difference between correct and incorrect following of a rule is not a difference that can be drawn at the level of an individual at a time. There is, in this case, no fact of the matter that determines the difference between correct and incorrect application of a rule. This shows that we cannot, here, talk of the *correct* application of a rule.

This will, of course, have epistemological consequences. If there is no fact of the matter determining that the person is following one rule rather than another then it will not be possible to know which rule the person is following since they are, in fact, *not* following one rule rather than another. Therefore, nor will it be possible to know if they are following a rule correctly or have made a mistake – because there is, in effect, nothing here to know. But the underlying problem is metaphysical rather than epistemological.

A natural temptation in the face of this problem is to resort to the *magical*. Somehow, we might be tempted to suppose, the whole application of a rule is presented to us:

> "It is as if we could grasp the whole use of a word in a flash." Like *what* e.g.? Can't the use – in a certain sense – be grasped in a flash? And in *what* sense can it not? The point is, that it is as if we could "grasp it in a flash" in yet another and much more direct sense than that. – But have you a model for this? No. It is just that this expression suggests itself to us.[7]

This suggestion, however, is bankrupt. It is not an answer to the question of which fact determines that we are following one rule rather than another. It is a simple assertion that there must be some such fact, a fact that involves "grasping the rule in a flash". But unless we can give an account of what this grasping consists in, we are no further down the road of identifying the fact that determines that a person is following one rule rather than another.

Wittgenstein's solution to the sceptical paradox makes no appeal to such strange processes. Instead, the paradox shows, he thinks, something quite different: "What this shews is that there is a way of grasping a rule which is *not an interpretation*, but which is exhibited in what we call 'obeying the rule' and 'going against it' in actual cases."[8] If following a rule is to be possible at all, then there must be a way of following a rule that does not consist in an interpretation of that rule, where, "We ought to restrict the term 'interpretation' to the substitution of one expression of the rule for another."[9] Instead, the following of the rule must somehow be exhibited in what we call obeying the rule or contravening it. Understanding this is the key to grasping Wittgenstein's views on the nature of meaning and understanding. Before we proceed to this, however, we need to look at an important implication of the sceptical paradox: the impossibility of a private language.

The private language argument

The attack on the inner process model, culminating in the sceptical paradox, throws into doubt the idea that meaning or understanding something by a sign could consist in a private, inner state of an individual. However, there is a certain area of language where, we are tempted to suppose, the meaning of a sign must consist in some private, inner item: that area of language where we talk about private, inner items – those words that we use to talk about our mental states. If we did use mental words to refer to private, inner states, and if the meaning of such words derived from their reference to such states, then, it seems, such a language would be *private*: it would be a language that could, in principle, only be understood by one person. Wittgenstein argues that such a language is logically impossible.

By *private language*, Wittgenstein is referring to a language that is logically rather than contingently private: "The individual words of this language are to refer to what can only be known to the person speaking; to his immediate private sensations. So another person cannot understand the language."[10] A contingently private language is one that is, in fact, understood only by one person but that could, in principle, be understood by more than one. A logically private language is one that can, in principle, only be understood by one person. Cornish, for example, is a language that is reputed to be spoken only by several hundred people at present.

Suppose this number were reduced to one. Then Cornish would be a contingently private language. However, there is nothing, in principle, that prevents it from being learned by other people. Cornish, like every other language, employs words that refer to public objects – birds, trees, rocks and the like – and learning the language involves learning what various words stand for, together with the syntactic rules that allow one to combine meaningful words in legitimate ways. A logically private language, however, is of a quite different order. A language where words get their meaning through referring to sensations, understood as private, inner entities, would be logically private. The meanings of the words of this language would be accessible only to the speaker since only the speaker would have access to the private sensations that constitute these meanings.

A logically private language, Wittgenstein argues, is impossible, even in principle. This is not, as is sometimes supposed, because no one else would be able to understand what the speaker of such a language was talking about. That may be true but misses the point. After all, that is what a logically private language is supposed to be – one that no one else can understand – so to use this as an *argument* against the possibility of a logically private language would be to beg the question. The real problem is that in a logically private language there is nothing that constitutes meaning or understanding something by a sign, *not even to the speaker of that language*. In a logically private language there can be no such thing as meaning or understanding something by a sign. Therefore, there can be no such thing as a logically private language.

Why can there be no such thing as meaning or understanding in a logically private language? Wittgenstein's argument, in essence, is an extension of the sceptical paradox. In order for meaning or understanding to be possible, there must be some distinction between correct and incorrect application of a word. And, in the case of a logically private language, no such distinction exists.

> Let us imagine the following case. I want to keep a diary about the recurrence of a certain sensation. To this end I associate it with the sign "S" and write this sign in a calendar for every day on which I have the sensation . . . I speak or write the sign down, and at the same time I concentrate my attention on the sensation – and so, as it were, point to it inwardly . . . in this way I impress on myself the connexion between the sign and the sensation. – But "I impress it on myself" can only mean: this process brings it about that I remember the connexion *right* in the future. But in the present case, I have no criterion of correctness. One would like to say:

whatever is going to seem right to me is right. And that only means that here we can't talk about "right".[11]

In order for "S" to mean the sensation S, or to be the name of that sensation, we would have to use "S" only in the presence of S. That is, we would have to follow a rule of the sort: *apply "S" only when S occurs.* However, this rule is, logically, a symbol, and, in order to determine linguistic behaviour, it must first have its meaning determined. For example, suppose someone regularly writes "S" in their diary upon the occurrence of S. One day, they (apparently) change their behaviour, and begin writing "S" upon the occurrence of a distinct sensation S*. If we could access what was going on in this private arena, we might want to say that they made a mistake: they were writing "S" when S was not present. However, they might reply that it is we who are mistaken. We are assuming that "S" picks out a state with a unique qualitative character, Q. But in fact, "S" picks out any state that has qualitative character Q before time t, and that has a distinct qualitative character Q^* after time t. That is, S is a state that is individuated by way of a time-indexed disjunctive qualitative character. So there are two possibilities: the person is following a rule that links "S" to a single qualitative character, or they are following a rule that links "S" to a time-indexed disjunctive qualitative character. If the former, then the person makes a mistake. If the latter, then they do not. The problem is: what determines whether the person is following one rule rather than another? The answer is: if we focus on the individual and their mental and behavioural state at a time before t, then *nothing at all* determines that they are following one rule rather than the other. There is no fact about that individual that determines that they are following the first rule incorrectly or the second rule correctly. This conclusion is obtained by parity of reasoning, which produced the sceptical paradox in the first place. That is, the behavioural facts about the individual, prior to t, are compatible with both rules. And the mental facts about the individual cannot be used to determine which rule is being followed since mental facts are themselves just further symbols, appeal to which will commit one to an infinite regress.

It is worth reiterating that this is not, primarily, an epistemological problem. Sometimes Wittgenstein's private language argument is rendered as an epistemological point about the unreliability of memory and, consequently, how the private diarist can know whether he is correctly applying "S" in any case. To understand Wittgenstein's argument in this way is to rob it of most of its importance and appeal, and invites the response that there is no *special* worry over the reliability of internal memory over that of external memory. But this response will not answer the real problem, for this is metaphysical not epistemological. Assume, if you like, that the private diarist's memory is infallible (whatever that means). Then, this still does not answer the question of whether they are making a mistake when they apply "S" to the sensation with Q^* rather than Q. Even if they correctly realize that $Q^* \neq Q$, this in no way alters the fact that there is nothing to determine which way they are using the rule, hence nothing to determine whether they are or are not making a mistake when they apply "S" to a sensation with Q^*. This is the real problem, not the anodyne worry about reliability of memory. And this worry is a special case of the general sceptical paradox: an application of the principles involved in generating the paradox to a language whose terms are supposed to refer to private, inner states of an individual.

Wittgenstein's solution to the sceptical paradox

Wittgenstein offers a solution to the sceptical paradox, one that centrally involves the notion of a *practice*:

> And hence also "obeying a rule" is a practice. And to think one is obeying a rule is not to obey a rule. Hence it is not possible to obey a rule "privately": otherwise thinking one was obeying a rule would be the same thing as obeying it.[12]

The solution involves a distinction between (merely) thinking that one is obeying a rule and actually obeying it. This distinction is logically dependent on the distinction between correct and incorrect application of a rule. In the absence of the latter distinction, there can be no former distinction. That is, where there is no distinction between correct and incorrect application of a rule, there is no difference between thinking that one is obeying a rule and actually obeying it. In order to draw this distinction, Wittgenstein claims, we need to understand that obeying a rule is a *practice*.

Wittgenstein uses the terms "practice", "custom" and "form of life" interchangeably. Wittgenstein's solution to the paradox involves connecting the notion of meaning with the capacity to act. To mean something by a sign is to know how to do something, to have an ability, to be master of a *technique*: "To understand a sentence means to understand a language. To understand a language means to be master of a technique."[13] The effect of this characterization is to forge a direct connection between meaning and use; meaning and understanding are essentially connected with use because they involve the capacity to do certain things with signs. The obvious question is: what things? It is here that the notion of a practice, custom or form of life assumes prominence. To mean or understand something by a sign is to possess the technique of adjusting one's use of that sign to accord with common practice.

> A person goes by a sign-post only in so far as there exists a regular use of sign-posts, a custom.[14]

> It is not possible that there should have been only one occasion on which someone obeyed a rule. It is not possible that there should have been only one occasion on which a report was made, an order given or understood, and so on. – To obey a rule, to make a report, to give an order, to play a game of chess, are *customs* (uses, institutions).[15]

Here, Wittgenstein is providing an alternative to traditional interpretational conceptions of meaning. Meaning something by a sign is not a matter of supplying an interpretation to that sign. Nor is it a matter of consulting something that might indicate what the meaning of the sign is. Rather, it is a matter of being able to adjust one's use of a sign to bring it into line with customary usage, to make it accord with common practice.

A custom or practice is something that becomes established not through the deliverances of reason but on the basis of tradition. Once established, adhering to the custom is not a matter of reason or reflection. It is simply what one does, unreflectively, blindly.

> How can he *know* how he is to continue a pattern by himself – whatever instructions you give him? – Well, how do I know? – If that means "Have I reasons" the answer is: my reasons will soon give out. And then I shall act without reasons.[16]

> When I obey a rule, I do not choose. I obey the rule blindly.[17]

In short, according to Wittgenstein, meaning something by a sign is a matter of possessing a technique of using the sign in accordance with a *practice, custom,* or *form of life*. And possession of such a technique, and exhibition of such use, is logically prior to any act of interpretation or reflection.

Practice: individual versus community interpretations

The concept of a practice, as it appears in Wittgenstein's work, is notoriously open to two, quite distinct, interpretations. We might call these the *individual* and the *community* interpretations. Obeying a rule is, let us accept, a practice. But is a practice something that can be constituted by or through the actions of a single person? An affirmative answer yields the individual interpretation, and a negative one yields the community interpretation. Two distinct issues arise in this connection. First, which provides the best interpretation of Wittgenstein? Secondly, which interpretation is most successful at accommodating the problems that prompt the introduction of the concept of a practice?

The first question is, I think, essentially contestable. On the face of it, the term "custom" might be thought to connote a pattern of behaviour adopted by a community as a whole. This connotation, however, is, perhaps, not shared by the term "practice". In favour of the community interpretation, the following passage from *Remarks on the Foundations of Mathematics* might be telling.

> Could there be arithmetic without agreement of those who calculate?
>
> Could a solitary man calculate? Could a solitary man follow a rule?
>
> Are these questions somewhat similar to this one: "Can a solitary person carry on a trade?"[18]

The suggestion seems to be that just as carrying on a trade presupposes a community, so too does following the rules constitutive of arithmetic. However, it is also true that Wittgenstein phrases this point interrogatively. And *Remarks on the Foundations of Mathematics* are, after all, a set of posthumously published notes that, there is every reason to suppose, Wittgenstein had no intention of publishing as they stood. These remarks are, therefore, very much a "work in progress". Textual evidence in support of the individual interpretation, on the other hand, includes the fact that Wittgenstein nowhere qualifies the words "custom" and "practice" with terms such as "community" or "social". One would have thought that Wittgenstein would surely have inserted these qualifying adjectives if he really intended to maintain a community-based view of meaning.

Adjudicating between individual and community interpretations of Wittgenstein is probably impossible on a textual level, so let us turn to what is, anyway, a far more important question: which interpretation is more successful at accommodating the problems that prompted the introduction of the notion of a practice in the first place? That is, which interpretation is most successful at solving the sceptical paradox?

The sceptical paradox arises because of the failure to identify any fact of the matter that could determine whether a given individual is using one rule rather than an alternative where both are compatible with his or her actual behaviour. That is, the mental and behavioural facts about an individual at a time are compatible with their following an indefinite number of rules. Therefore, these mental and behavioural facts taken at a time do not suffice to determine that the individual is following one rule rather than any of the alternatives. The dispute between the individual and the community interpretation of Wittgenstein, ultimately, comes down to this: are these facts insufficient because we are focusing on the individual, as opposed to the community, or are they insufficient because we are focusing on the individual at a time as opposed to the individual through time? If we regard the individual/community issue as crucial, we will be pushed towards a community interpretation. If we regard the at-a-time/through-time issue as crucial, we will be at liberty to adopt an individual interpretation of the notion of a practice.

Any account of rule-following must, Wittgenstein argues, allow for the possibility of incorrectly following a rule. Without such a possibility, there will be no distinction between an individual incorrectly following rule R and correctly following a distinct rule R^*. The community interpretation is introduced to safeguard the possibility of making a mistake in the following of a rule, without which, Wittgenstein argues, there can be no such thing as the correct following of a rule. The idea behind the community interpretation is that we can draw a distinction between correctly and incorrectly following a rule, not at the level of the individual, but only in the relation *between* an individual's behaviour and the behaviour of a community. Why does an individual's behaviour count as the incorrect following of R rather than the correct following of a distinct rule R^*? According to the community interpretation, it is because, and only because, R, rather than R^*, is the rule exhibited by the community as a whole. Hence we can accommodate the possibility of error in rule-following, and so can legitimately talk of correct rule-following.

Upon further analysis, however, the community interpretation seems powerless to stop the sceptical paradox. To see why, let us return to the mathematical rule "$n + 2$". This rule, we can suppose, has been exhibited in a consistent way at the level of a community, C. Suppose C is a community where mathematics is in its infancy and it has yet to develop the number system beyond three digits. Nevertheless, members of C are quite capable of developing mathematical progressions up to and including 999. So suppose a member of C, Jones, starts a progression, 2, 4, 6, 8, 10, 12, . . ., 994, 996, 998. Then he makes the breakthrough: 1000. After 1000, however, he does something that, by our lights, seems peculiar. He continues: 1004, 1008, 1012, ... His practice, let us suppose, catches on, and the community learns to continue sequences of numbers in the same way. The original sceptical paradox – applied to individuals – concerned whether there was any fact of the matter that determines that Jones was following the "$n + 2$" rule (and made a mistake) or the "$n + 2$ iff $n < 1000$, $n + 4$ otherwise" rule (and continued correctly). Now, however, it seems we have precisely the same problem applied to the community as a whole. Is there any fact of the matter that, prior to inventing the 1000 numeral and continuing sequences such as 2, 4, 6, 8, 10, . . ., the community was following the "$n + 2$" rule or the "$n + 2$ iff $n < 1000$, $n + 4$ otherwise" rule? If there is no fact of the matter in the case of the individual, then, by parity of reasoning, there should be no fact of the matter in the case of the community either.

It is true that, at the level of the community, it is not possible to talk of making a mistake in the following of a rule, a possibility that clearly does make sense for individuals. Whether the community continues the sequence 1002, 1004, 1006, . . . or 1004, 1008, 1012, . . . this is not a matter of their being mistaken in one case and correct in the other. However, this observation, one made frequently by Wittgenstein, is not, by itself, sufficient to avoid the sceptical paradox. Immunity from the possibility of error in following a rule does not, by itself, guarantee that there is fact of the matter as to which rule the community is following. Therefore, it seems that the community interpretation of the notion of a practice does nothing to solve or circumvent the sceptical paradox. Essentially the same paradox arises for both individuals *and* communities.

This leaves us with the individual interpretation of the notion of a practice. The community interpretation sought to ground the possibility of individual error in following a rule in terms of the relation between that individual and a wider community. The possibility of error is, thus, grounded in an essentially *synchronic* relation – a relation, at a time, between an individual and a community of individuals. The individual interpretation sees the possibility of individual error in following a rule as grounded in terms of an essentially *diachronic* relation between what an individual does with a sign at one time, and what that same individual does with that sign at later (or earlier) times. Note that it need not be the same individual that uses the sign on different occasions. Rather, the claim is that it *could* be the same individual who uses the sign on distinct occasions. This claim is what the community interpretation must deny. What is crucial to the individual interpretation is the repeated use of a sign, and the interpretation is indifferent as to whether it is one or more individuals that engages in this repeated use. This indifference, however, cannot be endorsed by the community interpretation. On the community interpretation, more than one individual *must* be involved. In short, the community interpretation sees the possibility of individual error in a rule to be grounded in the distinction between a solitary *individual* and the community at large, whereas the individual interpretation sees the relevant distinction as being between a solitary *occasion* of use of a sign and repeated occasions of use of that sign.

The most obvious objection to this can be seen by way of a suitably abstract description of the sceptical paradox. Any instance of rule-following, or apparent rule-following, is insufficient to yield a fact of the matter with regard to which rule is being followed because there are an indefinite number of rules that are compatible both with the behaviour contained in the instance and the state of mind of the individual engaged in this behaviour at that time. For example, writing down the sequence 2, 4, 6, 8, . . . is compatible with, literally, an infinite number of algebraic rules and it is impossible for the relatively impoverished contents of the agent's conscious (and unconscious) mind at the time of writing to rule out many, if any, of these possible interpretations. In suitably abstract terms, the problem is that the contents of the agent's mind and behaviour are, at any given time, strictly finite. As such, they are incapable of adjudicating between the infinity of possible rules that would provide an interpretation of the behaviour. If this is, indeed, the form of the paradox, then appeal to further occasions of use (e.g. continuing 10, 12, 14, 16, . . .) can do nothing to undermine the paradox, for no matter how many further instances of use of a rule we appeal to, this does not alter the fact that these instances are always finite. No matter how many occasions of rule-following we cite, no matter how many occasions we can compile as evidence for an interpretation, these occasions can never comprise more than a finite number. As such they will be incapable of adjudicating between the infinite number of rules that would provide an interpretation of the behaviour of an individual. Therefore, it might seem as if appeal to further occasions of use can do nothing to settle the issue of whether there is a fact of the matter with regard to which rule an agent is following.

However, if this is the problem, a possible solution now suggests itself. We appeal not just to further *actual* occasions of use; we also appeal to further *possible* occasions of use. That is, the distinction required by the individual interpretation is that between a solitary occasion of the use of a sign, an occasion characterized by the *actual* contents of a person's mind and behaviour, and repeated occasions of the use of that sign that can be characterized both by the actual contents of a person's mind and behaviour and by the *dispositional* contents of the mind and behaviour – what they *would* do and *would* think under appropriate circumstances. That is, the repeated occasions of use appealed to by the individual interpretation can consist of both actual occasions of use and occasions of use that *would* have resulted if conditions had been a particular way.

If this solution is going to work, however, then we will be committed to a certain view of the nature of dispositions: a person's dispositions to think and behave in various ways are not finite in the way that a person's actual thoughts and behaviour are. The dispositions to think and behave in certain ways given appropriate circumstances are as unlimited as the circumstances in which that person *might* be placed. Therefore, if the individual interpretation can make use of the idea that the repeated occasions of use that make up a practice comprise both actual and dispositional occasions, the individual interpretation might have the resources to solve the sceptical paradox. This view of dispositions is not uncontroversial but it is certainly defensible.

However, even if the necessary account of dispositions can be defended, there is a further problem, one that afflicts both individual and community interpretations of the notion of a practice. On either interpretation, Wittgenstein's solution to the sceptical paradox involves essential appeal to the idea of *what we do*. However, doing is a form of acting and, as such, is essentially connected to intentional states. That is, action is distinguished from bodily movement, at least in part, by way of its causal antecedents. Roughly, an action is a bodily movement that is caused by intentional states such as beliefs, desires and so on. However, beliefs and desires have content, and such content is essential to the identity of such states. But the content of a belief, desire or other propositional attitude is simply the meaning of the sentence that follows the *that*-clause used to ascribe such states. The content of the thought that the sky is blue is simply the meaning of the sentence "The sky is blue". Therefore, Wittgenstein's appeal to use as a solution to the sceptical paradox is in danger of being circular. The sceptical paradox is a paradox about how meaning is possible. Wittgenstein's appeal to practice implicitly presupposes the existence of states that have semantic content. Therefore, it seems to assume, rather than provide, an answer to this question.

Wittgenstein and externalism

Wittgenstein's appeal to the concept of a practice in solving the sceptical paradox is, therefore, not without its difficulties. In the eyes of many, his solution to the paradox is not as convincing as the development of the paradox itself, and, for this reason, Wittgenstein's negative conclusions concerning meaning are more widely accepted than his positive ones.

If Wittgenstein's negative arguments work, then they apply not just to meaning and understanding narrowly understood. They apply to any state that has intentional or semantic content. This includes all the so-called *propositional attitudes*. A propositional attitude is a type of mental state that is nominally characterized by way of its typical manner of ascription. Thoughts, beliefs, desires, hopes, fears, expectations and the like are all ascribed to individuals by way of a *that*-clause. For example, we ascribe a belief to an individual, Jones, by way of an expression of the form "Jones believes that ...", where the "..." is filled in with a sentence or proposition. The intentional or semantic content of a propositional attitude is identical with the meaning of the sentence that follows the "that". To the extent that Wittgenstein's arguments apply to meaning, they will also apply to any state that is essentially individuated by way of such meaning. His arguments, therefore, apply to all the propositional attitudes at least. In as much as meaning something by a sign is not an inner state or process, neither is intending something by a sign, nor is thinking, anticipating, desiring and so on. What started out as a comparatively narrow thesis about meaning has, in fact, much wider application.

Whether or not Wittgenstein's solution to the sceptical paradox works – and whether or not that solution is individualistic or communal – it is clear that Wittgenstein has put forward a devastating critique of the idea of meaning and understanding as inner states or processes. Meaning something by a sign is not a process whereby we project an inner content outwards, or give an inner content outer garb in the form of words and sentences. And understanding is not the converse process where an outer content becomes transformed into inner content. Rather, to the extent that meaning and understanding exist, they are closely connected to our abilities to do things in the world, to the technique of adjusting our use of signs to bring it into line with practice. As such, meaning and under-standing are not things that we do or achieve in our heads; they are things we achieve in the world.

Wittgenstein, therefore, provides us with a view that pretty clearly qualifies as externalist. Meaning and understanding something by a sign do not consist in inner states or processes. Of course, it is not exactly clear what, on Wittgenstein's view, these things do consist in, but the notions of *capacities* and *dispositions* are going to be centrally involved: capacities to adjust one's use of a sign to bring it into line with what is *customary* or *practice*, and dispositions to so adjust one's use of the sign in appropriate circumstances. There is a way of understanding capacities and dispositions as the internal structural state of an individual or object. However, given Wittgenstein's attack on the inner process model, this understanding is clearly not Wittgenstein's. Rather, capacities and dispositions are understood as essentially related to structures in the world: patterns of sign usage, whether instantiated in a single individual through time or across different individuals both at and through time. It is not possible for an individual to mean or understand something by a sign in the absence of such external structures, so Wittgenstein's position clearly involves a rejection of the Possession Claim. And since meaning and understanding do not, according to Wittgenstein, consist in inner states or processes, Wittgenstein's position also seems to involve a rejection of the Location Claim. This issue will be discussed further in Chapter 12.

Conclusion

Wittgenstein developed a devastating attack on the idea of meaning – and by extension, of understanding, intending, thinking, believing, desiring and so on – as consisting in some form of inner state or process. Meaning and understanding do not consist in inner states or processes and this is true whether the internal process is understood imagistically, experientially or in terms of the concept of a mental rule. It is also true whether the inner process is conceived of as a conscious one or an unconscious one. He supplemented this with a positive account of meaning and understanding that is, perhaps, slightly less convincing. But the central idea that meaning and understanding something by a sign is conceptually connected to our ability to do things in the world, as much as in our head, is surely a good one. In both his negative and positive accounts Wittgenstein develops a form of externalism about meaning, understanding and other intentional states.

In attacking the idea of meaning and understanding as inner states or processes, and in developing the idea that meaning and understanding are things we achieve, fundamentally, in the world rather than in our heads, Wittgenstein paves the way for some arguments developed in the 1970s by both Hilary Putnam and Tyler Burge. These arguments are classic statements of the position that has become known as *externalism*. We will look at these in Chapter 6.

CHAPTER 6
Content externalism

As we saw in Chapter 3, what Kant referred to as his "Copernican revolution" in philosophy was motivated by the *matching problem*. According to Kant, if our knowledge-acquiring faculties are capable of yielding knowledge of the world, as they certainly seem to be, then this must be because they must, in some way, match up to the world. There must be some sort of *fit* or *match* between the nature of our knowledge-acquiring faculties and the nature of the world. The question of how knowledge is possible, then, translates into a question about how this matching can occur. Kant's answer to this was his transcendental idealism. Our knowledge-acquiring faculties – the faculties of sensibility and understanding – match up, or mesh, with the world because the world, the phenomenal world of our everyday experience, is constructed by these faculties.

The Kantian, idealist, solution to the matching problem is, then, based on the idea that phenomenal or empirical items are not individuated independently of the activities of the mind. And they are not individuated independently of the activities of the mind because they are, in part, products of those activities. In the work of Sartre, examined in Chapter 4, we see the outlines of an alternative solution to the matching problem. Again, the solution is based on the idea that environmental items are not individuated independently of mental items. But, according to Sartre, this lack of individuative independence is for precisely the converse reason. Consciousness, for Sartre, is nothing more than directedness towards the world. It has no contents of its own, ones for which the question of the relation between their individuation and that of environmental entities might arise. Instead, consciousness is nothingness: nothing but a directedness towards the world that is transcendent to it. On Sartre's view, therefore, there is no question of consciousness being individuated independently of the world, for there are no world-independent contents in consciousness of which this might be true.

Consciousness is essentially permeated by the world, essentially shot through with the worldly entities that it is not, but in terms of which it is defined. In short, in Sartre's system, the matching problem is solved not by the Kantian idealist idea that worldly entities are constituted by consciousness but, rather, by the idea that consciousness is thoroughly penetrated by the world. This stance towards the matching problem is the stepping-off point for externalist views of the mind.

Twin earth

The most famous form of externalism is what we can call *content externalism*. Indeed, when people apply the rubric "externalist" to a position, it is typically content externalism that they have in mind. Content externalism was motivated by a series of now classic thought-experiments developed in the 1970s by Hilary Putnam and Tyler Burge. This section outlines Putnam's argument for externalism.

Putnam's argument is philosophical science fiction at its very best.[1] We are to imagine a planet that nearly duplicates our planet earth. Call this planet *twin earth*. Except for certain features, ones we will get to in a moment, twin earth duplicates earth in every detail. Inhabitants of earth have duplicate counterparts or doppelgängers on twin earth, and these counterparts are exact – and I mean exact – duplicates of their corresponding earthlings. So, your duplicate is physically identical to you – in a *qualitative* rather than *numerical* sense. That is, they are identical to you in the way that one can of Coca-Cola is identical to another. And this physical qualitative identity runs all the way down to the level of molecular structure. They are also functionally and behaviourally identical to you. Whatever behavioural history you have, your twin has precisely the same history. Whatever functional roles are instantiated in your brain, the same roles are there in your twin's brain too. They have had the same history as you – whatever you have done, your twin has done too, and at exactly the same time as you. Indeed, your twin – poor thing – is at this moment reading a twin copy of this book (a book written by my twin). Indeed, on one way of understanding the notion of experience, your twin has had precisely the same experiences as you. If you stubbed your toe at 4.15pm on 21 August 1988, and had a painful experience as a result, so too did your twin. What you have suffered, your twin has suffered, and what you have enjoyed, so too has your twin.

In short, you and your twin are type-identical in point of physical constitution, functional profile, behavioural dispositions and experiential history, where – and here's the catch – all these are identified *solipsistically*. To identify something solipsistically, in this case, is to identify it in a way that presupposes the existence of no entities external to, or separate from, you and your twin.

Let us look a little more closely at this notion of solipsistic identification, since it is important. Take a physical state of your body: a brain state, for example. There are various ways of identifying this state, some solipsistic, some not. For example, your brain may go into a certain state of activation as the result of someone standing on your toe. If you identified this state as the state that your brain went into as a result of someone stepping on your toe, then your identification would not have been solipsistic – it would presuppose the existence of something external to you; namely, the person who trod on your toe. We often identify states of a person in terms of their typical causes. And when these causes are external – as they often are – then our method of identifying these states is by definition not solipsistic. Similarly, we can identify functional roles and behavioural definitions both solipsistically and non-solipsistically. For example, pain is sometimes identified in terms of its typical causes. But there are two ways of understanding such causes. We can cite what are known as *proximal* causes or *distal* causes of pain. A proximal cause might be, for example, bodily damage. And if we assume that this occurs at or inside the skin of the subject of pain, and if we assume that both at or inside the skin of a subject is not external to the subject, then in identifying pain by way of this sort of cause, we have identified it in a way that presupposes the existence of no entities external to the subject of the pain. We have identified pain, therefore, solipsistically. Suppose, on the other hand, we identified pain in terms of its typical *distal* causes: sharp objects and the like. Then we would have identified it in a way that does presuppose the existence of entities external to the subject of the pain. Our identification would, therefore, not have been solipsistic.

How about experiences? Can we identify them solipsistically? For some types of experience – pain is an obvious example – there is no real problem. But for others, such as perceptual experiences, the possibility of solipsistic identification seems, at least on the face of it, unlikely. When we identify an experience as, for example, the seeing of a pink rose, are we not presupposing the existence of something external to the subject of that experience: the pink rose? However, there is also a way of talking about experience in which the same experience could be had even in the absence of the rose, for example, if the experience were a realistic hallucination or illusion. Therefore, having an experience in this sense – having the common experiential character that is shared by perceptions, illusions and hallucinations – does not require the existence of anything external to the subject of that experience. It might be possible, therefore, to provide a solipsistic identification of experience understood in this sense. We do so by identifying the experience by way of the properties that are common to veridical perception, illusion, hallucination and the like. In the above case, these would be the phenomenal properties associated with the rose: pinkish, prickly and so on.

You and your twin, therefore, are qualitatively identical with respect to your physical constitution, functional profile, behavioural dispositions and experiential history, where all these are, in the sense explained above, identified *solipsistically*.

There is one difference between earth and twin earth. The liquid on twin earth that runs in rivers and taps is not water. It is not water because it is not H_2O; it is not a compound made up of two atoms of hydrogen to one atom of oxygen. Instead, it is a very different substance, made up, let us suppose, of elements with which we are entirely unfamiliar. However, this substance is indistinguishable from water by any casual observational test. It looks, tastes, feels and so on exactly like water. In fact, the only way to distinguish it from water is by complex chemical and microstructural analysis. And let us suppose that at the time this thought-experiment is set, neither the inhabitants of earth nor their twin-earth doppelgängers have the means of carrying out such analyses. They have, that is, no way of distinguishing water from the corresponding substance on twin earth, a substance that we can call *retaw*. We can call it "retaw", but, of course, the twin earthlings do not. Being functionally and behaviourally identical to us, they speak twin English, and so refer to it with the term "water".

You might be tempted to suppose that because water and retaw are indistinguishable, and are used in the same way by earthlings and twin earthlings, they are in fact one and the same substance. If you are tempted to suppose this, don't be! Water is no more retaw than gold is fool's gold. The cases are not exactly the same. Fool's gold can, apparently, be distinguished from gold without chemical analysis (at least, it can if Hollywood has not been lying to me). But suppose iron pyrites was just a little more like gold than it is. Suppose that the only way of distinguishing it from real gold was by way of chemical analysis. It still wouldn't be gold. Gold, and water, are what are sometimes known as *natural kinds*, and part of what this means is that they are defined by a *real essence*: a constitution that marks them out as the substances they are. The real essence of water is that it is composed of two atoms of hydrogen and one atom of oxygen. The real essence of gold is that it has an atomic number of 79. Something that is not made up of two atoms of hydrogen and one atom of oxygen is not water, and something that does not have an atomic number of 79 is not gold, even if we are incapable of discerning these facts.

So far, we have two components of the twin-earth thought-experiment. First, there is the idea of twins that are type-identical in point of their physical constitution and functional, behavioural and experiential history – where all of these are specified solipsistically. Secondly, there is the idea that substances can vary from one planet to another without any corresponding ability of the inhabitants of the planets to detect such variation. What do we get when we put these ideas together?

Suppose $Emma_1$ is an English speaker on earth, and $Emma_2$ is her counterpart on twin earth. Neither knows the structure of what she calls "water" – and remember that $Emma_2$ will call retaw "water" since she speaks twin English. We can assume that the two Emmas are identical in point of (solipsistically specified) physical constitution, functional profile, behavioural dispositions and experiential history. Suppose $Emma_1$ says "water is wet", and $Emma_2$ utters something of the same phonetic form. Do the two Emmas mean the same thing? As Putnam has pointed out, it is difficult to see how they could mean the same thing. The form of words "water is wet" means something different depending on which Emma utters it. $Emma_1$'s utterance refers to, and is true of, water but $Emma_2$'s utterance refers to, and is true of, retaw, which she just happens to refer to with the term "water". The term "water" differs in reference from one planet to another, and so the sentence-form "water is wet" differs in truth-conditions from one planet to another. But a difference in reference for a word, and a difference in truth-conditions for a sentence, it is argued, add up to a difference in meaning for that word and that sentence. And, if this is right, then this indicates that the (solipsistically specified) physical, functional, behavioural and experiential properties of a speaker do not suffice to determine the meaning of what a speaker says (or writes). Or, as Putnam puts it, *meanings just ain't in the head!*

This may seem a strange and radical claim. And indeed it is. What could seem more natural than the idea that it is you who fix the meaning of the words you use, that it is you who determines the content of what you say and write? If Putnam is correct, however, this idea must be rejected. Nothing going on inside you is sufficient – enough – to fix the meaning of the words and sentences you utter. What also, at least partially, determines what you mean is the environment in which you are situated.

But we have only begun to scratch the surface of the implications of this view. Here is an implication that Putnam, in fact, did not point out. The point we have just made about the constitution of meaning can also be made about certain sorts of mental state too. The mental states in question are what are known as *propositional attitudes*. The term was coined by Bertrand Russell to refer to mental states that are ascribed in a certain way – by way of a *that*-clause containing an embedded proposition. Take belief, for example. We say Emma believes *that* water is wet. That is, we ascribe this belief to her using the word "that" followed by the proposition expressed by the sentence "water is wet". The same is true of thoughts, desires, hopes, fears, expectations, anticipations and so on. These, and many others, collectively constitute the category of propositional attitudes. They are contrasted with sensations, such as pain, that are not ascribed in this way.

When Emma thinks that water is wet, does she have the same thought as her twin-earth counterpart? Well, how can she? Her twin has never been in any sort of contact with water. Indeed, unless her twin is a philosopher with a penchant for twin-earth thought-experiments, the possible existence of water has probably never even occurred to her. Whenever she has had any thought that she would express using the term "water", it is retaw, not water, she has been thinking about; similarly, for the belief that water is wet. The belief seems to vary from one Emma to another. The belief of Emma$_1$ is a belief about water, but the belief of Emma$_2$ is one about retaw (which she simply happens to express to herself and others using the term "water").

So not only does the meaning of the two utterances differ, but so too do the contents of the beliefs, thoughts and other propositional attitudes that the two Emmas have about the substance on their planets. However, it is common to regard the contents of propositional attitudes as essential to them. For example, what makes the belief that water is wet distinct from the belief that the sky is blue? Precisely the contents of the two beliefs. The former is a belief about water and the relation it bears to the property of wetness. The latter is a belief about the sky and the relation it bears to the property of blueness. The beliefs are different because they are about different things, and this difference is reflected in the content of the beliefs – reflected, that is, in the meanings of the sentences embedded in the *that*-clause. So beliefs, it seems, differ precisely when, and because, their contents differ. And this apparently means that the content of a given belief is one of the essential determinants of the identity of that belief. The content, that is, is essential to the belief. The same applies to all the other propositional attitudes.

If this is right, then the contents of the beliefs of the two Emmas, the beliefs they would both express using the syntactic–phonetic form "water is wet", are different. But contents are essential to beliefs – if their contents differ, then the beliefs differ too. So the beliefs of the two Emmas are also different. But, *ex hypothesi*, everything going on inside the heads of the two Emmas is the same. The two Emmas share the same solipsistically specified physical, functional, behavioural and experiential properties: they are type-identical with respect to these properties. And, if this is right, then this indicates that the (solipsistically specified) physical, functional, behavioural and experiential properties of a speaker do not suffice to determine which beliefs, thoughts, desires and other propositional attitudes Emma and her twin have. Meanings are not in the head, but neither, so it seems, are thoughts, beliefs, desires and other propositional attitudes.

The thought-experiment is, of course, outlandish – of precisely the sort to make non-philosophers despair of philosophers. But, outlandish or not, it is being used as a graphic way of making a simple point. *If you fix everything that is going on in the head, and vary the environment, then meanings, thoughts, beliefs, desires and other propositional attitudes will vary with the changes in the environment even though nothing has changed inside the head.* Meanings and propositional attitudes are, in this sense, not "in the head". Their presence in a person is not determined purely by what is going on inside that person's head but also by what is going on in that person's world. And to identify what a person is thinking, believing, desiring and meaning we must look not just at what is inside their head, but also at the world that their head is inside.

Counterfactual earth

We are to imagine a person, call him Larry, who has a number of psychological states concerning arthritis. He believes that he has arthritis, for example, and believes that he has had it for years. He believes that arthritis can be very painful, but also that it is better to have arthritis than lung cancer. In addition to these beliefs, he also believes that he has arthritis in his thigh. This belief is, of course, a false one, since arthritis is an ailment that afflicts only the joints. However, what is important is that, despite Larry's misapprehension, we are still willing to count his belief that he has arthritis in his thigh as a belief about arthritis – it is just that it is a false belief about arthritis. What underlies our willingness to count this as a belief about arthritis is, almost certainly, the fact that Larry inhabits a linguistic community containing people who have various beliefs about arthritis, and that Larry would allow himself to be corrected in his use of the term "arthritis" by (at least some of the) members of this community. Then, given plausible constraints on interpretation, it seems we not only can, but must, interpret Larry's false belief about arthritis as a belief about arthritis.

We now imagine Larry in a counterfactual situation. Counterfactual Larry is type-identical with actual Larry in point of physical constitution, functional profile, behavioural dispositions and experiential history, where, just as in Putnam's twin-earth scenario, all of these are solipsistically specified. The counterfactuality in the situation touches only on Larry's linguistic environment. In the counterfactual situation, the phonetic or syntactic form "arthritis" – as used by physicians, lexicographers and competent laypersons – applies not only to an affliction of the joints but also to various other rheumatoid ailments. That is, in the counterfactual situation, the correct use of the term "arthritis" encompasses Larry's actual misuse. In this case, our intuitions seem to tell us that Larry, in the counterfactual situation, does not have arthritis beliefs at all. So too for other propositional attitudes – thoughts, desires, hopes, fears and so on – that Larry might have had about arthritis. That is, counterfactual Larry lacks the beliefs and other propositional attitudes that we, in the actual world, ascribe to people using the term "arthritis" (embedded in a sentence following "that"). For Larry in the counterfactual situation, unlike Larry in the actual situation, does not have the concept of arthritis; he has the concept of counterfactual arthritis (= arthritis + rheumatism, as we might say).

So Larry's beliefs vary between actual and counterfactual situations because the contents of those beliefs vary between the two situations. And the contents of the beliefs vary because of variations in linguistic usage. The differences between the beliefs are again the result of differences in the reference of the terms involved in the expression of the content of those beliefs but, in this case, the difference in reference stems from a difference in linguistic use, not, as in the Putnam thought-experiment, a difference in the physical environment. The physical environments are, in an important sense, the same between actual and counterfactual situations, but the differences in linguistic use mean that this same physical environment is conceptually "chopped up" differently in the two situations. So we distinguish arthritis from rheumatism but our counterfactual counterparts make no such distinction: they run the two together. It is this difference in conceptualization or categorization of the same physical reality that accounts for the difference in reference and so, ultimately, the difference in beliefs.

The above is an argument first developed by Tyler Burge.[2] What is interesting is the range of application of this argument. Some have argued that Putnam's argument turns on the natural-kind status of water. But Burge's way of developing the argument has no such restriction. Indeed, Burge claims that relevantly similar arguments can be constructed for "any notion that applies to public types of objects, properties or events that are typically known by empirical means".[3] Thus Burge's arguments, if successful, yield conclusions that are much more general in scope than those of Putnam.

There is another sense in which Burge's arguments are more general than those of Putnam: the considerations adduced by Putnam can be subsumed under those identified by Burge. Superficially, Putnam's and Burge's arguments seem quite different. Putnam's arguments turn on the nature of the physical environment, and Burge's arguments turn on the nature of the linguistic environment. But this is superficial. Burge's arguments do, of course, involve the linguistic environment, and the way words are used in this environment. But it is possible to incorporate Putnam's arguments within this general framework. Putnam's arguments turn on the notion of truth-conditions, whereas Burge's turn on the notion of linguistic use. We can render these arguments consonant by way of the claim that some words – natural-kind terms are the obvious example – are used to track items in the natural environment. That is, the way some words are *used* is sensitive to the *truth-conditions* of the sentences in which they occur. Meanings, on the Putnam model, are not in the head because the truth-conditions of sentences vary with changes in a subject's natural environment, and do so in a way that is independent of what is going on in that subject's head. But why should this be so? Because, it might be argued, words employed in those sentences are *used* in such a way – to track changes in the environment independently of what is going inside the subject's head – that makes the truth-conditions of sentences in which they occur sensitive to changes in the natural environment of a subject but independent of what is going on in the head of that subject. If we accept the idea that truth-conditions are determinants of meaning because, and only because, sentences are used in a given linguistic community to track truth-conditions, then Putnam's arguments become a special case of Burge's arguments.

Indexicals

Indexical expressions are ones whose reference depends on context. "Today", for example, changes its reference daily. Indexical beliefs, accordingly, are ones whose content depends on context. An important type of indexical expression is known as a *demonstrative*: an expression that acquires its reference through pointing. For example, "this" as in "This cat is on the mat" is a demonstrative expression. Similarly, there is a category of demonstrative beliefs: ones that acquire their content through pointing.

Certain treatments of indexicality recognize that indexical beliefs can be ascribed using sentences that have, as David Kaplan puts it, the same *character* but different truth-conditions.[4] For example, the sentence "Today is fine", while expressing the same character on each occasion of use, differs in truth-conditions on each day on which it is used. Similarly, the utterance "I am tired" possesses the same character on each occasion of use but differs in truth-conditions depending on the utterer and time of utterance. So suppose that my twin-earth doppelgänger and I both have a belief specified by the sentence "I am tired". Again, even if we assume that my twin and I are identical in point of (solipsistically specified) physical constitution, and behavioural, functional and experiential histories, we still do not share the same belief. The truth-conditions of my belief are that I am tired, while the truth-conditions of my twin's belief are that he is tired. Our beliefs share the same character but the contents of our beliefs, hence our beliefs, differ.

Individuation dependence and external individuation

As Colin McGinn has pointed out, the arguments for externalism seem to establish, at the very least, a claim of *individuation dependence* of the mental on the environmental.[5] The notion of individuation dependence derives from Peter Strawson and McGinn's development of the idea, which runs as follows.[6]

> *F*s are individuation dependent on *G*s if and only if:
> (i)   Reference to *F*s requires prior reference to *G*s.
> (ii) Knowledge of the properties of *F*s requires prior knowledge of the properties of *G*s.
> (iii) It is not possible for *F*s to exist in a world where *G*s do not exist.
> (iv) Possessing a concept of an *F* requires prior possession of a concept of a *G*.[7]

We can refer to these conditions as the *linguistic, epistemological, metaphysical* and *conceptual* conditions respectively.

The arguments for externalism, if correct, establish that propositional mental states are individuation dependent on the world in this sense. Let the *F*s be beliefs and the *G*s be objects and properties in the world. Then the significance of the arguments for externalism can be expressed in terms of the following four claims.

(i)   Reference to beliefs requires reference to appropriate worldly entities.

There is no way to specify what someone believes without specifying what worldly entities the belief is about. This is why *that*-clauses serve precisely to pick out beliefs by way of the non-mental entities those beliefs are about.

(ii) We cannot know what someone believes without knowing the non-mental objects and properties their beliefs are about.

One cannot know that someone believes the cat is on the mat without knowing that their environment contains cats, mats, spatial relations and so on. Interpretation of another person's beliefs, that is, must be based on antecedent knowledge of the nature of that person's environment.

(iii) It simply is not possible for a subject to hold a belief unless their environment contains the appropriate entities.

This is why your twin cannot entertain the belief that water is wet. Their belief is necessarily a belief that retaw is wet, not that water is wet, notwithstanding the phenomenological similarities between the two beliefs.

(iv) It is not possible to master the concept of a belief without already having mastered concepts for the worldly entities beliefs are about.

One could not, for example, master the concept of the *belief that the cat is on the mat* without having mastered the concept of *cat* and *mat*, since the former complex concept embeds the latter simple concepts.

One cannot fail to notice, of course, that the final three conditions – the epistemological, metaphysical and conceptual conditions – are the converse of the three conditions used, in Chapter 2, to characterize the notion of individuation *in*dependence that constituted what I called the internalist's Possession Claim. This was identified as one of the two defining features of internalism, as characterized in that chapter. Thus, the external individuation of at least some mental states – their individuation dependence on environmental items – entails the straightforward rejection of the Possession Claim partly constitutive of internalism.

One implication of the arguments for externalism, then, is that, if they are correct, they establish that at least some mental states are individuation dependent on worldly or environmental items. This entails rejection of one of the defining features of internalism: the Possession Claim. So this is one way in which the content externalism of Putnam, Burge and others is anti-internalist.

The arguments for externalism, then, entail the rejection of the Possession Claim because they establish, or seem to establish, that some mental states are *externally individuated*: individuation dependent on items that exist outside the heads or skins of the subjects of those states. That they establish this is relatively uncontroversial. However, with regard to the rest of the story – with regard to the other implications of the arguments for externalism – *nothing* is uncontroversial.

The dual component theory

The thought-experiments of Putnam and Burge, and the work on indexicals associated with Kaplan and others, threatens the Cartesian view of the mind as a self-contained entity located inside the skin of a subject. A natural (though certainly not necessary) assumption to make is that the mind is wherever its contents are; and among the contents of minds are, of course, mental states. The above arguments, if successful, threaten to undermine the view that mental states necessarily occur inside the heads – or skins – of things that have minds. And this threatens the view of the mind as a self-contained interiority.

It would be natural to expect, then, that a prominent early response to the arguments for externalism would be essentially defensive. The response acknowledges the force of the arguments but seeks to limit their significance. According to the response, propositional mental states – the sort of mental state impacted by the arguments – should be regarded as having two components: an internal component and an external one. An extended quotation from McGinn makes the point quite nicely.

> Our intuitive conception of belief-content combines two separable components, answering to two distinct interests we have in ascriptions of belief. One component consists in a mode of representation of things in the world; the other concerns itself with properly semantic relations between such representations and the things represented. I want to suggest that the former is constitutive of the causal-explanatory role of belief, while the latter is bound up in our taking beliefs as the bearers of truth. We view beliefs *both* as states of the head explanatory of behaviour, and as items possessed of referential truth-conditions.[8]

When I believe that water is wet, and my twin has a belief ascribable with a sentence of the same syntactic or phonetic form, we have, if the arguments for externalism are correct, distinct beliefs. Nevertheless, these beliefs seem to share important features. First, they dispose us to the same (solipstically specified) behaviour: if my twin and I desire a bath, I will fill my tub with water and my twin will fill his tub with retaw. Secondly, my belief that water is wet seems to function in inference in the same way as the corresponding belief of my twin. If I desire to get wet, for example, my belief that water is wet might cause me to infer that water is what I need to satisfy my desire. But my twin's belief that retaw is wet will function in the same way – leading him to conclude that retaw is what he needs to satisfy his desire. Thirdly, experientially, my twin's interactions with retaw seem pretty much the same as my interactions with water. What it is like to see retaw, for example, is the same as what it is like to see water. So, too, what it is like to taste retaw is the same as what it is like to taste water. So my belief that water is wet and my twin's belief that retaw is wet seem to share some key features.

This has suggested to many that we ought to regard beliefs, and other propositional mental states, as being made up of separable components. One component, often called the *internal* component, consists in the properties of a mental state in virtue of which it occupies a certain causal or functional role, and so plays a certain role in our behavioural economy, and in virtue of which it connects up with experience in the way it does. This component is identical with what many have called the mental state *narrowly individuated* or the *narrow mental state*. The other component, the *external* component, consists in the properties possessed by a mental state in virtue of which it represents a portion of the world. This component is, supposedly, irrelevant to the mental state's causal or functional role and independent of whatever experiential properties are commonly associated with the mental state. The combination of internal and external components makes up the mental state *widely individuated* or the *wide mental state*.

This strategy acknowledges the force of the arguments for externalism but seeks to limit their consequences. Specifically, the Cartesian idea of the mind as a self-contained interiority is preserved: the bounds are simply redrawn. The Cartesian mind is now made up of the internal components of mental states, and not of entire mental states as was envisaged by orthodox Cartesianism. Features such as privileged access, first-person authority and incorrigibility, which were thought, by orthodox Cartesianism, to characterize our access to our own mental states, can now be thought to characterize our access to the internal components of our own mental states. We may no longer know our own mental states first and best, but we still know the internal components of those states first and best. The bounds of the inner may have been reinterpreted by the dual component theory but they have not been abandoned.

This attempt to safeguard the Cartesian vision has one consequence for the interpretation of the dual component theory. Not only must each propositional attitude be made up of two components, but these components must be at least logically or conceptually separable. Someone who wants to deny the Cartesian interiority of even a component of the mind, for example, could accept with equanimity the idea that beliefs, thoughts and the like were composed, in part, of various internal factors or constituents. All that is required to undermine the Cartesian picture of the mind is the claim that the role these factors or components play in collectively constituting the belief cannot genuinely be factored into components that act in logically independent ways. Once this is granted, the idea of the mind as a *self-contained* interiority must be abandoned. If the role played by environmental factors in the construction of the mental cannot be even logically or conceptually separated from the role played by factors within the subject, then there is no prospect of identifying a component of the mind that is purely internally constituted, hence to which traditional Cartesian features such as privileged access, first-person authority, incorrigibility and so on, can be thought applicable. The limited defence of Cartesianism provided by the dual component theory, therefore, requires more than the claim that propositional attitudes are constituted by different components; it also needs the claim that the roles each of these components plays in constituting the mental are ones that are at least logically or conceptually separable from each other.

Narrow content

If the two components of propositional mental states, and hence the respective roles played by each component in constituting such states, are at least logically or conceptually separable, then it must be possible to identify each component independently of the other. That is, the logical separability of the roles played by each component in constituting the mental is underwritten by the independent identifiability of these components. Thus if the limited defence of Cartesian interiority supplied by the dual component theory is to be successful, there must be a way of identifying the internal component of any propositional mental state independently of the external component that also partly constitutes that state. What might this be?

Ordinary (i.e. wide) beliefs and other propositional attitudes are identified by way of their *content* – in terms of the meaning of the sentence that follows the 'that' by way of which they are ascribed. So a natural idea is that we might be able to do the same thing in the case of the internal component of beliefs. That is, we might be able to identify the narrow mental state – to narrowly individuate that state – by way of its content. This content would, then, be the *narrow content* of the belief. What might this narrow content be?

One approach to explaining narrow content exploits the connection between the narrow mental state and the phenomenological character associated with that state. When I believe that water is wet, and my twin believes that retaw is wet, our beliefs clearly seem to have something in common. We both believe that the colourless, odourless, transparent, drinkable liquid in front of us is wet. So it is natural to suppose that we might be able to specify the narrow content of the belief in terms of this sort of phenomenological character. That is:

Narrow content of belief   =   the colourless, odourless, transparent,
   that water is wet   drinkable . . . liquid is wet

Filling in the dots requires filling in whatever phenomenal qualities are deemed to be required to capture accurately the narrow meaning of "water is wet". On this suggestion, then, narrow content is identifiable with what we can call *phenomenal content*. Will this suggestion work?

One problem is immediately apparent. We have not successfully expunged all non-phenomenal terms from the above definition. The right-hand side of the definition, for example, makes use of the notion of a liquid. But this is a non-phenomenal term and, more importantly, seems susceptible to the twin-earth examples in the same way as water. Liquid is a natural-kind category and being a liquid consists in instantiating a certain molecular structure. Anything that does not instantiate such a structure is not a liquid, appearances notwithstanding. So suppose twin earth is identical with earth except that on twin earth there are no liquids. Instead, there are simple non-physical substances, whose existence and effects on human beings are preserved and controlled by God in much the same way that the idealist philosopher George Berkeley thought was true of the world in general. These substances, in virtue of God's beneficence on this liquidless planet, affect (or at least appear to affect) twin-earth human beings in the same way that liquids affect human beings. These substances are referred to on twin earth as "liquids", but it is clear that they are not liquids in the sense meant on earth. They are not even physical substances, let alone physical substances with a particular type of molecular structure. When you and your twin have a thought that you would both express to yourself using the syntactic–phonetic form "liquids are wet", you think different thoughts, despite the type-identity of your physical, functional, behavioural and experiential properties. Your thought is a liquid-thought: your twin's thought is, we might say, a tw-liquid thought.

In order to make the definition of narrow content in terms of phenomenal content work, we would have to make sure we have eliminated all terms that express concepts for which twin-earth examples could be run. Obviously, the hope is that we can either rely exclusively on purely phenomenal or observational concepts or, more plausibly, rely on these combined with concepts so general that they abstract across all differences on which twin-earth scenarios could possibly turn. Concepts such as that of substance, stuff, thing and so on *might* be sufficiently general to avoid twin-earth counter-examples.

These issues aside, however, the idea that narrow content can be reduced to a form of phenomenal content faces serious problems. To see this, recall the characterization of the concept of individuation dependence given earlier. As McGinn has pointed out, this characterization slides over a crucial difference, a difference he tries to capture in terms of a distinction between what he calls *weak* and *strong* externalism.[9] The claim that (some) mental states are externally individuated – individuation dependent on objects and properties external to the subjects of those states – covers two, quite distinct, types of case:

- the objects and properties are causally or environmentally connected to the subject of the state whose content they individuate;
- the objects and properties occur in the same possible world as the subject of the state they individuate.

Weak externalism, on McGinn's construal, is the thesis that a given mental state requires the *existence* of some non-mental item external to the subject of that state, and that its identity is dependent on that item. Strong externalism, on the other hand, is the thesis that a given mental state requires existence *in the environment of the subject* of some non-mental item external to the subject of that state, and that its identity is dependent on that item. Strong externalism ties mental states to a particular part of the world – the part that the subject inhabits – while weak externalism ties mental states to the world at large, whether or not the required non-mental entity exists in the vicinity of the subject.

If we accept the validity of this distinction, we seem forced to allow that a form of externalism applies to phenomenal contents: such contents are weakly, if not strongly, external. To see this, let us set up a modified twin-earth thought-experiment. Rufus lives in a world – the actual world – in which there exists the property of redness. So Rufus, on the basis of various patterns of experience can, correctly or incorrectly, attribute the property of redness to various objects. And Rufus can have thoughts with contents expressed by sentences like "This shirt is red", "I appear to be in a red-light district" and so on. Whether such thoughts are true or false, they are nonetheless thoughts about things that are red.

We now imagine a counterfactual situation. Counterfactual Rufus – whom we will call "Dufus" – lives in a world where different evolutionary pressures have had the following result. In this world, there is no property of redness. The evolutionary exigencies of Dufus's species have not caused them to distinguish what we regard as red from what we regard as green. Instead, they run the properties together into an indivisible whole – the property of "gredness".[10] The members of this counterfactual community do not regard the property of gredness as a composite property capable of being factored off into red and green components. Rather, although they might allow that gredness admits of shades (much as we do of redness) they regard gredness as a single property (again, much as we regard redness).

Now suppose that throughout their lives Rufus's and Dufus's phenomenal experiences have been identical: they have exactly the same history of encounters with coloured objects. It would still not be true to say that they possess the same intentional states. Rufus's beliefs are about red and green things; Dufus's corresponding beliefs are about gred things.

This is, of course, not a twin-earth experiment in the classic vein. It would be implausible to suppose, for example, that Rufus's and Dufus's internal constitution are the same if one can discern red from green things and the other cannot. But this is not essential to the point that the experiment makes. One of the entailments of McGinn's distinction between weak and strong externalism is that the question of whether a given mental state is externally individuated and the question of whether it is possible to set up a classic twin-earth thought-experiment for that state are logically independent of each other. A state can be weakly external even if it is not possible to set up a twin-earth scenario for that state. The point of the present thought experiment is that it simply is not possible for a subject to entertain a belief about, say, redness in a world where there is no redness. Thus if, in a possible world, no creature had ever evolved that was capable of distinguishing redness from greenness – and so, in effect, there was no property of redness – then it would not be possible for any creature to have beliefs about redness; and this is true even if their experience is phenomenally indistinguishable from ours when we have experiences of red. The possibility of entertaining a belief that x is P, requires that one inhabit a world where x exists and P exists. This is the force of the claim that mental states are weakly external.

The attempt to identify narrow content with phenomenal content, then, runs into the problem that phenomenal content is weakly external.

Therefore, it is not genuinely narrow. Phenomenal contents are externally individuated; it is just that they are weakly rather than strongly externally individuated. Phenomenal content, then, does not seem to be genuinely narrow. It is still individuated by items external to the subject of that content.

We might call the strategy for trying to express the narrow content of a mental state examined in the above paragraphs the *phenomenological strategy*. The strategy consists in trying to find a collection of concepts that are not externally individuated and providing a *narrow* construal of other concepts in terms of these. The strategy is *phenomenological* because the envisaged base solipsistic concepts are qualitative, observational or phenomenological in character. If, as McGinn would argue, even these concepts are (weakly) externally individuated, then the strategy, it would seem, fails.

There exists another strategy for trying to express the narrow content of a mental state; we might call this the *indexicalist strategy*. This involves treating belief-content indexically in a way that is assumed to presuppose the existence of no entities external to the subject of the belief. The strategy is associated with John Searle.[11] For example, Searle says that "water" is to be defined indexically as whatever is identical in structure with the stuff causing *this* visual experience. Thus, the narrow content shared by my twin and I is a content that can be expressed as follows: "Whatever is identical in structure with the stuff causing this visual experience is wet." There are at least two distinguishable problems with this view.

First, the concepts in terms of which this indexicalist criterion of narrow content are formulated seem themselves to be (strongly) externally individuated. Consider, for example, the notion of causation. It seems possible to set up a twin-earth scenario for this concept. Suppose that, in this world, Hume (or the standard interpretation of Hume) is correct. So when I have a belief attributable by a sentence of the form "causation is universal", then the external properties to which I will be related will be properties of contiguity, succession and constant conjunction. But I will not be related to any external property of natural necessity, for the simple reason that there is no such property. My twin, however, lives in a world where Hume is wrong, and what he calls "causation" is a matter of natural necessity. So when he has a belief attributable by a sentence of the form "causation is universal", as well as being related to external properties of contiguity, succession and constant conjunction, he will also be related to the external property of natural necessity. Hence, he has a different thought. The concept of causation, then, seems to be strongly externally individuated.

Secondly, the expression "causing this visual experience" fails to refer uniquely, and fails in a way that is impossible to rectify so that it satisfies the condition of narrowness. There are many things causing any given visual experience, and consequently causing beliefs formed on the basis of that experience, some of them external, some of them internal. For example, one of the causes of my visual experience of water, and consequently of my belief that there is water in front of me, is the pattern of neuron-firing in the optic nerve. But, presumably, we do not want to say that my belief that there is water in front of me is really a belief about a pattern of neural excitation in my optic nerve. To avoid the general conclusion that beliefs that appear to be about external objects are really beliefs about internal states and processes caused by those objects, we have, it seems, only one option. We must distinguish between the internal or *proximal* causes of beliefs and the external or *distal* causes of beliefs and then claim that the indexicalist strategy applies only to distal causes. This may help the indexicalist reconstruction of belief content but it is no help to the person wishing to use it to supply an account of narrow content. Since distal causes are external, any notion of content indexically constructed on their basis will, *ipso facto*, not be narrow.

Therefore, it is unlikely that the indexicalist strategy, just like the phenomenological strategy, yields any form of content that is genuinely narrow.

The inexpressibility of narrow content

The problems faced by phenomenological and indexicalist strategies for expressing narrow content are, I think, symptomatic of a more general difficulty: *narrow content is simply not the sort of thing that can be expressed*. The problem is pointed out by Fodor.

> So, in particular, qua expressions of English "water is wet" is anchored to the wetness of water (i.e. H_2O) just as, qua expressions of Tw-English, "water 2 is wet" is anchored to the wetness of water 2 (i.e. to the wetness of XYZ). And, of course, since it is anchored to water, "water is wet" doesn't – can't – express the narrow content that my water-thoughts share with my Twin's. . . . Narrow content is radically inexpressible because it is only content potentially; it's what gets to be content when – and only when – it gets to be anchored.[12]

The problem is clearest with indexicals. Suppose you say "I have a sore toe", and your twin utters a sentence of the same phonetic form. What is the content that the two utterances have in common? The answer is: you cannot say. When you use the word "I" this word is anchored to you, when your twin uses the word "I" it is anchored to him. Now, consider again Putnam's twin-earth case. Consider the thoughts had by me and my twin-earth counterpart, expressed by the sentence "water is wet". These distinct thoughts supposedly share the same narrow content. The question is: what is this content that the two thoughts have in common? As Fodor has argued, this question is ill-advised since it admits of no answer. An answer would require the uttering of an English sentence that expresses just what my water thoughts have in common with those of my twin. And this cannot be done. This is because the content that an English sentence expresses is *ipso facto* anchored content, hence *ipso facto* not narrow.[13]

Of course, this is not a problem that affects just English. Twin English and, indeed, any language whose terms are anchored will be equally affected. Whatever the means of anchoring involved – and different philosophers will give you very different stories – words have meaning because they are anchored. But narrow content would have to have a form of content that is not anchored, since only then could it be something that is common to more than one world. So narrow content does not seem to be a form of content at all. Narrow content is radically expressible because, as Fodor puts it, it is only content *potentially* – it is what gets to be content when, and only when, it becomes anchored.[14]

Nonetheless, Fodor argues that the notion of narrow content is still a potentially useful one. Most importantly, despite its inexpressibility, it is possible to supply a *criterion of identity* for narrow content – a criterion that specifies when two propositional attitudes are identical with respect to narrow content and when they are distinct. The idea is that referring expressions of English (or tw-English for that matter) can be used to pick out narrow contents via their hypothetical semantic properties. For example, the English expression "the thought that water is wet" can be used to *specify*, even if it cannot express, the content of a mental state that my twin and I share because the narrow content that water is wet is the *unique* narrow thought that yields the truth-condition water is wet when anchored to my earthly context and the truth-condition retaw is wet when anchored to his twin-earthly context. Thus we have an extensional criterion of identity for narrow contents: two narrow contents are identical only if they effect the same mapping of thoughts and contexts onto truth-conditions.[15]

It is one thing to provide a criterion of identity for narrow content – even if that criterion entails that narrow content is not really a form of content at all. It is quite another thing to show that the item identified by way of this criterion is logically or conceptually separable from ordinary wide semantic content. Not only does the criterion not demonstrate this latter claim, in fact it demonstrates the opposite. In Fodor's terms, we can identify narrow content either by way of sentences that express it or by way of sentences that *sneak up on it*. Narrow content, however, cannot be expressed by way of the sentences of any natural language, for such sentences are, necessarily, anchored ones. We can sneak up by *mentioning*, rather than *using*, sentences of a natural language that, as mentioned, pick out narrow contents via their hypothetical semantic properties (i.e. that pick them out as functions from thoughts and contexts to truth-conditions). But this means that narrow content can be identified only by way of sentences that express ordinary wide semantic content. We may have an extensional criterion of identity for narrow content, but narrow content is still individuation dependent on wide content. Thus, narrow content does not seem to be logically or conceptually separable from wide content. And, therefore, the appeal to narrow content does nothing to support the limited defence of the Cartesian picture provided by the dual component theory. It does nothing, that is, to support the idea of a separate portion of mental reality to which the Cartesian picture could be applicable.[16]

Narrow mental states as syntactic properties

Since we identify ordinary wide mental states by way of their content, it is natural to suppose that we might expect to do the same with narrow mental states. However, this expectation has proved to be unfulfilled. There is no way of expressing the narrow content of a mental state using sentences of a public language – and what other sort of language would there be? – since such a language uses terms that express concepts that are wide or, as Fodor puts it, *anchored*. The alternative is to *sneak up on* the narrow content of mental states by *mentioning*, rather than using, sentences of a natural language, where mentioning a sentence can be used to pick out narrow content via its hypothetical semantic properties. However, while this may provide us with an extensional criterion of identity for narrow contents, it does not do so in a way that provides any support to the Cartesian view that we can separate off a portion of mental reality that is logically independent of the external world. Narrow content, understood as a function from thoughts and contexts onto truth-conditions is, pretty clearly, individuation on wide semantic content in that the only way we have of identifying the former is by way of sentences that express the latter. Therefore, it seems that any attempt to bolster the Cartesian conception of the mind by way of the notion of narrow content is doomed to failure.

There is, however, an alternative way of identifying the narrow mental state – one that proceeds not by appeal to the notion of content but by way of the notion of *syntax*. Recall Putnam's twin-earth thought-experiment described earlier. One of the temptations to say that Emma and her twin had the same mental state, when they both had mental states that they would express to themselves by way of the phrase "the thought that water is wet", stemmed from the fact that both states seemed to play an identical functional role in the two Emmas' psychologies – at least when these functional roles were solipsistically specified. Thus, they also had precisely the same consequences for the behaviour of the two Emmas.

This prompts the idea that narrow mental states are individuated by way of their functional roles. Emma's thought expressed by the sentence-form "water is wet" is identical with twin Emma's thought expressed by the same sentence-form, because the two mental states are identical with regard to their functional roles, solipsistically specified of course.

How does the concept of functional role link up with the concept of syntax? Basically, the notion of syntax, while not entirely unambiguous, is the notion of a *higher-order physical property of a state in virtue of which it has a functional role*. A key, for example, has a certain shape, and in virtue of this shape it is capable of opening a certain lock and not others.[17] The shape of the key, that is, is a (partial) determinant of the causal powers of the key. However, it is not the shape *in toto* that determines the causal powers of the key with respect to a lock. It is only a certain aspect, or certain parts, of the shape of the key that are relevant – specifically, those parts of the shape that interact with the relevant features of the lock it is supposed to open. Any part of the shape of the key that does not interact with the lock is irrelevant to the lock-opening causal powers of the key. Thus, the syntax of the key is not the shape *simpliciter* of the key, but a certain higher-order feature of that shape. How do we identify this higher-order feature? The most natural way is to individuate it *functionally*. That is, the syntax of the key consists in those features or aspects of the shape of the key in virtue of which it interacts with a lock in such a way as to open (or lock) it. That is, the syntax of the key is a functionally individuated higher-order feature of the shape of the key.

It is also possible to talk of the syntax, or syntactic features, of mental states. Such talk is most natural within the apparatus of what are known as *mental representations*. Some mental states – specifically the propositional attitudes – are often thought of as relations to mental representations. That is, to have a propositional attitude is to stand in a certain relation to a mental representation. What relation? It depends on the propositional attitude. To have a belief is to stand in the belief relation to a mental representation. To have a desire is to stand in the desire relation to a representation. What makes this relation a belief relation, or a desire relation? The usual story is a functional one. A belief that *P* has a very different functional role from a desire that *P*. Desires for things typically make their possessor go after those things, for example, whereas beliefs can play a role in deciding how best to satisfy desires.

However one ultimately understands the nature of the relation to a representation, this is very different from the nature of the representation itself. A mental representation is usually understood as a structure instantiated in the brain of a mental subject. However, what makes this structure a representation is not, typically, thought to be its neural properties but rather certain other higher-order properties. Of course, for a structure in the brain to count as a representation, it must actually represent something. That is, it must be about something; it must have what is known as *intentionality* or *aboutness*. The belief that water is wet is about water, and about its relation to wetness. If, therefore, this belief is a relation to a representation, then the representation must somehow be about water and wetness. One way of putting this is to say that the representational must have representational properties; it must have certain properties in virtue of which it is about something other than itself.

There is no philosophical consensus on exactly what the representational properties of representations are. Usual accounts focus on some sort of causal, nomological or teleological, relation. On the first view, a representation *R* is about some state of affairs *S* only if *S* typically causes *R*. On the second view, a representation *R* is about *S* only if *S* and *R* enter into an appropriate lawlike relation of the form, "Necessarily, *R* only if *S*". On the third view, *R* is about *S* only if *R* is supposed to occur only in the presence of *S*, where "supposed" is typically explained in terms of some sort of history of selection. There are problems with all three accounts.

In addition to representational properties, mental representations are usually regarded as having other, non-representational, properties. This stems from the fact that beliefs, desires and other propositional attitudes can enter into causal relations with each other. A desire combined with a belief, for example, can cause another desire, a desire that is believed to be a necessary condition of satisfying the first desire. Therefore, propositional attitudes must have properties in virtue of which they can enter into causal relations with each other. They must, that is, have properties in virtue of which they have a certain functional role in a mental subject's psychology. These properties are typically conceived of as higher-order physical properties of the neural structures that constitute representations. These are the *syntactic* properties of representations.

We arrive at the view that every propositional mental state has both representational or semantic properties and formal or syntactic properties in virtue of being a relation to a representation that has both semantic and syntactic properties. This has been, and pretty much still is, the orthodox view of propositional mental states.

If we accept that content-based attempts to explain the notion of a narrow mental state do not work, then we are left with formal or syntactic attempts. The narrow mental state, on this view, is the mental state individuated according to its formal or syntactic properties, or, more accurately, according to the formal or syntactic properties of the representation to which it is a relation.

Is the syntactic individuation of mental states sufficient to safeguard the Cartesian vision of the mind as an internally constituted reality? It can do so only if it is possible, at least logically, to separate the causal roles of mental states from the wider world in which those roles are situated, for it is in terms of these roles that we individuate the syntactic properties of mental states and hence arrive at the mental state narrowly individuated. The natural idea, here, is that to separate the functional roles of mental states from the wider world in which they are situated is to provide a solipsistic specification of those functional roles. If a solipsistic specification of those roles is possible, so too is the separation required by a limited defence of Cartesianism.

Consider a belief, for example. To preview an important discussion in Chapter 9, suppose this is the belief that the Museum of Modern Art is on West 53rd Street. On an ordinary understanding of the functional role of this belief, this role is patently non-solipsistic. Specification of this role, for example, will advert to what typically causes it: for example seeing the museum while walking down West 53rd Street. It will also advert to the typical behaviour that, in combination with other mental states, issues from it. Thus, in combination with the desire to see Picasso's Les Demoiselles d'Avignon, it might result in the behaviour of entering the building whereas, in combination with an aversion to any art after the Impressionists, it might result in one scuttling off down the street. The typical causes of the belief and the typical behaviour that issues from it all involve items that are clearly external to the subject of the belief. Therefore, to understand the role of the belief in this way is to understand it non-solipsistically.

There is, however, another way of understanding the functional role of the belief. This involves restricting the typical perceptual causes and the typical behavioural effects of the belief to proximal episodes occurring at or inside the skin of the subject of the belief. For example, instead of regarding a typical cause of the belief as the museum itself, we might construe it as a pattern of light energy distributed across the retina. And instead of regarding a typical behavioural effect as entering the building, we might regard it as a bodily movement of a certain sort, one that can, in principle, be identified independently of the museum itself. In this sort of way, it might be thought, we could provide a solipsistic specification of the functional role of the belief and thus underwrite the limited defence of Cartesianism suggested by the dual component theory.

There are, I think, profound difficulties with this project. Particularly pressing is the problem of providing the relevant solipsistic specification of behaviour.[18] For example, for obvious reasons, we cannot describe the behaviour as walking towards the building. But even walking seems to entail the existence of (i) a body and (ii) space within which that body can move. And, at least (ii) and, on some versions of internalism, (i) are external to the subject of the behaviour. So we could set up a twin-earth thought-experiment, along the lines of the *Matrix* example described earlier. Your twin lives in a pod and is fed the liquefied remains of his or her neighbours. However, due to some nifty virtual-reality pyrotechnics on the part of the machines, your twin has lived a life experientially indistinguishable from yours (on a solipsistic way of individuating experience, of course). Nevertheless, your twin has never walked. To describe your behaviour as walking falls foul of a twin-earth scenario, and so to describe it in this way is not to describe it solipsistically.

It is difficult to see, then, what the requisite narrow specification of behaviour would be like. In the absence of this, there is no reason for supposing that the appeal to syntax in an attempt to explicate the idea of the narrow mental state is going to work. However, this is only to scratch the surface of the problems with the idea that we can specify functional roles narrowly. In Chapter 9 we shall look at another way of developing the idea of externalism, a way that does not depend on, or derive from, the content of mental states. This is an externalism, not of the *contents* of cognition but of the *vehicles* of cognition. As we shall see, there is an intimate connection between the notion of a vehicle of cognition and the concept of functional role. The possibility of this further form of externalism – *vehicle externalism* – drives another nail into the coffin of the idea that we can safeguard a limited form of Cartesianism by appeal to the concept of syntax or functional role.

Conclusion

Content externalism derives from the thought experiments of Putnam and Burge, and from work on indexicals associated with Kaplan. Content externalism applies to mental states – the propositional attitudes – that are individuated according to their semantic content. If the arguments of Putnam, Burge and Kaplan are correct, then, at the very least, such mental states are externally individuated. This means that they entail, at the very least, the rejection of the Possession Claim that, in part, defined the concept of internalism.

The dual component theory is an attempt – Cartesian in spirit – to restrict the impact of these arguments by redrawing the bounds of the inner to encompass the internal components of mental states, or mental states narrowly individuated, rather than mental states traditionally understood. If this attempt is to work, the internal component must be at least logically separable from the mental state widely individuated. And this entails that it must be possible to identify the former independently of the latter. Attempts at such independent identification either involve the notion of the narrow content of a mental state or the notion of a solipsistic specification of the functional role of that state. Prospects for either strategy, however, seem grim.

CHAPTER 7

The scope and limits
of content externalism

Chapter 6 examined the arguments for content externalism and an essentially defensive reaction to those arguments – a reaction that is Cartesian in spirit – based on the dual component theory, along with the associated idea of the mental state narrowly individuated. It was argued that this Cartesian reaction to the arguments for externalism faces serious difficulties. Nonetheless, we have not yet worked out the implications of the arguments themselves. If an essentially Cartesian strategy to limit their scope does not work, we have, as yet, done nothing to work out what that scope is. This is the task of this chapter.

Externalism and content

The arguments for content externalism turn, of course, on the *content* of mental states. That is, if they apply to a given class of mental states then this is in virtue of the fact that those mental states possess semantic content. In fact, in order for the arguments to work, not only must the mental states possess semantic content, but they must possess this content *essentially*. That is, this content must enter into the identity conditions of mental states. If not, all the arguments for content externalism would show is that certain of the inessential features of mental states are not determined exclusively by what occurs inside the skin of any given individual but depend on the nature of the physical and/or linguistic environment of that individual. But this is very different from showing that the mental states themselves are, in this sense, environmentally dependent. This latter claim will go through only if we assume that the content of mental states is essential to them.

The upshot is that the arguments for content externalism will work only for propositional attitudes, and then only if we assume that propositional attitudes possess their contents essentially. Propositional attitudes are a class of mental states composed of *cognitive* states such as beliefs and thoughts and *affective* states such as desires and fears. Roughly, a cognitive state is one that carries information about the way the world is whereas an affective state is one that pertains to the way the subject would like the world to be (or not be). The category of propositional attitudes includes both sorts of state.

The mind, of course, is made up of much more than just cognitive and affective states. In particular, there are two types of mental item that do not fall within this category. First, there are *cognitive processes*: processes such as perceiving, thinking, remembering, reasoning and so on. The connection between cognitive processes and cognitive and affective states is not a simple one. But, pretty clearly, cognitive states can be the result or culmination of cognitive processes. A belief, for example, can be the result of a process of perceiving (I believe that the cat is on the mat as a result of perceiving that the cat is on the mat) or reasoning (there is something on the mat, and since I am sure I locked the door when I went out, it is probably the cat). Affective states, while not usually the simple result or culmination of cognitive processes, can interact with cognitive processes in a variety of ways. Often, for example, they can initiate cognitive processes. I desire to get the cat off the mat but, fearing its hissing and spitting demeanour, I devise an elaborate strategy involving a dummy mouse and a piece of string, or whatever.

Cognitive and affective states can link up with cognitive processes in a variety of ways. However, cognitive processes are not the same thing as cognitive and affective states. What I believe is one thing; how I came to believe it is quite another. And what I desire is one thing, but the cognitive consequences of this desire are quite another. For our purposes, it is important to note that cognitive processes do not seem to be semantically evaluable in the way that cognitive and affective states are. Or at least one way of understanding cognitive processes is that they are not semantically evaluable. For example, I might remember that the cat is on the mat, and my memory is, thus, semantically evaluable: it has the content expressed by the sentence "the cat is on the mat". But it is not clear that the cognitive process itself has this semantic content. We shall return to this in the next section.

The second category of mental item to which the arguments for content externalism do not apply is the category of what are known as *sensations*. This category includes such things as pains, tickles, itches, orgasms, feelings of warmth or cold and the like. These sorts of mental state do not seem to be *about* anything – at least not in the same way that thoughts, beliefs and desires are about things. They are not intentional or representational states and so are not states that possess semantic content, essentially or otherwise. The arguments for content externalism, therefore, do not apply to them for the simple reason that they do not possess content.

The first restriction on the scope of content externalism, then, is that it applies only to mental items that possess semantic content and possess such content essentially. This incorporates the class of cognitive and affective states known as the propositional attitudes, but excludes other important mental items – notably cognitive processes and sensations.

Cognitive states and cognitive processes

On the face of it, it might seem that cognitive processes do possess semantic content. Suppose I desire to get the cat off the mat and I reason that if I let the dog into the room he will chase the cat off the mat. This is a process of reasoning, albeit rudimentary. My process of reasoning, however, seems to be made up largely of a belief, and so, it might be thought, the process is semantically evaluable since the belief is. The same thing also seems to apply to more complex reasoning processes. Here, for example, is the sort of thing Sherlock Holmes was very good at.

> I instantly reconsidered my position when . . . it became clear to me that whatever danger threatened an occupant of the room couldn't come from either the window or the door. My attention was speedily drawn, as I have already remarked to you, to this ventilator, and to the bell-rope which hung down to the bed. The discovery that this was a dummy, and that the bed was clamped to the floor, instantly gave rise to the suspicion that the rope was there as a bridge for something passing through the hole, and coming to the bed. The idea of a snake instantly occurred to me and when I coupled it with my knowledge that the Doctor was furnished with a supply of creatures from India I felt that I was probably on the right track.[1]

This is, clearly, a process of reasoning and, hence, a cognitive process. However, it seems to be composed largely of states that are semantically evaluable. In reality, however, what we have here is a succession of processes all of which culminate in a semantically evaluable state and which, when taken together, yield the (semantically evaluable) conclusion-belief that Holmes wants. Thus, a process results in Holmes becoming clear (i.e. believing with a certain degree of conviction) that the danger to the occupant of the room could come from neither window nor door, another process (his attention being speedily drawn) results in a belief that the bell-rope was the vehicle through which the attack took place and so on. At each stage of the reasoning process, a semantically evaluable state (belief, etc.) results, but the process itself is distinct from this state: the process is what results in the state and is not the state itself. When we talk of cognitive processes not being semantically evaluable, we observe this firm distinction between process and state that is the culmination of the process. Cognitive processes are not semantically evaluable, even if their products are.

What are cognitive processes? At an extremely abstract level, cognitive processes can be understood as *functions*: functions relating environmental input to cognitive or behavioural output. Take reasoning, for example. Holmes is presented with certain data as input: dummy bell-rope, bed clamped to the floor and so on. This input is combined with various principles of rational inference (principles that Holmes is peculiarly good at employing) to yield an output: the assassin used a snake, which crawled down the bell-rope. Reasoning is, then, a process by which input is transformed into output. To understand reasoning is to understand how this transformation is brought about.

Similarly, take perception: visual perception, say. According to the traditional account, input is provided in the form of stimulation of the retina (specifically the rod and cone cells of the retina). This stimulation, and the resulting pattern of activity, is propagated to the visual processing centre of the brain (the visual cortex), where it is combined with various operations occurring in the visual cortex. The culmination of all this activity – at least if all goes well – is a perception of whatever object it is that caused the stimulation. Thus, visual perception is a process that transforms sensory input into output that consists in a perception. To understand perception is to understand how this transformation takes place.

At this extremely abstract level, cognitive processes can be understood as functions whereby one thing or quantity is transformed into another. To understand a cognitive process is to understand how the transformation peculiar to it is achieved. But how do we understand this? The usual story is that to understand a function of this sort involves breaking it down into simpler and simpler sub-functions, and showing how these sub-functions can be performed or accomplished by way of certain identifiable mechanisms. To understand cognitive processes, it is claimed, is to be able to effect this sort of functional and mechanistic decomposition.

As an example of this general approach, consider David Marr's well-known model of vision.[2] Marr adopts the traditional understanding of vision as beginning with stimulation of the retina and culminating in a visual perception. Stimulation of the retina takes the form of electro-magnetic energy – measured in pixels – distributed over an array of different locations on the retina. This pattern of stimulation is often referred to as the *retinal image*. The starting point for vision is, thus, the retinal image. The retinal image, however, is not equivalent to a visual perception. Images are flat, static and open to a variety of interpretations. Visual perception, on the other hand, yields a three-dimensional, mobile and interpreted world. It seems, therefore, that visual perception must involve processes that go beyond the information present in the image. The image, in order to yield a perception, must be processed in some way. Therefore, to understand vision, according to Marr, is to understand the processes whereby the retinal image is transformed into a visual perception of the world.

To understand these processes, Marr recommends the sort of functional–mechanistic decomposition outlined above. According to Marr, three distinct theoretical levels need to be recognized in order to understand a complex information-processing task such as visually perceiving the world. For any process (and vision consists of very many such processes), we must first formulate a *computational* theory. Such a theory will specify what is being processed or computed and why. The next level consists of *algorithms* for achieving the computation. Finally, there is the level that describes the implementation of the algorithm. This is, broadly speaking, the level of mechanism.

The input for visual processing consists in a retinal image, where this is characterized in terms of light intensity distributed over an array of locations on the retina. The distribution of intensity values is created by the way in which light is reflected by the physical structures that the observer is viewing. The goal of early visual processing, according to Marr, is to create from the retinal image a description of the visual structures – the shapes of surfaces and their orientations and distances from the observer – that are being observed.

The first stage in early visual processing consists in the construction of what Marr calls the *primal sketch*. The primal sketch describes the intensity changes present in the image and makes some of the more global image structures explicit. Construction of the primal sketch consists of two stages. First, there is the construction of the *raw primal sketch*. The raw primal sketch is a representation of the pattern of light distributed over the retina in which information about the edges and textures of objects is made explicit. This information is expressed in a set of statements about the edges and blobs present in the image, their locations, orientations and so on. Secondly, the application of various grouping principles (e.g. proximity, similarity, common fate, good continuation, closure and so on) to the raw primal sketch results in the identification of larger structures, boundaries, regions and so on. This more refined representation is known as the *full primal sketch*. Further processing – specifically, analyses of depth, motion, shading and so on – results in what Marr calls the 2½D sketch. This is the culmination of early visual processing and describes the layout of structures in the world from the vantage-point of the observer. A further, and equally essential, aspect of vision is recognition of objects. In order to recognize the object to which a particular shape corresponds, a third representational level is needed, a level centred on the object rather than the observer. This level consists in what Marr calls 3D object representations. This stage of visual processing utilizes a stored set of object descriptions. Three-dimensional model representations are, according to Marr, the culmination of visual processing.

I include Marr's account of vision, not because I think it is correct but, rather, because it provides a very good illustration of the method of functional and mechanistic decomposition at work. Visual processing is broken down into early and late processing. Early visual processing is broken down into the construction of the primal sketch and the 2½D sketch. Construction of the primal sketch is broken down into the construction of the raw primal sketch and the full primal sketch and so on. The goal of this functional decomposition is to arrive at functions that are simple enough to be realizable by identifiable mechanisms – this, in Marr's terminology, being the level of physical implementation. The same methodological approach is embodied in Dennett's distinction between *intentional*, *design*, and *physical* stances.[3]

To understand vision, on this sort of approach, is to be able to effect the correct functional–mechanistic decomposition of the process whereby visual sensation is transformed into visual perception. This sort of decomposition is carried out or defined by processes that are almost universally regarded as internal. The starting point for vision is the retinal image, and this is something that occurs inside the skin of the perceiving organism. Since this image contains relatively little information, it must, in order to be transformed into a visual perception, be *processed*. This processing is conceived of as information processing, processing of the information contained in the retinal image. Since the retinal image occurs inside the skin of the perceiving organism, the information processing necessary to produce visual perception is also thought to occur inside that organism's skin. Vision, then, is a process that begins at the skin but takes place exclusively inside the perceiving organism.

Thus, the cognitive–affective aspect of mentality can be broken down into states and processes. The former consist in semantically evaluable states such as beliefs and desires. These are individuated according to their content and the arguments for content externalism can, accordingly, be applied to them. Cognitive processes, on the other hand, consist in operations whereby one semantically evaluable state, or group of such states, is transformed into another state or group of states. These operations are conceived of as information-processing operations: functions whereby one informational item is transformed into another. This sort of information processing is, still, almost universally thought of as something that occurs inside the skin of cognizing subjects. Thus the orthodox view is that although the arguments for content externalism might apply to the cognitive states that result from these information-processing operations, they do not apply to the operations themselves. Therefore, if the distinction between cognitive states and cognitive processes can be maintained, an externalist account of the former is perfectly compatible with an internalist story of the latter. This combination of internalism and externalism is still pretty much the orthodox view.

Psychotectonics and psychosemantics

A distinction that might help clarify and explain this peculiar combination of internalism and externalism is one between two crucially distinct ways of understanding the mind. The distinction is between what we can call *psychotectonics* and *psychosemantics*.

> *Psychotectonics*: the project of working out how to build a system capable of cognition.

Psychotectonics is an investigation into how psychological systems are constructed and by what design principles of cognitive capacities are forged. Since a system that is capable of cognition is a system to which semantic content can be attributed, psychotectonics is simultaneously the project of working out how to build a system that can sustain the attribution to it of such content. This project, however, should be clearly distinguished from that of psychosemantics.

> *Psychosemantics*: the project of working out the conditions under which the attribution of semantic content to a system is warranted.

In engaging in psychosemantics one would, presumably, have to pay attention to how the system in question is constructed, what design

129

principles are followed and so on. This is because whether or not the attribution of content to the system is warranted depends, in part, on such matters. Nevertheless, an investigation into the principles involved in building a system capable of sustaining the attribution to it of semantic content is not the same as an investigation into the conditions under which the attribution of such content to that system is warranted. The former is an engineering project, concerned with what is often called cognitive *architecture*. It is a project whose goal is to investigate how the edifice of the mind is erected from the ground up, so to speak. The latter is, for want of a better word, an *interpretive* project, concerned with the conditions under which it is legitimate to employ a particular sort of interpretation of the behaviour of a system.

The arguments for content externalism, since they turn on the content of mental states, can show only that the project of psychosemantics must be environment-involving. The arguments show that we cannot know whether a given attribution of a contentful state to an organism is warranted unless we focus, at least in part, on the environment of that organism, and specifically on the objects, properties, events and so on that exist in the world or the environment of that organism. This is not simply an epistemological problem. If the arguments for content externalism are correct, whether or not a given attribution of a content-based state is correct – irrespective of our knowing this – depends on the nature and contents of the environment. This, however, implies nothing whatsoever about the (putatively) internal processes, mechanisms or architectures that, in part, underwrite the attribution of contentful states to subjects. If content externalism is true, and if certain mental states have their contents essentially, then some form of externalism must be true of those states as well as of their contents. However, this is perfectly compatible with the claim that an organism to which the attribution of content is warranted also possesses purely internal mechanisms – mechanisms in which are instantiated internal events and processes – and that these mechanisms form the structural basis of mental states. Such mechanisms would form the cognitive architecture of the organism, the architecture that allows the organism to cognize and, when placed in a suitable environment, sustain the attribution of contentful states.

Externalism about content in no way impugns the possibility of mental states possessing this sort of internal structural basis or architecture. Thus, a psychotectonic investigation of this structural architecture can afford to focus purely on what is internal to the cognizing organism. This is true even if the project of psychosemantics is essentially environment-involving.

In other words, externalism about the content of mental states is compatible with the following claim.

The capacity of an organism to process the information it needs to interact successfully with the environment can be explained purely in terms of internal mechanisms and internal operations defined over those mechanisms.

This claim of the internality of cognitive architecture is just about constitutive of all but the most recent theorizing about the nature of cognitive processes. In Chapter 9, we will look at reasons for thinking that the claim is false. For present purposes, we should simply note that this claim of the internality of cognitive architecture and the cognitive processes instantiated in that architecture is compatible with the claim that cognitive (and affective) states – the results of such processes – possess content that is externally individuated.

We have now properly identified the first major restriction on content externalism. Content externalism applies to cognitive and affective states; since these are individuated according to their semantic content. However, it does not apply either to the cognitive architecture that allows a creature to cognize, or to the cognitive processes, run on such architecture, that culminate in the production of semantically evaluable cognitive and affective states. Content externalism applies to cognitive and affective states, but not to cognitive architecture and not to cognitive processes.

Experiences

In addition to cognitive processes, it is also plausible to suppose that at least some types of *experience* are immune to the arguments for content externalism. This will be true if, as many argue, experiences are not essentially characterized by semantic content. This claim is widely accepted for one category of experience: the category of bodily *sensations*. This category includes things such as pains, tickles, itches and nausea. The majority view is still that these sorts of experience are non-representational in character, hence do not have semantic content. A pain, for example, is not *about* or intentionally directed towards anything in the way that a belief is. Therefore, the orthodox view is that pain is not the sort of thing that can be characterized in terms of semantic content.[4] If this is correct, the arguments for content externalism cannot apply to pain and other bodily sensations.

In addition to bodily sensations, the category of experience also includes perceptual experiences: seeing or seeming to see a red rose, hearing a loud trumpet, tasting Rocky Road ice cream and so on.

Perceptual experiences are very different from bodily sensations in that the former have, but the latter lack, an intentional object. Visual experiences, for example, can be about things; we distinguish between a visual experience and what it is an experience of but we do not make this distinction in the case of pains. Visual experiences represent the world a certain way, but pains have no such representational content. Nevertheless, bodily sensations and perceptual experiences are often classified together because they are both, at least according to many, defined by their *phenomenology*: by the way it seems or feels to undergo them. That is, an orthodox view of the nature of both bodily sensations and perceptual experiences is that what it is to undergo them is a matter of *what it is like* for the subject of those states.

The claim that bodily sensations and perceptual experiences are both characterized by their phenomenology or phenomenal properties does not, by itself, rule out their being subject to content externalism. An increasingly popular position, for example, is that the phenomenal properties of an experience can be reduced to its representational properties or, equivalently, that the phenomenal content of an experience is identical with its representational or semantic content. This claim is more plausible for perceptual experiences than it is for bodily sensations; but has been made for both.[5] But even for perceptual experiences there are well-known problems involved in trying to reduce phenomenal content to representational content. The problems are illustrated in a thought-experiment developed by Ned Block, a variation on the Putnam twin-earth experiment.[6]

Block's strategy involves trying to show the possibility, with respect to a set of experience tokens, of a variation in the representational properties of those experiences without a corresponding variation in their phenomenal properties. If this type of possibility is genuine, Block argues, the phenomenal properties of experiences cannot be constituted by their representational properties. To this end, Block imagines what he calls *inverted earth*.

On inverted earth, everything has a different colour from the colour it has on earth. The sky is yellow, grass is red, the sun is blue and Coca-Cola cans are green. Thus, if you visited inverted earth, you would see the sky as yellow, the grass as red and so on. However, the vocabulary of the residents of inverted earth is also inverted. Thus, in talking of the colour of the sky, they use the term "blue"; and in talking of the colour of grass, they use the term "green" and so on. Furthermore, because of the differences between earth and inverted earth, the intentional or representational contents of the propositional attitudes and experiences of inverted earthlings are themselves inverted. Thus, when a resident of inverted earth wonders, as he would put it, "Why is the sky blue?", he is not wondering why the sky is blue, he is wondering why the sky is yellow.

Suppose, now, you are taken to inverted earth. Then, under normal circumstances, the sky would appear yellow and the sun would appear blue. However, suppose that during your transportation, scientists fit you with colour-inverting lenses (fill in the necessary details yourself: you are unconscious during transportation, your body pigments are altered so you don't have a nasty shock when you wake up and so on). The lenses cancel out the inverted colours on inverted earth, so when you wake up on inverted earth, you notice no difference. The yellow sky looks blue to you, the blue sun looks yellow. And all the inverted earthlings around you describe the yellow sky as "blue". So from the point of view of phenomenal character of your experiences nothing is any different from the way it would have been had you stayed on earth. Initially, the representational contents of your experiences and propositional attitudes would also be the same. The causal rooting of your colour words is grounded, it seems, in your prior use on earth. So on your first day on inverted earth, for example, when you think that, for example, the sky is as blue as ever, you are expressing the same thought as you would have expressed on earth; it is just that in this case you are wrong. Moreover, your thought is not identical with the one a native of inverted earth would express with the same words. However, it is plausible to suppose that after a suitable period of time, the representational contents of your experiences and attitudes would change. After sufficient time has been spent on inverted earth, your embedding in your new physical and linguistic environment would come to dominate, and your representational contents would, accordingly, shift so as to be the same as those of the natives.

Thus, we seem to have a logically possible situation in which the representational properties of your experiences alter without any corresponding alteration in the phenomenal properties of those experiences. And, if this is correct, the phenomenal properties of experiences cannot be constituted by the representational properties of those experiences.

The inverted earth thought-experiment is, perhaps, not decisive. There are various ways of replying to it, or attempting to avoid the conclusions it invites us to draw.[7] These issues are complex and we cannot adjudicate them here. Therefore, we will have to state the second restriction on content externalism in conditional form. *If*, as is still the orthodoxy, the phenomenal content of experiences cannot be reduced to representational content, and *if* experiences possess their phenomenal content, but not their representational content, essentially, then experiences are not subject to content externalism.

Simple and complex concepts

The scope of content externalism is restricted to states that possess semantic content essentially – states for whom their semantic content plays a role in determining their identity as the particular states they are. This is not surprising. Content externalism is, in the first instance, a thesis about semantic content, and the determination of such content by the environment. It is no wonder, then, that it should apply only to states that have such content essentially.

However, even when we focus on mental states that have semantic content essentially – which I will assume, for present purposes, are all and only the propositional attitudes – we still find fairly conspicuous limitations on the scope of content externalism. One limitation turns on the distinction between *simple* and *complex* concepts and a resulting difference between simple and complex propositional attitudes.

Is it possible to grasp the concept of H_2O in a world where there is no such thing? Actually, it seems so. H_2O is a complex concept, and so all one needs in order to grasp it is a grasp of the concept of hydrogen, a grasp of the concept of oxygen, and a grasp of the notion of molecular combination. Even if one lives in a world where hydrogen and oxygen never combine in this way, one can still grasp the concept of the state that would result from a combination of the two, as long as one grasps the idea of each individual component and of the mode of combination by way of which they might – even if, in fact, they never do – combine together. Thus, one does not need to live in a world where there is H_2O in order to have the concept of H_2O. Therefore, one does not need to live in a world where there is H_2O in order to have thoughts about, or more generally propositional attitudes directed towards, H_2O. All that is required is that one inhabit a world where there is hydrogen and oxygen and a way, consistent with the laws of nature, of combining the two. Even weak externalism is, therefore, not true of a complex concept such as H_2O.

The moral seems to be that externalism – even in a weak form and *a fortiori* in a strong form – is true only of concepts that are simple rather than complex.[8] The scope of content externalism is, therefore, restricted to propositional attitudes that express contents that are composed of concepts that are simple. Most thoughts and other propositional attitudes are, therefore, exempt from the arguments for content externalism.

External individuation and external location

The scope of content externalism is being revealed to be progressively more and more restricted. It applies neither to cognitive processes nor to the cognitive architecture in which such processes are realized. And in the absence of a reduction of phenomenal content to semantic content – a reduction that, I think it is fair to say, has yet to be successfully demonstrated – it does not apply to sensations or perceptual experiences. Moreover, even when we restrict our attention to propositional attitudes, we find that content externalism applies only to a sub-category of these: those attitudes whose content is constituted by at least one simple, as opposed to complex or derived, concept. There is one further restriction on the scope of content externalism, perhaps the most significant of all. Even in the case of propositional attitudes whose contents are constituted by concepts that are simple, the arguments for content externalism show only that such attitudes are externally *individuated*, not that they are externally *located*. That is, while the arguments for content externalism entail rejection of the Possession Claim that is partially definitive of internalism, these arguments, by themselves, are not sufficient to entail rejection of the Location Claim.

Recall McGinn's characterization of individuation dependence discussed in Chapter 6. According to McGinn:

Fs are individuation dependent on *Gs* if and only if:
(i)   Reference to *Fs* requires prior reference to *Gs*.
(ii) Knowledge of the properties of *Fs* requires prior knowledge of the properties of *Gs*.
(iii) It is not possible for *Fs* to exist in a world where *Gs* do not exist.
(iv) Possessing a concept of an *F* requires prior possession of a concept of a *G*.

We referred to these conditions as the linguistic, epistemological, metaphysical and conceptual conditions respectively.

The arguments for externalism, if correct, establish that propositional mental states are individuation dependent on the world – externally individuated – in this sense. Let the *Fs* be beliefs and the *Gs* be objects and properties in the world. Then, as we have seen, the significance of the arguments for externalism can be expressed in terms of the following four claims.

(i)   Reference to beliefs requires reference to appropriate worldly entities.

(ii)   We cannot know what someone believes without knowing the non-mental objects and properties their beliefs are about.
(iii) It simply is not possible for a subject to hold a belief unless their environment contains the appropriate entities.
(iv)   It is not possible to master the concept of a belief without already having mastered concepts for the worldly entities beliefs are about.

One implication of the arguments for externalism, then, is that if they are correct they establish that at least some mental states are individuation dependent on worldly or environmental items. These items usually occur outside the heads or skins of mental subjects and are, in this sense, external to those subjects. Therefore, the arguments for externalism establish that some mental states are *externally individuated*: individuation dependent on items that exist outside the heads or skins of the subjects of those states. Consequently, these arguments entail rejection of the Possession Claim for internalism.

However, this is very different from establishing that such states are *externally located*. To see this, consider an analogy. The property of being a planet seems to be an externally individuated property, in that it satisfies the sorts of conditions specified by McGinn. That is:

(i)   specification of which planet something is requires reference to the star that it orbits;
(ii)   one cannot know which planet something is unless one knows which star it orbits;
(iii) it is not possible for something to be a planet unless it orbits a star;
(iv)   one could not master the concept of a planet unless one had also mastered the concept of a star (and the concept of an orbit).

Thus, the property of being a planet clearly seems to be externally individuated; it is individuation dependent upon the property of being a star (and the property of being an orbit).

Nevertheless, even though the property of being a planet is externally individuated, this does not mean that an instance of this property – an individual planet – is located, even partly, where its star and orbit are located. The property of being a planet can be externally individuated without individual planets – instances of that property – sharing the same location as stars and orbits. In a similar vein, it would seem that mental properties – for example, the property of being propositional attitude *P* – can be individuation dependent on environmental objects and properties, and so can be externally individuated, without instances of that property – individual propositional attitudes of this type – being located, even in part, where those environmental objects and properties are located. The arguments for content externalism, that is, seem to establish only that mental properties are externally individuated. They do not establish that individual propositional attitudes – instances of those properties – are externally located.[9]

Armed with this distinction between external individuation and external location, we might distinguish between what we can call *reactionary* and *radical* forms of content externalism. Reactionary content externalism is the view that some propositionally individuated mental properties are externally individuated. Radical content externalism is the view that tokens or instances of some propositionally individuated mental properties are externally located. Reactionary content externalism is a thesis about mental properties and entails rejection of the internalist Possession Claim. What makes it reactionary is its preservation of at least one core aspect of the Cartesian conception of the mind: the idea that the mental is, ontologically speaking, an internal entity, one located, in one way or another, inside the skins of mental subjects. Radical content externalism, on the other hand, is a thesis about instances or tokens of mental properties. It entirely abandons this ontological aspect of Cartesianism, and consists in the rejection of both the Possession Claim *and* the Location Claim that jointly define the ontological character of internalism.

Radical content externalism is, intuitively, a much more surprising thesis than its reactionary cousin. Token mental states are literally not located entirely inside the heads or skins of mental subjects. Such states are *not in the head* in the quite literal sense that they are spatially located, at least in part, in the world. Reactionary content externalism, on the other hand, is a far less literal view, one whose force is accordingly somewhat attenuated: mental properties are individuation dependent on what is in the world.

The arguments for content externalism, however, seem to establish only the reactionary form of content externalism, understood as a thesis concerning the external individuation of mental properties rather than the external location of their instances. In this sense, content externalism is a far less surprising, and in many ways a far less exciting, doctrine than initial proclamations concerning the mind not being in the head and so on might have suggested. In later chapters, however, we will look at alternative ways of developing externalism's attack on the Cartesian conception, ways that are far more radical than the view we are licensed to believe by the arguments for content externalism themselves.

Conclusion

Examination of content externalism has shown it to be a view with severe scope limitations. To start with, it is restricted to states that have propositional content essentially: states that are individuated by way of their propositional contents. Thus, the thesis of content externalism does not apply to cognitive processes. Nor does it apply to the cognitive architecture or mechanisms that underwrite such processes. Moreover, it does not apply – at least not without a lot of further argument – to sensations, and other mental states defined by their qualitative rather than their propositional content (as perceptual experiences are often taken to be). And even when we restrict our attention to propositionally individuated mental states, the restrictions on content externalism are still severe. First, content externalism applies only to those propositional attitudes whose contents are constituted by at least one concept that is simple as opposed to complex or derived. Secondly, even when restricted to such attitudes, the arguments for content externalism establish only that such attitudes are externally individuated; they do not show that instances of such attitudes are externally located.

In other words, the thesis of content externalism applies only to a vanishingly small proportion of what passes for the mental. And even restricted to this small category of states, it seems to establish something far less exciting than might initially be expected. What we need to look at in the following chapters are ways of extending the general attack on Cartesianism intitiated by content externalism beyond the severely circumscribed limits of that view. We need to look, in other words, at whether there are ways of extending the general insights of content externalism to items – cognitive processes, cognitive architectures, sensations – that are not defined by way of propositional content. If this can be done, then content externalism is not a worthless doctrine. Rather, it would be the *thin end of the wedge*: the view that allows more robust and far-reaching anti-Cartesian arguments on to the stage. This, I shall try to show, is the best way of understanding the significance of content externalism.

This task will be attempted in Chapters 9 and 10. Before that, however, we need to look at an important issue surrounding content externalism, one that has, as yet, received only passing mention. This concerns the epistemological aspect of Cartesianism. We shall now turn to the implications that content externalism has for the idea that we know our own minds first and best.

CHAPTER 8

Externalism and first-person authority

The Cartesian conception of the mind, as we have seen, is composed not just of ontological theses concerning the nature of mental phenomena, but also epistemological theses concerning our knowledge of, or access to, such phenomena. These latter we summed up in the slogan: "each person knows his or her mind *first* and *best*" – the principle of *epistemic internalism*. This chapter examines the implications of content externalism for this principle.

Descartes and first-person authority

It is pretty clear that Descartes is committed to at least some version of the principle of epistemic internalism. Consider, for example, the following from the *Regulae*, §8: "Nothing can be known before the mind, because knowledge of all other things depends on the mind and not the other way around."[1] This is, of course, a clear statement of the claim that our knowledge of our minds is logically prior to our knowledge of other things including the external world. Knowledge of things outside the mind must be built up from our knowledge of what is going on in our minds, and the former is, therefore, dependent upon the latter. This is reiterated in, for example, the *Principles*, Part 1, §8, where he writes:

> the notion that we have of our soul, or of our thought, precedes the notion we have of our body, and it is more certain in view of the fact that we still doubt the existence of things in the external world while we know with certainty what we think.[2]

Here Descartes combines the claim that we know the contents of our own mind *first* – that is, that knowledge of the contents of our own mind is logically prior to knowledge of anything else – with the claim that we know the contents of our own mind *best* – that knowledge we have of these contents is more certain than our knowledge of anything else. Therefore, knowledge of things outside of our mind is, for Descartes, logically posterior to, logically dependent on and less certain than the knowledge each of us has of his or her own mind. The access each of us has to the contents of his or her own mind is, thus, in some sense *special* or *privileged* access, relative to our knowledge of all other things.

As we saw in Chapter 1, this idea of privileged access or, as it is often called, *first-person authority*, can be understood in several logically distinct ways, some of which are more plausible than others.

- *Infallibility*. On one interpretation, first-person authority consists in the infallibility of your knowledge about your own thoughts and other mental states. If you claim sincerely to be thinking that the cat is on the mat, then you cannot be wrong – not over whether the cat is on the mat, but over whether you are thinking that thought. This was probably Descartes's view, although it attracts few adherents today.
- *Incorrigibility*. A somewhat less extreme view is the claim that first-person authority consists in the incorrigibility of your first-person judgements about your own mental states. Incorrigibility is not infallibility. Rather, to say that your judgements about your own mental states are incorrigible is to say that they are not subject to correction by others. You may not be an infallible authority concerning the contents of your own mind, but you are, nonetheless, the *highest* authority.
- *Self-intimacy*. Another alternative is to understand first-person authority in terms of the idea that the contents of your own mind are immediately or transparently available to you, or *self-intimating*; if you are, in fact, thinking that the cat is on the mat, then you know you are thinking this. And this does not require that we are either infallible or incorrigible about the contents of our minds.

Obviously, these three interpretations of first-person authority can be combined in a variety of ways. A more general idea underlying all of them is that knowledge of the contents of your mind is a priori in a way that knowledge of most other things (apart from logical truths and so on) is not. That is, if your knowledge of the contents of your mind is incorrigible and self-intimating, and perhaps even infallible, this entails, and may be grounded in, the fact that this knowledge is a priori. You may need to conduct an investigation of the world in order to find out if the cat is on the mat and your knowledge of this state of affairs is, consequently, a posteriori. But you need conduct no such investigation in order to work out whether you are thinking that the cat is on the mat. The knowledge you have of this latter fact about yourself is knowledge that is peculiarly self-intimating, and your corresponding judgement incorrigible. And this is because this knowledge is a priori. Content externalism provides a threat to first-person authority because it provides a threat to the idea that our knowledge of our own minds is a priori in this way.

Content externalism and privileged access: the problem

Content externalism threatens the idea of first-person authority in all its forms, and does so because it calls into question the idea that the access we have to our own mental states is privileged in the way required for such authority. Privileged access, it is thought, requires a priori knowledge, and content externalism entails that the knowledge we have of at least some of our mental states is not a priori. To see this, recall Putnam's twin-earth scenario described in Chapter 5. Emma, let us suppose, is thinking that water is wet. If the knowledge she has of her thought conforms to any version of Cartesian first-person authority, then this entails:

1. Emma knows a priori that she is thinking water is wet.

However, the moral of the twin-earth scenario is that Emma's ability to think this thought necessarily depends on her environment being a certain way. Twin Emma, for example, cannot think that water is wet since she inhabits a world where there is no such thing as water. Her corresponding thought may be subjectively indistinguishable from Emma's but it is, nonetheless, the thought that retaw is wet and not the thought that water is wet. Therefore, suppose we express the relevant condition of Emma's environment as follows: "Water is instantiated in the environment of Emma". Let us refer to this proposition by way of the letter E (E for "environmental" proposition). Then, it would appear to follow that:

2. The proposition that Emma is thinking that water is wet necessarily depends on E.

That is, in a world where E is false, it would seem that the proposition "Emma is thinking that water is wet" is also false. However, what is the epistemic status of the proposition E? How, that is, would one establish the truth of E? Quite clearly, E could be established only a posteriori. That is:

3. The proposition E cannot be known a priori, but only by way of empirical investigation.

Therefore, the truth of the proposition "Emma is thinking that water is wet" is necessarily dependent on the truth of the proposition E. But the truth of E can be established only a posteriori, by way of suitable empirical investigation. This therefore casts doubt on the claim that the truth of the proposition "Emma is thinking that water is wet" can be established a priori, *even when this proposition is entertained by Emma herself*.[3]

In other words, Emma cannot know whether she is thinking that water is wet unless she knows whether her environment contains water or retaw (that is, unless she knows whether she is on earth or twin earth). But the nature of her environment is not something that she can know a priori; this knowledge requires empirical investigation of the world. Therefore, since Emma's knowledge of what she is thinking can only be had on the basis of empirical investigation of the world around her, her knowledge of what she is thinking cannot be a priori.[4]

Neither, therefore, can it be self-intimating. She can know that she is thinking water is wet only if she knows the nature of her environment. But this latter knowledge is not in any way self-intimating. Therefore, it is difficult to see how the former knowledge could be self-intimating either. Nor, it is argued, is she in any position for her knowledge of what she is thinking to be incorrigible. To know what she is thinking she needs to know what is in her environment, and she is no more an incorrigible authority on this than any other person. Someone, for example, who knew that Emma had, unbeknown to her, been transported to twin earth would almost certainly be a higher authority on the content of her thought, hence of the thought itself, than would Emma. For similar reasons, therefore, there is no way Emma's knowledge of what she is thinking is infallible.

In short, since the content of Emma's thought depends on the nature of her environment, then so too does which thought Emma is thinking. Her knowledge of this, then, can be no more infallible, incorrigible or self-intimating than her knowledge of the nature of her environment. Since her knowledge of her environment is none of these things, neither is her knowledge of which thought she is thinking.

There is a useful way of making this problem graphic.[5] Suppose Emma were periodically transported back and forth between earth and twin earth. Being drugged, or whatever, she knows nothing of her transport. On earth, Emma would entertain thoughts about water. When she first arrives on twin earth, her thoughts, anchored as they are in an earthly context, would continue to be about water. However, after enough time on twin earth, once she has become sufficiently anchored in a twin-earthly linguistic context, her thoughts would switch to being retaw thoughts. However, if she is unaware of her removal to twin earth, she would also be unaware of the shift in her thoughts. As far as she is able to tell, the water thoughts she used to have are type-identical with the thoughts (about retaw) that she now has. And if she were transported back and forth between earth and twin earth, her thoughts would undergo this sort of *slow-switching* even though she is incapable of discerning any difference.

So, at time t, we might suppose, Emma has the thought that water is wet. At time t^*, after her transport to twin earth, Emma has the thought that retaw is wet. But she is completely incapable of telling this apart from her earlier water-thought. Indeed, she takes it to be a water-thought. Therefore, it seems Emma, at any given time, is incapable of identifying whether she is having a water-thought or a retaw-thought. Therefore, her judgement as to the thought she is having could be neither infallible nor incorrigible. Nor is the presence to her of one thought rather than another in any way self-intimating: what is present to her consciousness is insufficient for her to distinguish between a water-thought and a retaw-thought. Thus, if she has knowledge of which thought she is having, this could not be knowledge that was acquired a priori. She could acquire it only subsequent to empirical investigation of her environment.

A dialectical intermission

The argument for the claim that content externalism is incompatible with first-person authority is quite clear. In the eyes of many, however, what the argument establishes is far less clear. We can divide the protagonists into two broad camps. *Compatibilists* claim that content externalism is perfectly consistent with first-person authority (in at least some of its forms).[6] *Incompatibilists* claim that the views are inconsistent.[7]

The motives of these various protagonists in this debate are diverse. One common thread running through much of the debate is that the incompatibility of content externalism with first-person authority is, at least prima facie, a problem for externalism; the presupposition being, of course, that the fact of first-person authority is so obvious that any view that entails its negation is implausible. The (alleged) incompatibility of content externalism and first-person authority, therefore, is often advanced, and defended, by incompatibilists as an *objection* to content externalism.[8] Conversely, one often finds compatibilism defended by those who, to a greater or lesser extent, are sympathetic towards content externalism.[9]

The position I am going to defend in the rest of this chapter is a qualified incompatibilism: content externalism and first-person authority are, in the final analysis, incompatible. However, this is not a problem for content externalism. This is where the qualification comes in. In Chapter 8 we saw that the thesis of content externalism was severely restricted in scope. It does not apply to cognitive processes, cognitive architecture, sensations, and propositional attitudes whose contents are made up of complex, rather than simple, concepts. Therefore, even if content externalism is true, and even if it is incompatible with first-person authority, this still leaves room for first-person authority about all of the above. While no one, presumably, would want to claim that we have first-person authority over our cognitive architecture, and few would want to claim that we have first-person authority over all of our cognitive processes, the claim that we have such authority over our sensations and at least some of our propositional attitudes is, I think, significant. Indeed, I think it is significant enough to deflect most of the force of the counter-intuitiveness accusation levelled against content externalism on the basis of its incompatibility with first-person authority. Before we get into this, however, let us look more closely at the compatibilist position.

Davidson's compatibilism

Donald Davidson develops an influential argument in favour of the compatibilism of content externalism and first-person authority.[10] Central to his case is the contention that the appearance of incompatibility between content externalism and first-person authority derives from two assumptions, ones that are closely associated with such externalism but ones that are, Davidson argues, mistaken. Content externalism entails neither assumption; it can therefore usefully jettison them and the appearance of incompatibility with first-person authority, accordingly, disappears. The two assumptions are:

1. If a thought is identified by a relation to something outside the head, it is not wholly in the head.
2. If a thought is not wholly in the head, it cannot be "grasped" by the mind in the way required by first-person authority.[11]

Consider assumption 1. Davidson, correctly, points out that the inference from a thought being identified by a relation to something outside the head does not entail that the thought is not wholly in the head. Sunburn, for example, is identified by the external factors that produce it, but this does not mean that sunburn is not a condition of the skin (that it is located outside the skin). We encountered this objection in Chapter 7, and this is what occasioned the last, and possibly most significant, restriction on content externalism. The property of being a planet is identified by relation to external items such as stars and orbits. But this does not mean that a planet is located where its star and orbit are. This is why we cannot move from a claim of external *individuation* – individuation dependence on external items or factors – to a claim of external *location* – sharing the spatial position of those items or factors. Davidson is surely correct on this point. However, the question is: does this have any relevance to the issue of first-person authority? And the answer, I think, is clearly: *no*. The question of whether we have first-person authority over our thoughts is logically independent of the question of the location of those thoughts.

To see this, let us accept the minimal content externalist thesis that thoughts are externally individuated, but deny, as we did in Chapter 7, that this means they are externally located.[12] This makes not the slightest difference to the question of our authority over which thoughts we are thinking, for this authority is sensitive to the way in which those thoughts are individuated and not where they are located. To see this, consider our "authority" over the condition of our skin. We wake up one morning and find ourselves with no memory of the preceding days and with darker than usual skin. Do we have "authority" over what this darker hue is? Can we, for example, determine whether it is a suntan, or an expertly applied artificial tan? If the artificial tan were expensive enough, probably not. Thus we have no authority over the condition of our skin and this is so despite the fact that this condition is clearly *not* externally located.

It is the way in which thoughts, and other mental states, are individuated, and not where they are located, that is germane to the issue of first-person authority. Thus, the first assumption Davidson urges us to reject, although he is correct in his urging, has no bearing on whether content externalism is compatible with first-person authority.

Davidson backs his rejection of assumption 1 with the following argument. Those who think that the way in which a thought is identified – that is, by reference to factors outside the skin – has implications for the location of that thought – that is, as outside the skin – are, in essence, confusing thoughts with the descriptions we give of those thoughts. Thus, if we find a difficulty for first-person authority in the claim that thoughts are identified by reference to external factors, then, similarly, we are confusing thoughts with their descriptions. There is, however, an additional worry with this line of argument. It overlooks the fact that the authority that a subject has with respect to their thoughts cannot, plausibly, be regarded as independent of the manner in which the subject represents those thoughts; this manner is precisely the sort of thing that will be represented by way of a description.

As McKinsey asks, what would a case of description-independent first-person authority be like? Presumably Davidson's idea is that we can have authority with respect to the thought itself, but not with respect to the description we might give of that thought. Then, exactly what is it with respect to which we have authority? In such a case, McKinsey argues, we would have no access even to the fact that the episode with which we are acquainted is an episode of thought, rather than, say, indigestion.[13] Contrast this with the traditional conception of first-person authority. On this view, we have authority not just over whether our thoughts occur as some or other indeterminate episode; more importantly, we have authoritative access to the fact that these thoughts have certain contents – the thought that water is wet or that the cat is on the mat. But this, it seems, is precisely to have authority over our thoughts as satisfying certain descriptions. Davidson's attempt to render content externalism compatible with first-person authority by way of the distinction between thoughts and their descriptions, therefore, does not work. It overlooks the fact that the description of a thought is crucial to the question of whether we have first-person authority over that thought.

Now consider assumption 2. What underlies Davidson rejection of assumption 2 is the idea that the perceived incompatibility of content externalism and first-person authority stems not from content externalism as such, but from the mistaken metaphor of thoughts as things to be "grasped" by the mind. The problem, that is, derives from the idea that thoughts and other mental states exist as mental objects that, so to speak, lie before the mind's conscious gaze. First-person authority, as Davidson sees it, then rests on the idea that these objects are entirely transparent to the mind's eye: that each such mental object is what it seems and seems what it is. As he, correctly, points out, "There are no such objects, public or private, abstract or concrete."[14]

In rejecting the idea that thoughts are mental objects, transparent to the mind's eye, Davidson is, I think, entirely correct. Where he is not correct, however, is in thinking that this has any essential bearing on the issue of first-person authority. The idea of introspection as a form of inner observation has been falling progressively out of favour in recent years. However, the question of whether content externalism is compatible with first-person authority arises even if this model is rejected.

To see this, consider a caricature of an alternative account of our introspective faculty. The idea, associated (in non-caricatural form) with Fred Dretske and others, is that access to our own mental condition arises through a form of *displaced perception*.[15] I will consider a hopelessly simplified version of this position, since if we can show that an issue of first-person authority arises even here, then it will also surely arise for more sophisticated versions.

According to the caricatural version of the displaced perception model, the access we have to our own mental condition is an access to mental facts, rather than mental states, that we instantiate. We have access to such facts by way of a displaced perceptual access to the world. The principle is much like having access to the condition of one's petrol tank – whether it is full, empty, or whatever – by way of displaced perceptual access to the petrol gauge. In its caricatural form, let us suppose this is all there is to introspection. We look around, for example, at the cat that is on the mat, and get from this by way of displaced perception to the fact that we believe that the cat is on the mat. This is not a very plausible view, admittedly,[16] but we are using it for a reason. Here we have no suggestion of there being mental objects that lie before the mind's eye. Do we still have a problem of first-person authority? It should be pretty clear that we do. If we were on twin earth, a world where there were no cats but only robots that looked very much like cats, then this sort of displaced perception would not give us access to the mental fact that we believed there was a cat in front of us. We do not see a cat, therefore displaced perception cannot give us access to the fact that we believe there is a cat on the mat. If our access to the mental facts we instantiate is the result of our displaced perceptual access to the world then, if the world is altered, the mental facts to which we have access automatically change also. Therefore, we again have a problem of first-person authority with respect to the mental facts we instantiate.

So we seem forced to accept that the issue of first-person authority does not, in any way, logically depend on the mistaken model of thoughts as mental objects lying, transparently, before the mind's eye. It arises even for theories – caricatural or otherwise – that explicitly repudiate this model. Therefore, Davidson's rejection of assumption 2, while in itself correct, does not automatically effect a reconciliation of content externalism and first-person authority.[17]

Burge's compatibilism

Tyler Burge has also attempted to reconcile content externalism with first-person authority.[18] Recall the three propositions listed earlier that we used to delineate the contours of the dispute.

1. Emma knows a priori that she is thinking water is wet.
2. The proposition that Emma is thinking that water is wet necessarily depends on E.
3. The proposition E cannot be known a priori but only by way of empirical investigation.

The incompatibility of content externalism and first-person authority is thought to derive from, or be reflected in, the collective mutual inconsistency of these three propositions. However, Burge argues that there is a reading of propositions 1–3 that renders them consistent.

Burge's argument turns on the expression "necessarily depends" in proposition 2. Specifically, if this is interpreted as an expression of *metaphysical* dependence, propositions 1–3 are, in fact, consistent. The notion of metaphysical dependence derives from the work of Kripke and denotes a relation of broad logical necessity without the associated idea that this necessity should be knowable a priori.[19]

Consider, for example, the following example of logical necessity, one peculiarly beloved of philosophers: "No bachelor is married." This is what is known as a logical or conceptual truth. The statement is not only true; it must be true, in virtue, roughly, of the meanings of the terms employed in it. The truth of the statement holds with what is known as *logical* or *conceptual* necessity. Moreover, the truth of this statement is knowable a priori, knowable independently of empirical investigation of the world. All that is required is that one knows the meanings of the relevant terms. Thus, there exists a long-standing association of logical necessity with a priori knowledge.

Contrast a logical truth of the above sort with another sort of statement: "The cow did not jump over the moon." This statement is also true, and also seems to hold with some sort of necessity. Compare it with another, grammatically similar, statement: "The cow did not jump over the hedge." The latter statement may also be true. However, the former statement, in addition to being true, seems, in some sense, necessarily true. Not only did the cow, in fact, not jump over the moon, the cow *couldn't* – in some sense of couldn't – jump over the moon (whereas, assuming we are dealing with a relatively small hedge or athletic cow, it could have jumped over the hedge). Therefore, both the statements "No bachelor is married" and "The cow did not jump over the moon" are, in addition to being true, necessarily true. However, there seems to be a significant difference in the type of necessity attaching to each statement. If we claim that some bachelors are married we are, in effect, contradicting ourselves. If we claim that a cow did jump over the moon, we are not committing the same sort of mistake. The claim that there exists a cow who did jump over the moon is incompatible with natural laws – the laws of nature that govern the physical world – but it is not logically inconsistent in the way that "Some bachelors are married" is logically inconsistent.

In short, there is no logical contradiction involved in the claim that a cow did jump over the moon, just a profound ignorance of the laws of nature. Yet both statements seem to be, in some sense, necessarily true. The commonalities and differences between the statements are captured by way of a distinction between two sorts of necessity. The statement "No bachelors are married" is said to hold with logical necessity, meaning that if you were to deny it, you would, broadly speaking, be committing a logical contradiction. However, the claim "The cow did not jump over the moon" is said to hold with *natural* or *nomological* necessity. Denying this statement does not involve a logical contradiction, but it is inconsistent with the known laws of nature. Statements that hold with natural or nomological necessity are not, typically, statements whose truth can be discovered a priori; their truth, in almost all cases, is knowable only a posteriori.

Some types of necessary relation, however, seem to conform to neither of these sorts. For example, identity is a necessary relation. If $X = Y$, then, it is necessary that $X = Y$. Thus, if $X = Y$, then it is not possible for $X \neq Y$. This is more than merely natural or nomological necessity. There is no possible situation or world where water is not H_2O. That would simply be a situation or world where there is a substance superficially indistinguishable from water, but that really is not water, and this substance is not H_2O. In this respect, the identity of water with H_2O seems to be akin to logical necessity. However, it is also true that this sort of identity cannot be discovered a priori. Water is identical with H_2O, but this identity is not the sort of thing that can be discovered by any sort of a priori reasoning – for example, through analysis of the concept expressed by "water". Rather, the identity of water to H_2O is something that can be discovered only a posteriori – through empirical investigation of the world. Therefore, the issue of the necessity of the relation of water with H_2O is logically independent of the issue of the epistemic status – a priori or a posteriori – of our knowledge of this relation.

When Kripke and others invoke the notion of metaphysical necessity, what they are alluding to is a relation of determination that is stronger than mere natural or *nomological* necessity, but does not have the a priori epistemic status usually associated with logical necessity.

This idea of metaphysical necessity provides the basis of Burge's claim that propositions 1–3 are consistent. More precisely, Burge argues that, providing we understand the expression "necessarily depends on" as an expression of metaphysical, as opposed to logical, necessity, proposition 2 can be rendered compatible with both proposition 1 and proposition 3. As we have seen, a proposition that expresses a relation of metaphysical dependency does not entail that this proposition be knowable a priori. Similarly, just because a proposition that is knowable a priori metaphysically depends on another proposition, this does not entail that this latter proposition be knowable a priori.

Thus, take the proposition "Emma is thinking that water is wet". Having first-person authority, Emma knows this proposition a priori. However, this proposition, on Burge's interpretation, is metaphysically dependent on the environmental proposition E: "Water is instantiated in the environment of Emma." However, since metaphysical dependence has no epistemic consequences, the metaphysical dependence of the first proposition on the second does not entail that Emma knows a priori that her environment contains water. That is, Burge argues that proposition 2 should read:

2*. The proposition that Emma is thinking that water is wet is metaphysically dependent on E.

And since metaphysical dependence does not entail a priori knowledge, propositions 1, 2* and 3 are mutually consistent. Therefore, Burge argues, content externalism is compatible with first-person authority.

The problem with Burge's reconciliation of content externalism and first-person authority is that his reading of proposition 2 as proposition 2* is implausible. Metaphysical dependence of the sort invoked by Burge is far too broad to be suitable for the purposes of the content externalist. In particular, as McKinsey has argued, invoking metaphysical dependence in this context will have a rather unfortunate consequence: it will entail that *all* psychological states of *any* kind are wide.[20]

For example, it is plausible to suppose that it is metaphysically necessary that each human being has just the parents they in fact have. Any two people born from different parents, no matter how similar they are, would be different people. This is a widely accepted truth that is thought to hold with metaphysical necessity. Therefore, Emma's thinking that water is wet is metaphysically dependent on Emma's parents existing (at some time or other). In fact, Emma having *any* thought at all is metaphysically dependent on the existence of her parents. Thus, if thoughts are wide, or externally individuated, in virtue of their metaphysical dependence of external objects, then *all* of Emma's thoughts would be wide. Indeed, all of her psychological, physical and behavioural states are metaphysically dependent on her parents. So, presumably these would also have to qualify as wide or externally individuated.

Thus, reading proposition 2 as proposition 2*, in terms of the concept of metaphysical dependence, would render the thesis of content externalism utterly trivial. So this is obviously not the sense of external individuation relevant to content externalism. Emma's thinking that water is wet may, indeed, be metaphysically dependent on the existence of her parents, but it cannot, surely, be externally individuated for *this* sort of reason. In short, Burge's attempt to reconcile content externalism and first-person authority rests on an interpretation of external individuation in terms of metaphysical dependence. But this interpretation cannot be correct and Burge's attempt, therefore, fails.

First-person authority and the scope of content externalism

Defenders of content externalism often take it to be incumbent upon them to fashion some sort of reconciliation with first-person authority because, as they see it, the denial of such authority is sufficiently counter-intuitive to count as an objection to content externalism. I think this argument has little force and, accordingly, the best strategy for the content externalist is to simply reject first-person authority for those states to which content externalism applies. This is a form of incompatibilism, but its scope is severely circumscribed. And its scope is severely circumscribed precisely because, as we saw in Chapter 7, the scope of content externalism is also severely restricted.

As we have seen, content externalism applies only to those mental states that have propositional content essentially: states that are *individuated* by way of their propositional contents. Thus, the thesis of content externalism does not apply to cognitive processes. Nor does it apply to the cognitive architecture or mechanisms that underwrite such processes. Moreover, it does not apply – at least not without a lot of further argument – to sensations and other mental states defined by their qualitative rather than their propositional content (as perceptual experiences are commonly taken to be). Thus, there is nothing in content externalism that rules out our having first-person authority over these sorts of items. Of course, it would be a strange view that held that we have first-person authority over our cognitive architecture, or even many of our cognitive processes, but the reasons we rule out first-person authority for these items has nothing whatsoever to do with content externalism.

The threat to first-person authority posed by content externalism, therefore, probably applies only to propositional attitudes. But, more than this, it applies only to *some* of these. As we also saw, even when we restrict our attention to propositionally individuated mental states, the restrictions on content externalism are still severe. In particular, content externalism applies only to those propositional attitudes whose contents are constituted by at least one concept that is simple as opposed to complex or derived.

Suppose, for example, Emma is thinking that diamonds are a girl's best friend. Suppose also (what may or may not be true) that "diamond" simply means "allotrope of carbon". In line with her first-person authority, Emma knows a priori that she is thinking that diamonds are a girl's best friend. Unfortunately Emma lives in a world where there are no diamonds. So she obviously cannot know a priori that she lives in a world where diamonds exist. She cannot know this at all, since in Emma's world the proposition "diamonds exist" is false. Is the a priori character of Emma's knowledge of what she is thinking compatible with the absence of diamonds in her world? Clearly it is, as long as she lives in a world where there are carbon atoms that, consistent with the operative laws of nature, could combine to form diamonds, even if none ever have. Therefore, if Emma's a priori knowledge of her thought does not require even knowledge of the existence of diamonds in her environment, it clearly does not require *a priori* knowledge of diamonds in her environment.[21]

One reason content externalism is thought to have implausible consequences with respect to the first-person authority we have over our mental states is because it is often associated with claims such as:

(i)   Emma cannot think that water is wet in a world where there is no water.

(ii) Emma cannot think that diamonds are a girl's best friend in a world where there are no diamonds.

Both these claims are false. What might be true, however, is that:

(ia) Emma cannot think that water is wet in a world where there is no hydrogen and/or oxygen or where the operative laws of nature do not allow for these elements to combine with each other.

(iia) Emma cannot think that diamonds are a girl's best friend in a world where there is no carbon, or where the operative laws of nature do not allow the formation of this particular allotrope of carbon.

But, even claims (ia) and (iia) have problems. The term "carbon" tracks an item that can be broken down into protons, neutrons, electrons and so on arranged in certain appropriate ways. And these can, in turn, be broken down into further, more basic, constituents. Who knows where this sort of analysis will stop. That, in essence, is the point. If we do not know where the analysis will stop, then why should Emma? We should probably reformulate the above claims to something like:

(ib) Emma cannot think that water is wet in a world where ontological analysis does not reveal the appropriate basic constituents.
(iib) Emma cannot think that diamonds are a girl's best friend in a world where ontological analysis does not reveal the appropriate basic constituents.

But why should this, in any way, be thought to impugn Emma's first-person authority over the contents of her mind? What it entails, presumably, is that statements of first-person authority always have be to hedged, or qualified, in the following sort of way.

1*. Emma knows a priori that, if the world turns out a certain way, she is thinking that water is wet.

Crucially, in order for proposition 1* to be true, there is no requirement that Emma knows how the world turns out. That the world be an appropriate way is a background or limiting assumption of Emma's a priori knowledge of her thought. But it is not as if Emma has to conduct an empirical investigation of the world in order to find out whether she has a priori knowledge of this sort.

In other words, what Emma has first-person authority over is this: that she is thinking something that, if the world turns out to be a certain way, will be the thought that water is wet. Moreover, in having first-person authority over this, she will also have such authority over the various experiential accompaniments that go with having a thought of this sort. Combining these, I think, we find all the first-person authority we could reasonably expect. If content externalism is incompatible with our having any more authority than this, then this is not an objection to content externalism.

Conclusion

Content externalism is thought by many to be incompatible with first-person authority. Attempts to reconcile the two positions along compatibilist lines fail and a qualified incompatibilism is the best option. However, this incompatibilism is severely restricted in scope for the simple reason that content externalism is severely restricted in scope. Content externalism does not apply to cognitive architecture, cognitive processes and sensations. Therefore, such externalism does not rule out first-person authority over these sorts of item (although claims of authority, for architecture and many processes, would be implausible on other grounds). Moreover, content externalism does not apply to propositional attitudes whose content is composed exclusively of complex concepts. Recognition of this latter fact allows the threat to first-person authority posed by content externalism to be, effectively, nullified for most of the propositional attitudes too. In particular, the sort of authority we have over most of our attitudes can be rendered thus: S knows a priori that, if the world turns out to be a certain way, he or she is thinking that P. It is not clear that there need be anything more to first-person authority than this. Therefore it is not clear that content externalism jeopardizes first-person authority in any sort of realistic way.

CHAPTER 9

Vehicle externalism

Content externalism, as we have seen, is best understood as the thesis that some of those mental states that possess their content essentially – namely, propositional attitudes – are individuation dependent on objects, properties, relations and so on occurring outside the skins of the subjects of mental states. As such, content externalism is severely restricted in both its scope and force. It applies neither to cognitive processes nor to the architectures or mechanisms in which those processes are realized. It does not apply to phenomenal states – experiences of various forms – at least not if the essential properties of these states are phenomenal or qualitative rather than propositional or semantic. It applies to some, but only some, propositional attitudes: those whose content is composed of at least one simple rather than complex concept. And even where it does apply, it shows only that these propositional attitudes are externally individuated and not that they are externally located. Content externalism, that is, entails rejection of the internalist Possession Claim but not of the Location Claim.

In Chapters 9 and 10 we look at attempts to broaden the scope and augment the force of externalism. Chapter 10 looks at the possibility of applying externalist principles, broadly understood, to conscious experiences. This chapter, however, focuses on cognitive processes and the architectures that underwrite them. Externalism applied to such items often goes by the name of *vehicle externalism*: externalism about the *vehicles*, rather than the *contents*, of thoughts.[1]

Cognitive states, processes and architectures

In order to understand the difference between content and vehicle externalism, we need to understand the difference between the contents and vehicles of cognition. The distinction is essentially a simple one: a distinction between content and what has that content. In the case of sentences, for example, the distinction is fairly obvious. The sentence "The cat is on the mat" has a certain content; namely, that the cat is on the mat. And this content is had by, or attaches to, something: the syntactic–phonetic sentence form, "The cat is on the mat".

So one way of developing the distinction between vehicles and contents of thought is by enforcing a parallel distinction for the case of thoughts. This, in effect, is to invoke the apparatus of representations we looked at in Chapter 6. Suppose that any given thought is a relation to a representation. This is usually understood as a structure instantiated in the brain. As we saw, what is crucial to representations is that they are *symbols*. They have both formal or syntactic properties and semantic or representational properties. The latter properties constitute their content. And, roughly, very roughly, the former properties are what make representations vehicles of thought. This is only a rough approximation for, as we shall see, the notion of a vehicle of thought is not unambiguous. But it is a reasonable place to start.

So far, we have arrived at the idea of a vehicle of thought by following up the analogy with sentences. Thoughts, like sentences, possess both formal and semantic properties, and it is the former that constitute the vehicle of thought and the latter that constitute its content. The formal or syntactic properties of representations, as we saw in Chapter 5, are made up of various higher-order physical properties. It is these higher-order physical properties that determine which causal relations a given representation, hence a given thought, can enter into with other representations. These properties, therefore, determine the functional role that a representation, hence a thought, has in a mental subject's psychology.

Therefore, as a first approximation, we can say that the content of a thought consists in the semantic properties of the associated representation, and the vehicle of the thought consists in the syntactic properties of that representation: the higher-order physical properties that determine the functional role of that representation in an agent's psychology. Now let us try to refine this a little.

First of all, the apparatus of representations with formal and semantic properties was introduced at, and has its most natural home in, a time when thought was conceived of as essentially linguistic: that is, where the vehicles of thought were regarded as linguistically structured entities. This *language of thought* hypothesis has fallen on hard times recently, and justifiably so. So the first thing we need to do is emphasize that when we talk of representations possessing formal and semantic properties, we are not conceiving of these representations as linguistic, or quasi-linguistic, entities. That is, we are using the concepts of *formal* and *semantic* in a much wider sense than that in which they are traditionally employed. In this wider sense, a picture, for example, which is not a linguistically structured entity, can have formal and semantic properties. Its semantic properties consist in what it depicts (or, more accurately, those properties that determine what it is that it depicts) and its formal properties consist in a subset of its causal properties, that subset which determines how it might interact with other pictures in ways that we deem relevant.

Let us regard a thought as a typical example of a cognitive *state*, as a relation to a representation of some sort, where this representation does not have to be a linguistically structured entity. The formal or syntactic properties of this representation, accordingly, do not have to be regarded as linguistically structured either. What we are left with is the simple idea of higher-order properties in virtue of which one representation will interact, in ways relevant to cognition, with others. And let us refer to this broad notion of a formal property as the *cognitive architecture* of or underlying a thought. Cognitive architecture, then, consists in the mechanisms – understood as higher-order physical properties of structures – that allow us to cognize: to relate distinct thoughts to each other in appropriate ways and produce new thoughts on the basis of this interaction. The vehicles of thought, therefore, consist in cognitive architecture.

The externalism we have looked at so far has been externalism about the contents of thoughts. Now we turn to a form of externalism that is wholly more radical: externalism about the vehicles of thought – externalism about the cognitive architecture that allows us to cognize.

Our cognitive architecture consists in the cognitive mechanisms that allow us to cognize. They allow us to cognize because they allow us to run, implement or engage in various sorts of *cognitive process*. There is actually little consensus as to what makes something a cognitive process. Often, the class of processes that we regard as cognitive is defined by ostension. Cognitive processes include such processes as perceiving, remembering, thinking, reasoning and the processes involved in the production and understanding of language. Underlying this ostension is the somewhat vague idea that these are the processes in virtue of which we can accomplish cognitive tasks: perceiving the world, remembering perceived information, employing such remembered information in contexts of reasoning and the like. That is, the notion of a cognitive process is defined in terms of the notion of a cognitive task. There is also the, again vague, idea that cognitive processes involve some form of *information processing* – roughly, transformation of information-bearing structures – or, sometimes, that cognitive processes are essentially computational ones.

Attempts of this sort to render more precisely the concept of a cognitive process founder on the fact that we really have very little idea of what information is or of what computation is.

Most standard accounts of information – for example, accounts based on the idea that information consists in some form of nomic dependence – entail that information is essentially ubiquitous. If so, then it seems that information-processing operations will also be, similarly, ubiquitous. Thus, for example, information is contained in the food I eat in virtue of nomic dependencies between the properties of this food and other properties. When my digestive juices break down this food, the information contained in it is, accordingly, transformed. But, clearly, digestion does not count as a cognitive process.

These are difficult issues, and I do not pretend to know how to solve them. To avoid them, in so far as this is possible, I propose to take the notion of a cognitive task as basic, and as defined by ostension – by pointing. That is, cognitive tasks are those tasks we say are cognitive. Cognitive processes, then, consist in those information-processing operations that are essential to the solution of cognitive tasks. Digestion, presumably, is not essential to the accomplishing of a memory task, since the task can be accomplished irrespective of what is going on in one's digestive tract.

If externalism is true of cognitive architecture – as vehicle externalism claims – then it will also be true of the processes that run on such architecture. Thus, vehicle externalism is the claim that both cognitive architecture and cognitive processes are not purely internal entities, and that the latter are not purely internal because the former are not purely internal. This chapter deals with vehicle externalism in this sense.

It is worth noting that if vehicle externalism turns out to be true, then this also closes off the limited defence of Cartesianism that we encountered towards the end of Chapter 5. The suggestion was that we could explain the notion of a narrow mental state in terms of the formal or syntactic properties of its associated representation. The narrow mental state, on this view, is the mental state individuated according to its formal or syntactic properties of the representation to which that state is a relation. This opportunity to defend a limited form of Cartesianism is closed off if we accept vehicle externalism, for if we accept that externalism is true of the formal or syntactic properties of representations, then – being themselves wide – there is, of course, no way they can be appealed to in the explanation of the narrow mental state.

The parity principle

In their justifiably influential paper "The Extended Mind", Andy Clark and David Chalmers develop the case for vehicle externalism by way of what they call the *parity principle*.[2] In illustrating this principle, they use the following example. The cognitive task in question is one involving rotation of a shape. For example, we might want to rotate a certain shape in order to see if it will fit with another – the mental equivalent of doing a jigsaw puzzle. There are three strategies that we might use to accomplish this task.

1. The first strategy is a standard mentalistic one. We form a mental image of the shape, then mentally rotate it to see if it will fit. This is, on the face of it, a textbook example of a cognitive process. We form an internal representation of the shape and then perform internal operations upon this representation. In doing so, we transform the information contained in the image, rendering it more amenable to the solution of the task: seeing if the shape fits. So we would have no hesitation in regarding this process as a cognitive one.
2. The second strategy involves our accomplishing the same task, but doing so by way of a computer screen and a program that allows us to rotate images on the screen. On the face of it, this seems to be an equally straightforward example of a process that we would *not* regard as cognitive, at least not one of *our* cognitive processes. Even if we were tempted to say that the computer was engaging in cognition – and we probably should not be tempted to say this – there seems little temptation to suppose that what is going on in the computer is part of our cognitive processes. What we do is manually manipulate the computer by way of its keyboard. And whatever the computer then does because of this, this surely is not an element of our cognition.
3. The third strategy involves a combination of the other two. Suppose that the mechanisms in the computer that allow it to rotate images on the screen were taken out of the computer and placed in one's brain. We can suppose, for the sake of realism, that the computer is a neurally plausible one, modelled on a yet-to-be-designed descendant of current neural network models, for example. The neurally realistic computer hardware forms a sort of neural implant, and in virtue of this hardware we are now able to run the program that allows us to rotate images. Let us suppose, also, that engaging this implant allows us to rotate images faster than we could do using our innate biological hardware.

The third strategy, Clark and Chalmers argue, provides us with an interesting puzzle. On the one hand, it seems to be a reasonably straightforward – if less than textbook – example of a cognitive process. The sort of hardware chauvinism that would allow us to deny its cognitive character simply because the implant is not organic has been in disfavour for some time. It is generally thought that replacement of neurons in a brain by silicon chips, for example, would not automatically entail the death of the cognizing subject. Indeed, if the chips were capable of replicating the functions of each individual neuron they replace – and, admittedly, that is a big *if* – then we would have good reasons for supposing that the cognitive processes that the purely organic subject was undergoing before the replacement could be the same as the ones he is undergoing in his partly inorganic post-replacement state. So we should not, it seems, rule out the neural implants subserving cognitive functions simply because they are not original, or organic, parts of the cognizing subject's brain. As long as function is preserved, cognition is preserved, or so widespread intuition seems to go.

However, if the operation of the implant when it is inside the brain is a cognitive operation, why should it not count as a cognitive operation when it is outside the brain? In both cases, the process involves the transformation of information-bearing representations. These transformations are effected, or brought about, by a cognizing subject in order to accomplish a cognitive task. If we would have no hesitation in describing the implanted device as underwriting a cognitive process, then why deny that the non- or pre-implanted device is underwriting a cognitive process? Is this denial warranted?

Of course, we could just stipulate that when it is not implanted in the brain the device is not performing a cognitive function because it is not located *inside* the skin of the cognizing subject. We can stipulate anything we want. However, in the present context this stipulation would be question-begging. What we are trying to work out is whether there is any justifiable reason for supposing that cognitive processes are restricted to what occurs inside the skins of cognizing subjects. We cannot assume a stipulative characterization of cognitive processes according to which, in effect, they just are. Nor would it help to remove the reference to the skin of the cognizing subject, and stipulate that cognitive processes must occur inside the cognitive subject, for if we assume that the cognizing subject is wherever its cognitive processes are, then the question of the location of the cognizing subject – whether it is located exclusively inside its skin – is something that is open to question, and cannot be assumed at the outset by simple stipulation.

This provides an example of what Clark and Chalmers call the *parity principle*. There is an abundance of structures, mechanisms, devices and so

160

on located in the environment of a cognizing subject such that, *were they located inside that subject*, we would have no hesitation in regarding the processes they underwrite as cognitive processes. Consequently, we would have no hesitation in regarding these structures, mechanisms or devices as examples of cognitive *vehicles* or cognitive *architecture*. The question, then, is whether denying the status of cognitive to these structures is anything more than a stipulation – anything more than an undefended Cartesian prejudice.

Part of the problem, of course, lies in the lack of clarity surrounding the concept of a cognitive process. However, as we have seen, it does seem fairly clear that the notion of a cognitive process is defined, in part, in terms of the notion of a cognitive task. A cognitive process is one that plays a fairly central role in allowing a subject to accomplish a cognitive task. And the notion of a cognitive task is defined, partly, by way of ostension: by pointing to stereotypical examples of cognitive tasks. There is more to a cognitive process than this, of course. Another component of the concept seems to be that cognitive processes somehow centrally involve information, and the manipulation and transformation of structures that carry information. This, in turn, presumably derives from the nature of cognitive tasks, which are typically seen as ones whereby the organism acquires and/or uses information about the environment. Of course, if we knew what information was, matters would be considerably clearer, but we do not and they are not. Nevertheless, we have a clear enough concept of information to appreciate the force of Clark and Chalmers' parity principle.

On the traditional interpretation, the information-bearing structures whose manipulation and transformation constitute cognitive processes are regarded as exclusively internal items: mental representations, in the orthodox sense. Clark and Chalmers's parity principle is based on the idea that there exist plenty of external structures that carry information relevant to the accomplishing of cognitive tasks and are manipulated and transformed by organisms to allow them to accomplish those cognitive tasks. Such structures seem to satisfy all of our rough-and-ready conditions for being cognitive except location. Thus, if they were to be somehow located inside the cognizing organism, we would have no hesitation in regarding them as cognitive structures underwriting cognitive processes. The charge is then that the denial that these external structures are cognitive, given that they satisfy most of the criteria for counting as cognitive except internal location, amounts to nothing more than a Cartesian prejudice.

Defence of the parity principle, of course, requires more than these programmatic considerations. It requires a detailed examination of cognitive processes and the external structures that are arguably centrally involved in them. However, before we turn to this, it is worth noting that the vehicle externalist account of cognitive architectures, and the processes they underwrite, can be supported by some quite general and, I think, powerful evolutionary considerations. It is to these that we now turn.

Beaver and superbeaver

Beavers build dams. That is what they are good at. The evolutionary explanation of this is that the presence of a dam increases the distance the beaver is able to travel by water, which is both safer than travelling by land and easier for transporting food. If a beaver lived on a stream, the supply of food trees lying on the bank would be quickly exhausted. By building a dam, the beaver creates a large shoreline that affords easy foraging without the beaver having to make long and hazardous overland journeys. So the building of dams has been incorporated into the beaver's evolution.[3]

Things, of course, could have happened differently. Instead of employing dam-building behaviour, the evolution of the beaver might have involved investing in ways that facilitated the beaver's ability to travel overland. Suppose that in the dim and distant evolutionary past the ancestors of the beaver had started to evolve in two alternate ways. The first of these involved adopting dam-building behaviour, and culminated in common-or-garden beaver with which we are familiar today. The second strategy, however, completely neglected the dam-building option, and instead concentrated on making the beaver stronger, quicker and more intelligent, thus increasing its efficiency in evading predators and transporting food. This strategy, then, involved investing in features such as increased muscle mass, larger brain, more powerful legs and torso. So, in this thought-experiment, evolution results in two very different types of beaver: the ordinary dam-building beaver, and the stronger, smarter, speedier *superbeaver*.

The tasks that the beaver's ancestor had to accomplish were, first, the location and/or transport of food and, secondly, evasion of predators. We can call the conjunction of these tasks T. The beaver and the superbeaver have attempted to accomplish T through the adoption of two alternative strategies, which we can call S_O, the ordinary strategy, and S_S, the super-strategy. And let us suppose that the beaver and the superbeaver are, by way of their respective strategies, equally competent in the performance of T. That is, statistically speaking, the ability of the ordinary beaver and superbeaver to transport food by way of their respective strategies is equal. What this means, very roughly, is that the same proportion of beavers and superbeavers die in the performance of these tasks.

Does the equality in survival rate with respect to T entail that, with respect to T, the beaver and superbeaver are equally fit? Actually, it does not. All other things being equal, the superbeaver, in fact, would turn out to be less fit than the beaver. The reason is that the ability of the superbeaver to transport food and evade predators has been bought at greater cost than the corresponding ability of the beaver. What the notion of *cost* amounts to here is, very roughly, the amount of genetic material and energy that must be put into a strategy in order to get it to work. In order to get their respective strategies to work, the beaver and superbeaver must invest a certain amount of genetic resources into building the structures and mechanisms that allow each of them to implement their strategies. In the case of the beaver, the structures will, primarily, be big, strong teeth and a flat tail. How about the superbeaver?

It seems that the structures that must be developed by the superbeaver will be much more extensive, hence much more expensive. The superbeaver will require more powerful, hence bigger, muscles, both to escape from the predators it is likely to meet and to transport food it will hopefully find on the long overland journeys it is obliged to make. Thus, its limbs and torso must become more powerful (i.e. larger). To evade predators successfully, it might have to become more intelligent. At the very least, its sensory modalities would have to improve, allowing it earlier and more reliable detection of predators. This would require some form of *encephalization*: an increase in the size of its brain. If this should happen, costs will start to multiply. Encephalization entails a larger brain, which, in turn, requires a larger head, which, in turn, leads to more weight at the front of the body. This must be balanced by added weight elsewhere, which, in turn, requires stronger (i.e. larger) muscles and so on.

The cost to the superbeaver of adopting its strategy will, accordingly, be much greater than that to the beaver. Both the genetic resources the superbeaver must put into developing the necessary structures, and the energy it must put into maintaining those structures once in existence, will be greater than the genetic–energetic resources the beaver must put into implementing its strategy. And this fact will impinge on the overall fitness of the superbeaver. The reason is that the genetic and energetic resources available to a creature are finite, and, therefore, greater expenditure in one area will necessarily show up as a deficit somewhere else.

Consider, for example, aphids. Even within sub-species, winged aphids are less fertile than wingless aphids. Why? Resources that have been invested in wing development are then not available to be invested elsewhere, in this case in reproductive processes. This also explains why female ants, which sprout wings for their nuptial flight, follow consummation by biting or breaking them off at the roots. It would seem that if anything conferred an evolutionary advantage on something it would be wings, so, once you have them, why get rid of them? You never know when they might come in handy. The answer is that wings have their costs as well as their benefits. And in certain circumstances, as in the case of the queen ant, those costs outweigh the benefits.

The same is even true, in certain circumstances, for another apparently advantageous adaptation: the brain. The juvenile sea squirt, for example, spends its days navigating its way along the ocean floor. To facilitate this, it possesses a rudimentary brain and nervous system. However, upon reaching maturity it fastens itself to a rock where it spends the rest of its life. Having done this it then proceeds to eat its own brain! Why doesn't it hang on to its brain, given that it already has one? Wouldn't it be a good thing to have, just in case? The answer, again, is that brains have their costs as well as their benefits, and in certain circumstances, as in the sea squirt's transition to maturity, those costs can outweigh the benefits.[4]

The costs of the superbeaver's strategy far outweigh those of the beaver's strategy. But the benefits are, we have supposed, equal. Therefore, the additional costs faced by the superbeaver will, inevitably, show up as a deficit elsewhere, in the superbeaver's ability to reproduce, for example. Therefore, all other things being equal, the superbeaver will, in fact, be less fit than the beaver.

Examples of this sort – manipulation of the environment so as to reduce the costs of accomplishing a given task – abound throughout the natural world. Consider just one more example. This is a limiting case where the environment of an organism is just another organism: parasitism. Some parasites have a life-cycle involving an *intermediate* host, from which they have to move to a so-called *definitive* host. Such parasites often manipulate the behaviour of their intermediate host to make it more likely to be consumed by the definitive host.

For example, there are two species of acanthocephalan worm, *Polymorphus paradoxus* and *P. marilis*, which both use a freshwater shrimp, *Gammarus lacustris*, as an intermediate host, and both of which use ducks as their definitive hosts. The definitive host of *P. paradoxus*, however, is generally a mallard, which is a surface-dabbling duck. *P. marilis*, on the other hand, specializes in diving ducks. *P. paradoxus*, then, should benefit from making its shrimps swim to the surface, while *P. marilis* should benefit from its shrimps avoiding the surface. Uninfected shrimps tend to avoid the light, and, therefore, stay close to the lake bottom. However, when *G. lacustris* becomes infected with *P. paradoxus* it behaves very differently. It then stays close to the surface, often clinging stubbornly to surface plants. This behaviour makes it vulnerable to predation by mallards.[5]

Polymorphus paradoxus might – in some sense of might – have evolved in a different way. Instead of developing a capacity to manipulate the behaviour of its intermediate host, it might instead have developed structures and mechanisms that enabled it to make its way to its definitive host under its own steam, so to speak. But think of what successful adoption of this alternative strategy would involve. First, *P. paradoxus* would have to develop structures that enabled it to break out of its intermediate host. Secondly, it would require structures that enabled it to move, under its own power, to the place where its definitive host is to be found. Thirdly, since it would then be obliged to journey from its intermediate to its definitive host, it would also perhaps have to develop some means of evading any predators that are non-suitable hosts. It seems fairly clear that this alternative strategy can be bought only at considerably higher cost than the actual strategy. The genetic–energetic costs of developing the necessary structures, maintaining these structures once in existence and actually employing these structures are, intuitively, much higher than the alternative of producing a certain chemical that gets something else – the unlucky *G. lacustris* – to do all the work for you.

As in the case of the superbeaver, these extra costs would have to show up as a deficit somewhere else. Therefore, all things being equal, the strategy of "*superparadoxus*" – that breaks its way out of its host, fights it way to the surface, staves off any predators, and so on – would make it less fit than ordinary *P. paradoxus*, even if the two strategies allowed "*superparadoxus*" and *P. paradoxus* to find, and invade, definitive hosts with the same statistical regularity. Therefore, all things being equal, "*superparadoxus*" will, in fact, be less fit than *P. paradoxus*.

Secret agents and barking dogs

The beaver relies on the external environment – admittedly an environment that has been shaped by the beaver – to bear some of the burden of its tasks. That is, some of the work that must be done in order for the beaver to accomplish its twin tasks of transporting food and evading predators is work that is, in effect, carried out by the environment. Accordingly, the beaver has less work to do itself. The superbeaver, on the other hand, attempts to do all the necessary work itself, and therefore has more to do than the beaver. The superbeaver, accordingly, must invest more resources – genetic and energetic resources – into accomplishing these tasks. And, therefore, the superbeaver has less resources left over for the accomplishing of other tasks.

Underlying the manipulation and exploitation of the environment carried out by the beaver, therefore, is a simple principle. If you have some work to do in order to accomplish a certain task, then the more you can get someone or something else to do that work for you, the less you will have to do yourself. This assumes, of course, that the work you have to do in order to get this someone or something else to do work for you is less than the work they thereby do for you.

Andy Clark encapsulates the essential insight here by way of what he calls the *007 principle*.

> In general, evolved creatures will neither store nor process information in costly ways when they can use the structure of their environment and their operations upon it as a convenient stand-in for the information-processing operations concerned. That is, know only as much as you need to know to get the job done.[6]

I, on the other hand, named the underlying principle after an old adage: why keep a dog if you are going to bark yourself? Or, closer to the present point, if you do have a dog, then you can get it to do your barking for you, and, consequently, save yourself a lot of time, energy and sore vocal chords. More precisely:

> *The Barking Dog Principle*: If it is necessary for an organism to be able to perform a given adaptive task *T*, then it is selectively disadvantageous for that organism to develop internal mechanisms sufficient for the performance of *T* when it is possible for the organism to perform *T* by way of a combination of internal mechanisms and manipulation of the external environment.[7]

Given the "choice" of two strategies for accomplishing a given task – one that involves the development of internal structures and mechanisms that, by themselves, will allow you to accomplish the task and another that involves a combination of internal structures plus an ability to manipulate and exploit the environment in appropriate ways – the second type of strategy makes better evolutionary sense. Fitness, basically, comes down to this: *resource controlled versus resource expended*. In getting the environment to do some of the work for you, you expend less resources per resource controlled. Your fitness would, accordingly, be greater than if you had not adopted an exploitative strategy.

This broad principle applies almost universally, covering most adaptive tasks that evolution sets animals and plants. The barking dog principle covers activities as diverse as predation (e.g. angler fish), evasion of predators (e.g. beaver), reproduction (e.g. canary, cricket), rearing of young (e.g. cuckoo), feeding and gaining access to food (e.g. sponge) and locating suitable habitats (e.g. parasites). In each case, the strategy of environmental manipulation can be adopted at less evolutionary cost – genetic, energetic or both – than strategies that do not involve such manipulation. The *manipulate-the-environment* strategy is, from an evolutionary point of view, an extremely cost-effective method of accomplishing a given, evolutionarily specified, task. Thus, typically, a strategy that involves manipulation of the environment in order to accomplish some adaptively specified task is more selectively advantageous than a strategy that eschews such manipulation. The crucial point is that when an organism adopts a manipulative strategy, the organism can get the environment to do much of the necessary work for it, and so the resource-controlled:resource-expended ratio is greater than it would have been were a non-exploitative strategy adopted.

Consequences for cognition

The structures and mechanisms that allow us to cognize – our cognitive architectures – are also, it seems overwhelmingly likely, items that have been produced by way of evolution. They are the culmination of a long history of random mutation enforced by natural selection. Therefore, if the barking dog (or the 007) principle is correct, as a general account of the relation between evolutionarily produced structures and the environment they were produced in, we should expect the principle to apply to the architecture that supports cognition, as well as to the architecture that supports other evolutionarily specified tasks.

If this is correct, we should expect the internal structures in an organism that support that organism's capacity for cognition to be structures that have evolved in conjunction with, and therefore function in conjunction with, abilities of the organism to manipulate and exploit its environment appropriately. Cognitive processes would accordingly be distributed across both internal structures and mechanisms and external structures and mechanisms. The architecture of cognition would incorporate more than the internal; it would also encompass those environmental structures that allow the organism, in combination with the activity of suitable internal mechanisms, to accomplish cognitive tasks.

The application of the barking dog principle to cognitive architecture is likely to meet with resistance. And the principal source of this resistance will probably stem from the idea that the principle is committed to some illicit form of *adaptationism*. The principle, some might object, assumes that all structures and mechanisms relevant to cognition are ones that have evolved through natural selection. But this, it will be argued, is not in general true. For example, Gould and Vrba write:

> The brain, though undoubtedly built by natural selection for some complex set of functions, can, as a result of its intricate structure, work in an unlimited number of ways quite unrelated to the selective pressure that constructed it. . . . Current utility carries no automatic implication about historical origin. Most of what the brain does now to enhance our survival lies in the domain of exaptation – and does not allow us to make hypotheses about the selective paths of human history.[8]

An adaptation, according to Gould and Vrba, is "any feature that promotes fitness and was built by selection for its current role". Exaptations, on the other hand, are "characters . . . evolved for other uses (or for no function at all), and later 'coopted' for their current role". It might be argued, then, that the structures and mechanisms responsible for human cognition are exaptations, rather than adaptations. And, if this were so, it might be thought that arguments concerning cognitive architecture based on evolution have no force.

Happily, however, the arguments from evolutionary efficiency do not presuppose that the structures and mechanisms presently responsible for cognition evolved for that purpose. The distinction between adaptations and exaptations is simply irrelevant to these arguments. The claim is that when a structure or mechanism takes on the role of underwriting a cognitive process – whether it originally evolved for that purpose or not – then it is best, from the point of view of evolutionary cost, for that mechanism to fulfil its role in conjunction with manipulation of the environment. One must never forget that evolution acts not just to produce structures and mechanisms; it also acts to maintain them in existence once they have been produced. A structure or mechanism that is maintained because of the role it plays in underwriting certain cognitive processes, even though it was not originally developed for this role, is an evolutionary product no less than a structure that was originally produced for that role. Both adaptations and exaptations are products of evolutionary processes; considerations of cost apply equally to both of them. Whether a feature has been adapted for a role in underwriting cognition, or coopted for this role, it is better, from the point of view of evolutionary cost, for it to fulfil its role in conjunction with manipulation on the part of the organism of relevant structures in the environment.

Once we remove this common misunderstanding concerning the relevance of the phenomenon of exaptation, there is, I think, little obstacle to regarding cognitive architectures – the states and mechanisms that underwrite cognition – as evolutionary products. This means, assuming the barking dog principle is correct, that such architectures will have been produced – or coopted – to function in conjunction with manipulation, on the part of the organisms that possess them, of relevant environmental structures. That is, cognition will be underwritten or realized not just by internal mechanisms of organisms, but by manipulation of structures in the environment of those organisms. As such, cognitive processes will straddle both internal processes and external ones. Cognition will be, in part, distributed on to the environment. Cognitive processes are not purely in the head.

Perception

The sorts of evolutionary arguments described above are not conclusive. The barking dog principle and/or 007 principle are concerned with specifying the most efficient way for an organism to accomplish a given task. Their application to cognitive architectures and processes amounts to this: the most evolutionary efficient way for an organism to develop the capacity for cognition is by way of a combination of internal mechanisms plus manipulation of environmental structures. However, there is no guarantee that the most efficient method of accomplishing tasks set by evolution will always, or indeed ever, be adopted. The development of cognitive architecture in humans, for example, might not have followed the most efficient route. Therefore, there is no guarantee that the barking dog principle applies to human cognitive architecture, since there is no guarantee that the development of this architecture followed the most efficient route. This means that the evolutionary arguments need to be backed up by a detailed examination of cognitive processes – an examination that will, hopefully, unearth evidence to suggest that the development of the necessary cognitive architectures did, in fact, follow the most efficient route and, accordingly, does involve the manipulation of environmental structures.

Consider a fairly central example of a cognitive process: visual perception. Traditional approaches to visual perception are organized around the following framework.

1. Perception begins with stimulation of the retina by light energy impinging on it.

2. This results in a retinal image, characterized in terms of intensity values distributed over a large array of different locations.
3. Retinal images carry relatively little information, certainly not enough to add up to genuine perception.
4. In order for perception to occur, the information contained in the retinal image has to be supplemented and embellished (i.e. processed) by various information-processing operations.
5. These information-processing operations occur inside the skin of the perceiving organism.

Thus, perception begins at the retina (skin) and all the essential operations involved in it occur inside the perceiver. We looked at a good example of the traditional approach in Chapter 7, in Marr's theory of vision.

A very different approach, one that provides a good example of a vehicle externalist approach to perception, is to be found in James Gibson's *ecological approach*.[9] In order to understand this, it is necessary to understand the concept of an *optic array*. Light from the sun fills the air – the terrestrial medium – so that it is in a "steady state" of reverberation. The environment is, in this way, filled with rays of light travelling between the surfaces of objects. At any point, light will converge from all directions. Therefore, at each physical point in the environment, there is what can be regarded as a densely nested set of solid visual angles, which are composed of inhomogeneities in the intensity of light. Thus, we can imagine an observer, at least for the present, as a point surrounded by a sphere, which is divided into tiny solid angles. The intensity of light and the mixture of wavelengths vary from one solid angle to another. This spatial pattern of light is the optic array. Light carries information because the structure of the optic array is determined by the nature and position of the surfaces from which it has been reflected.

The optic array is divided into many segments or angles. Each of these contains light reflected from different surfaces and the light contained in each segment will differ from that in other segments in terms of its average intensity and distribution of wavelength. The boundaries between these segments of the optic array, since they mark a change in intensity and distribution of wavelength, provide information about the three-dimensional structure of objects in the world. At a finer level of detail, each segment will, in turn, be sub-divided in a way determined by the texture of the surface from which the light is reflected. Therefore, at this level also, the optic array can carry information about further properties of objects and terrain.

The realization of the importance of the optic array is, in many ways, Gibson's essential insight. The rest of his ecological approach really stems from placing the optic array in its proper position of conceptual priority. The optic array is an *external information-bearing structure*. It is external in the quite obvious sense that it exists outside the skins of perceiving organisms, and is in no way dependent on such organisms for its existence. It also carries information about the environment. Indeed, according to Gibson, there is enough information contained in the optic array to specify the nature of the environment that shapes it. Information, for Gibson, is essentially nomic dependence. The structure of the optic array depends, in a lawlike (i.e. nomic) way on the structure of the physical environment that surrounds it. In virtue of this dependence, the optic array carries information about this wider environment. The optic array is, as Gibson puts it, *specific* to the environment. Because of this, an organism whose perceptual system detects optical structure in the array is thereby aware of what this structure specifies. Thus, the perceiving organism is aware of the environment and not the array and, more importantly, is in a position to utilize the information about the environment embodied in the array.

Once we allow that the optic array is an external structure that embodies information about the environment, we are, of course, forced to admit that some of the information relevant to perception exists in the environment of the perceiver. And this, in itself, leads to an important methodological conclusion. Suppose we are faced with a particular perceptual task. If we accept the concept of the optic array, we have to allow that at least some of the information relevant to this task will be located in the array. Perhaps, as Gibson seems to suggest, this information will be sufficient for us to accomplish the task. Perhaps not – in which case we might find it necessary to postulate some form of internal processing operations that somehow supplement or embellish the information contained in the array. Even if this is so, however, one thing is clear. We cannot begin to estimate what internal processing an organism needs to accomplish unless we already understand how much information is available to that organism in its optic array. The more information available to the organism in its optic array, the less internal processing the organism needs to perform. Understanding of the internal processes involved in visual perception is logically and methodologically secondary to understanding the information that is available to the perceiving organism in its environment.

The next stage in understanding visual perception, then, would be to provide an account of how a perceiving organism is able to make the information contained in the optic array available to it. Here we find another distinctively Gibsonian element: the emphasis on *action*. As Gibson points out, perception is inextricably bound up with action. Perceiving organisms are not, typically, static creatures but, rather, actively explore their environment. And, movement, for Gibson, is essential to seeing. The fact that perceiving organisms actively explore their environment allows crucial information from motion perspective to tell them not only about structures in the world, but also about their own positions and movements relative to such structures. When an observer moves, the entire optic array is transformed and such transformations contain information about the layout, shapes, and orientations of objects in the world.

The optic array is a source of information for any organism equipped to take advantage of it. But the optic array does not impinge on passive observers. Rather, the living organism will *actively sample* the optic array. The organism obtains information from the array by actively exploring it and, thus, actively appropriating the contained information. One way of doing this is by moving and thus transforming the ambient optic array. By effecting such transformations, perceiving organisms can identify and appropriate what Gibson calls the *invariant* information contained in the optic array. This is information not in any one static optic array as such but in the transformation of one optic array into another. Invariant information, therefore, takes the form of higher-order variables. Consider, for example, what is known as the *horizon ratio relation*. The horizon intersects an object at a particular height. All objects of the same height, whatever their distance, are cut by the horizon in the same ratio. This provides an example of invariant information, information that can be made available only through the transformation of one optic array into another. Thus, an organism can detect such information only by moving and, hence, effecting transformations in the optic array. Information, in this sense, is not something inside the organism. Rather, it exists as a function, a nomic consequence, of changes in the organism–environment relation or, equivalently, a function of the persistences and changes in the organism–environment system.

What is crucial here is that: (i) the optic array, a structure external to the perceiving organism, is a locus of information for suitably equipped creatures; and (ii) a creature can appropriate or make this information available to itself through acting upon the array, and thus effecting transformations in it. What the perceiving organism does, in effect, is *manipulate* a structure external to it – the optic array – in order to make available to itself information that it can then use to navigate its way around the environment. And the notion of *making information available to itself* can be understood in terms of the idea of the organism rendering information susceptible to detection by itself.

If information relevant to perception is contained in the array, then manipulating the array to make this information available is, in effect, a form of information processing. If we want to think of visual perception in terms of the concept of information processing, then this is where the information processing relevant to visual perception begins: not in the organism but in the world. Or, if we do want to think of visual perception in terms of the concept of information processing, then there is no good reason for insisting that information processing occurs only inside the skin of the perceiving organism. When an organism manipulates the optic array, it appropriates and makes available to itself the information contained therein. There seems to be no sound theoretical reason for denying that this process is one of information processing. This, in effect, is the force of Clark and Chalmers's parity principle. If the sort of operations an organism performs on the information-bearing optic array – transformation and resulting appropriation of information – were somehow performed inside the head of that organism, we would have no hesitation in regarding what is going on as a form of information processing.

One could, of course, always *stipulate* that the concept of information processing is to be restricted to processes occurring inside the skins of organisms. One can stipulate anything one likes. However, given that information is embodied in structures external to organisms, and given that an organism can manipulate these structures in order to appropriate the contained information, it is difficult to see the point of this restriction. In other words, there seems to be no great theoretical divide between manipulating *internal* information-bearing structures and manipulating *external* information-bearing structures in order to make available to oneself the information that results. To claim that only the former constitutes genuine information processing seems little more than an internalist prejudice.

For similar reasons, there seems little principled reason for denying that the processing of information contained in external structures, via the manipulation and transformation of such structures, constitutes a form of cognitive process. The manipulation and transformation of external structures is, *ipso facto*, manipulation and transformation of information via the structures that carry it. As a result of such transformation, information is made available to the organism that was, otherwise, not directly available. Such information can often be, at least practically, indispensable to the solution of a cognitive task. Thus, the role played by manipulation and transformation of external structures seems to meet the classic conditions for counting as a cognitive task. Again, any decision to deny that this is a cognitive operation would seem to amount to nothing more than an internalist prejudice.

Memory

Let us now turn our attention to another central example of a cognitive process: *remembering*.[10] What role can be found for environmental manipulation in such a process? It is arguable that at least two distinct roles can be found: one pertaining to day-to-day operations of remembering, and the other to the way in which the type of memory distinctive of modern literate human beings came into existence. Consider, first, day-to-day operations of remembering.

The idea of using external cues to aid memory is pretty mundane. Tying a knot in one's handkerchief, writing down a shopping list, marking calendars, asking someone to remind you to do something, leaving something in a particular place where it will be encountered at the time it needs to be remembered and so on all constitute a small subset of the total number of external memory aids people employ. These are typically viewed precisely as *external aids* to memory: as extrinsic devices that might help trigger the real process of remembering, itself a purely internal operation. However, the dichotomy between external aid to memory and internal process of remembering is not as straightforward as one might suppose.

Cole *et al*. describe a case where a child is seeking an ingredient for baking a cake.[11] The child does not need to remember exactly where the ingredient is located. Instead, they simply go to the shelf and work their way along it until this ingredient is found. In this case, part of the external world – the shelf – stands in, or goes proxy, for a detailed internal memory store. Examples of this sort can be extended indefinitely. Suppose I want to find a book at the library. I have seen the book before, but I can remember neither the title nor the author. Moreover, I do not remember exactly where it is in the library, but I do remember the floor, and I also remember that it is on a shelf with a peculiar distinguishing feature, a red tray at the end, say. Therefore, I go to the correct floor, look for the shelf with the distinguishing feature and then work my way along the shelf until I find the book. In this case, the library floor and the shelf together seem to go proxy for a complex internal memory store. The role that this sort of internal store would play in my locating the book is taken over by my ability to manipulate an appropriate structure in the environment. Similar remarks would apply to the process of navigating one's way around the environment by way of remembered landmarks (I cannot remember exactly where X lives, but I know that if I turn right by the lake, go on as far as the pub and then take a left . . .). In this case, it is my ability to locate serially each landmark and use this to direct me to the next one that takes over the role of a detailed internal memory store.

Suppose I am reading a book and come across an interesting argument that may prove relevant to my own work at some point. Having a propensity to forget arguments, I make no serious attempt to commit it to memory. Since I have no facility for remembering page numbers either, I instead remember something much simpler – I remember approximately where on the page the argument appeared. Then, when I want to consider the argument again, I flip through the book, scanning the relevant part of each page, until I come across the argument. In this case the book itself seems to stand in for a detailed memory store. My remembering where the argument is seems to be a process formed from the combination of an internal representation of the location of the argument on a page together with actual physical manipulation of the book itself.

What do these various scenarios have in common? First, there is the idea that the function of an internal representation can, in certain circumstances, be taken over by an environmental object or structure. This structure, we might say, stands in, or goes proxy, for the internal representation. This external structure is relevant to the accomplishing of the cognitive task – for example, remembering the location of an item – in question. What makes it relevant? Well, essentially, it seems to be a structure that carries information that will allow, in suitable circumstances, the cognitive task to be accomplished. Secondly, this information can be extracted and identified through *acting* on the structure. The library shelf, for example, carries information relevant to the location of the book. This information is not immediately available to the book seeker, but can be appropriated by the seeker if they act on the self in an appropriate way (essentially, by working their way along it book by book). In this case, what we essentially have is known as an *action loop*: a series of iterated operations involving feedback between organism and environment. This action loop is characterized by the following.

1. It is, in the circumstances, an operation essential to the accomplishing of a cognitive task.
2. It involves the manipulation and transformation of information-bearing structures.
3. These structures are external to the cognizing agent.

If we took just points 1 and 2, we would have little hesitation in saying that the process involved was cognitive, and that the information-bearing structures formed part of the cognitive architecture of the agent. The factor that blocks such identification is point 3: the fact that the structure in question is not an internal one, and hence the operations performed on it are not internal ones. Once again, we find ourselves with Clark and

Chalmers's parity principle. If the shelf and our operations on it were modelled by some form of computer simulation, and then this simulation somehow implanted in the brain so that the agent was able to activate the simulation and find the book, we would have little or no hesitation in calling the resulting internal process a cognitive one. What seems to underlie our hesitation in the normal case, then, seems to be nothing more than an internalist bias.

Manipulation and exploitation of information-bearing environmental structures are centrally implicated not only in our contemporary exercise of our memory abilities but also in the historical development of those abilities. Consider the consequences that the existence of an external information store will have for the development of memory. Given the availability of a relatively permanent external information store, in what sort of direction should we expect memory capacities to develop? Consider a simple case of visuographic representation: *kvinus*.[12] *Kvinus* are a system of knots that were used in ancient Peru, China, Japan, among other places. In Peru they were used for a variety of tasks, including the recording of chronicles, transmission of instructions to remote provinces, recording information about the state of the army and so on. A *kvinu* officer was assigned to the task of tying and interpreting *kvinus* and the system was eventually developed and standardized to the extent that it could be used to record all the major matters of state.

Invention of this visuographic system will have had a profound effect on the development of strategies of remembering employed by those who were familiar with them. To see this, compare the memory of an African envoy, transmitting word for word the lengthy message of his tribal chief, with the memory of a Peruvian *kvinu* officer. The African envoy has to remember not simply the content of the message, but, much more difficult, the precise sequence of words uttered by his chief. The Peruvian *kvinu* officer, on the other hand, does not have to remember the information contained in the knot he has tied. What he has to remember is simply the "code" that will allow him to extract this information. Once he has done this, he is able to "tap in" to the information contained in his knots. Moreover, whereas the African envoy must employ his episodic memory resources each time he learns a message, the *kvinu* officer need employ his episodic memory only once, in the learning of the code. A potentially unlimited quantity of information then becomes available to him without any further employment of episodic memory.

Once an external information store becomes available, it is easy to see how memory is going to develop. Episodic memory – our memory for specific, concrete and detailed episodes – becomes a lot less important, restricted to the learning of the code necessary for appropriation of information in the external information store. This is why, according to Luria and Vygotsky, in the course of cultural development the outstanding episodic memory of primitive man tends to wither away. The evolution of memory is, in this sense, also *involution*: constituted not only by an improvement in certain areas, but also by retrograde processes whereby old forms shrink and wither away. This is an absolutely pivotal point in the development of modern memory. Internal development has now become external.

Our ability to manipulate external information-bearing structures often plays a central role in the present-day exercise of memory capacities. This is not surprising; such manipulation has been inextricably bound up with the historical development of those capacities. The reason why we have the sorts of memory capacities we do is precisely because of the role played by our manipulation and exploitation of external information-bearing structures. Our memory capacities have been shaped and forged by the information in the world around us and, accordingly, we cannot separate off, in any principled way, our ability to remember from our ability to exploit this ambient information.[13]

Reasoning

Another type of cognitive process that seems often to involve manipulation and transformation of external structures is *reasoning*. A now classic example is provided by Rumelhart *et al.*, and concerns mathematical reasoning (and, by extension, formal reasoning in general).[14] In a fairly simple case of a mathematical operation, say multiplication (e.g. 6×6), most of us can learn to just see the answer. This, Rumelhart *et al.* suggest, is evidence of a pattern-completing mechanism of some sort. But for most of us the answer to more complex multiplications will not be so easily discernible. For example, 343×822 is not easy to do in the head. Instead, we avail ourselves of an external formalism that reduces the larger task to an iterated series of smaller steps. Thus, we write down the numbers on paper and go through a series of pattern-completing operations (2×2, 2×4, etc.), storing the intermediate results on paper according to a well-defined algorithm. Rumelhart *et al.*'s point is that if we have a cognitive system that is capable of acting on, and transforming, its external environment in this way, then much of the cognitive burden faced by the organism is carried by, or distributed upon, the environment. Tasks that the cognizing organism would otherwise have to perform can now, it seems, be borne by the environment.

Similar remarks apply to spatial reasoning, rather than formal reasoning, tasks. Consider a jigsaw puzzle.[15] Imagine how difficult completing a jigsaw puzzle would be if you were not allowed to pick up and physically manipulate the pieces. In these circumstances, the role played by physical manipulation of the pieces would have to be taken over by mental manipulation. That is, one would have to form a mental picture of each piece and work out, by way of various image rotation techniques, whether one piece would fit with another. In practice, of course, we do things very differently. We might first make a rough mental assessment of the shape of the piece, but certainly do not form any sort of detailed representation. Then we physically manipulate the piece, to try to fit it with other pieces that our rough mental assessments have told us are promising candidates for a fit. Physical rotation and manipulation remove the need for mental analogues of these processes. Moreover, before we even begin the rough mental assessment of the shape of each piece, we might physically rotate the piece to make the task of forming an image easier; that is, physical rotation takes the place of mental rotation even before the process of image formation begins. Thus, we have a complex and iterated process whereby internal processes lead to (and in some cases are preceded by) actions that in turn change or simplify the tasks that must be accomplished by internal processes.

Action loops

The concept that underlies and unites the preceding discussion of perception, memory and reasoning is the concept of an *action loop*. A cognitive task – perceiving the world, remembering perceived information, employing this information in reasoning contexts – confronting an organism can often be accomplished by a combination of internal processes and manipulation of the external environment. This external manipulation can both obviate the need for certain sorts of internal process and even change the sort of task that the remaining internal processes must accomplish. Thus a process of manipulation of external structures in these sorts of action loops is an often practically indispensable feature of cognitive operations. It is also a process that involves the manipulation and transformation of information-bearing structures. The results of such transformation consist in information that would, otherwise, have remained unavailable to the organism. So the manipulation of external structures in these sorts of action loop is (i) the manipulation of information-bearing structures that (ii) yields information that would otherwise have remained unavailable to the organism, where (iii) this information is, at least practically, indispensable to the solution of the cognitive task facing the organism. Given that all this is so, what reasons could there be for denying the status of cognitive to external components of the action loop? Nothing more, it seems, than an internalist bias.

There is a well-known distinction, first drawn by Kirsh and Maglio, that allows us to formulate this point quite nicely.[16] The distinction is between *pragmatic* and *epistemic* action. Pragmatic action is action undertaken with a view to altering the world so as to satisfy some physical goal (e.g. one must go to the refrigerator in order to get beer). Epistemic action, on the other hand, is action that is taken to alter the character of our own mental tasks. When we physically rotate the jigsaw piece so that we do not have to rotate an internal analogue mentally, we are engaging in epistemic action. The actions described in the foregoing paragraphs in connection with perceiving, remembering and reasoning are all species of epistemic action. Epistemic action is action that allows us to distribute the cognitive *burden* imposed on us by a cognitive task out on to the world. Thus the burden that we might have had to bear ourselves is divided between us and the world, broadly construed. In these terms, the claim of the vehicle externalist is a simple one: *division of epistemic burden requires division of epistemic credit*.[17] If the burden of a cognitive task is, partly, distributed out on to the world, then that task is itself something that is, partly, distributed out on to the world.

Cognitive states

While vehicle externalism is a view that, perhaps, finds its most natural home in connection with cognitive processes and the mechanisms or architectures that underwrite such processes, Clark and Chalmers have, importantly, argued that it can also be extended to cognitive states.[18] This extension of vehicle externalism is likely to arouse even more hostility than its application to cognitive processes.

Clark and Chalmers describe the following case, involving a cognitively normal Inga and an Otto who is suffering from Alzheimer's disease. Inga hears that a certain exhibition is running at the Museum of Modern Art. Wanting to see it, she thinks for a moment, recalls that the museum is on West 53rd Street, and goes there. It seems clear, Clark and Chalmers claim, that Inga has the belief that the museum is on West 53rd Street, and she had this belief even before she consulted her memory. Prior to the memory act, of course, the belief was not *occurrent*. But most beliefs are like this. The belief was somewhere in memory, waiting to be accessed.

Otto, like many patients with Alzheimer's disease, relies on information contained in the environment to facilitate his day-to-day life. Otto carries a notebook with him wherever he goes and, upon learning new information, he writes it down. So whenever he needs old (i.e. previously acquired) information, he looks it up. Otto's notebook, in effect, plays for him the sort of role usually played by a biological memory. Otto hears about the exhibition at the Museum of Modern Art and, wanting to see it, looks in his notebook. This tells him that the museum is on West 53rd Street, which is where he duly goes.

According to Clark and Chalmers, "it seems reasonable to say that Otto believed the museum was on 53rd Street even before consulting his notebook".[19] This parallels the claim that Inga possessed the belief prior to her act of memory, for, according to Clark and Chalmers:

> in relevant respects the cases are entirely analogous: the notebook plays for Otto the same role that memory plays for Inga. The information in the notebook functions just like the information constituting an ordinary non-occurrent belief; it just happens that this information lies beyond the skin.[20]

The alternative, of course, is to invoke an extra step in the explanation of Otto's behaviour. Otto, we might suppose, has (i) an occurrent desire to go to the museum, (ii) a belief that the location of the museum is recorded in his notebook and (iii) the accessible fact that the notebook says the museum is on West 53rd Street. But why would we introduce this extra step? It is not as if we would make the analogous step in the case of Inga. That is, it is not as if we would explain Inga's behaviour in terms of (i) her occurrent desire to go to the museum, (ii) a belief that the location of the museum is recorded in her memory and (iii) the accessible fact that her memory store says that the museum is on West 53rd Street. This would be to complicate the explanation unnecessarily. So why should we similarly complicate the explanation in the case of Otto? The reason, again, seems to be an internalist bias.

There are, of course, differences between the cases of Otto and Inga. But it is far from clear that these differences are such as to disqualify Otto's notebook entries from qualifying as beliefs. First, one might argue that Inga has more *reliable* access to the information contained in her memory than Otto does to the information contained in his notebook. Someone might steal Otto's notebook, for example, but Inga's memory is a lot more secure. But this difference is one of degree, not kind, and there are easily imaginable circumstances in which the reverse is true. A surgeon might remove the relevant part of Inga's brain, for example, or she might have too much to drink. Conversely, we might imagine Otto's notebook being surgically grafted on to a part of his body in such a way that its removal is very difficult. Being a highly circumstance-sensitive difference of degree, it does not seem that lesser reliability of Otto's access to his notebook entries is sufficient to disqualify those entries as beliefs.

A second difference is that Otto's access to his notebook comes and goes. He showers without the notebook, for example, and cannot read it when it is dark and so on. But, again, this in itself cannot be decisive. Inga's access to her belief also comes and goes, the latter when she is asleep or intoxicated. Temporary disconnections do not seem to be decisive; what is crucial is that the information is easily available when the subject needs it, and this condition is met equally in both cases.

Perhaps the crucial difference is that Inga has *better* access to the information than Otto does. But, again, this difference does not seem to be decisive. Inga's friend Lucy, a museum-goer but also, let us suppose, a severe alcoholic, might, as a result of her condition, have an extremely inefficient link to her central memory system. Processing might be less efficient in Lucy's case, but assuming she can access the information, in a not too prolonged period of time, Lucy clearly believes that the museum is on West 53rd Street. Of course, if Lucy had to struggle for an overly long time to access the information, or if a psychotherapist's aid were required, we might be reluctant to ascribe the belief to Lucy. But such cases are disanalogous to the case of Otto, whose access to the necessary information is quick and easy.

Another suggestion for the crucial difference might turn on the different types of access Otto and Inga have to the information; Otto's access is perceptual, Inga's is not. However, it is unclear what this is supposed to show. If the supposed relevance turns on the idea that perceptual access is necessarily access to outer items, then the suggestion begs the question, for Clark and Chalmers are, in effect, arguing that Otto's internal processes and his notebook form, in effect, a *single* cognitive system. Thus, Otto's perceptual access to his notebook is not, thereby, access to anything external to his cognitive system. There is, of course, a distinctly perceptual phenomenology that attaches itself to Otto's access to his notebook. But this, again, cannot be decisive. First, why should the nature of the associated phenomenology make a difference to the status of a belief? Identity conditions for beliefs, it is almost universally accepted, do not involve phenomenological or qualitative properties. Secondly, it is imaginable for a cognitive system to have access to its beliefs that is perceptually phenomenological. Consider, for example, the Arnold Schwarzenegger

Terminator films. When Arnie recalls some information from memory, it is "displayed" before him in his visual field. The fact that his memories are recalled in this, by our lights, non-standard way does not impugn their status as beliefs.[21]

In short, the proposed features that supposedly disqualify Otto's notebook entries from counting as beliefs cannot be decisive. Thus, the differences between Otto's and Inga's cases are all shallow differences. What tempts us into elevating these shallow differences to the status of crucial or decisive can, again, be nothing more than a residual internalist prejudice.

Conclusion

Vehicle externalism is a way of extending the central externalist insight – that the mind is not restricted to what lies inside the skin of mental subjects – beyond the severely circumscribed limits of content externalism. The restriction of externalism to mental states that possess their contents essentially is abandoned by vehicle externalism. This form of externalism is externalism applied, in the first instance, to cognitive *architectures* – the mechanisms or vehicles of cognition – and then, on the basis of this, to the *processes* underwritten by such architectures. The arguments for vehicle externalism can, in the final analysis, also be applied to cognitive *states* – beliefs for example – that are the products of such processes. The arguments for this position are wide-ranging. Some turn on essentially *evolutionary considerations*; some revolve around *detailed analysis of specific cognitive processes*; and others are dialectically more subtle, seeking to show that rejection of vehicle externalism in the face of certain sorts of evidence is a violation of the *parity principle*, and, therefore, a form of residual *internalist bias*.

If we combine these sorts of arguments in the right way, we have, I think, a cogent and compelling case for the extension of externalist principles far beyond the initial (and still paradigm) cases of mental states that have their content essentially. If these sorts of arguments ultimately prove successful, then the scope of externalism has expanded to cover far more of the mental than we might have initially supposed. And it now covers this significant portion in a far stronger – more *radical* – sense. Vehicle externalism entails rejection not only of the internalist Possession Claim, but also of the Location Claim. Many mental phenomena, if vehicle externalism is true, are not merely *individuation dependent* on what is going on in the environments of their subjects, but they are also, in part, *located* in those environments.

CHAPTER 10

Externalism and consciousness

In Chapter 6 we saw that the scope of traditional content externalism seemed to be quite narrow. In particular, two central features of the mental seemed untouched by the arguments for content externalism. The first of these, cognitive processes and the architectures that underwrite them, were discussed in Chapter 9, where it was argued that a suitable extension of externalism – from content to vehicle externalism – would underwrite the externality of cognitive processes and architectures. The second feature of the mental arguably untouched by the arguments for content externalism is consciousness, and this is the subject of this chapter.

Consciousness and the internalism/externalism debate

Phenomenal consciousness is perceived by many to provide the principal threat to materialist accounts of the mind. This threat has been developed, in somewhat different ways, by a lineage of writers from Nagel, through Jackson and Levine to McGinn and Chalmers.[1] Attempts to explain precisely what phenomenal consciousness is tend to rely on a number of devices, linguistic and otherwise.

- *Example*. The way things look or sound, the way pain feels and, more generally, the experiential properties of sensations, feelings and experiences. Sensations and feelings will include things such as pain, itches, tickles, orgasms and so on. Experiences will include perceptual experiences, i.e. of colour, shape, size, brightness, loudness and so on. What motivates these sorts of examples is simply that anyone who has had any of the above experiences will know that they *feel* or *seem* a certain way, that there is *something that it is like* to undergo them.

- *Rough synonyms.* The concept of phenomenal consciousness is sometimes explained, and I use the term loosely, by way of terms that are roughly synonymous with the original expression. Thus, phenomenally conscious states are ones that have, or are defined by, a *phenomenology*, which have a certain *qualitative feel* or *qualitative character*. Such states are *experiential* or *subjective* ones. They are states that essentially possess *qualia*. Most importantly, perhaps, for any phenomenally conscious state, there is *something that it is like* to be, or to undergo, that state.
- *Just do it!* The third device embodies what we might call the Nike™ approach. Just do it! More precisely, one is invited to construct the circumstances that will produce in one states with a particular form of phenomenal consciousness (e.g. "pinch yourself").

Let us assume that these sorts of device are sufficient to allow to us to know what we are talking about when we talk about phenomenal consciousness: an assumption by no means granted by all. Then the question arises as to the location of such consciousness in the internalism/externalism debate. The traditional, and still widely accepted, view is that phenomenal consciousness is an internally determined feature of organisms. That is, phenomenal consciousness is a locally supervenient feature of organisms, a feature that supervenes on events and processes occurring inside the skins of conscious organisms.

This traditional view is coming increasingly under attack. One source of this attack lies in content externalism. Some have argued that the arguments for content externalism do, in fact, apply to phenomenal consciousness because, appearances notwithstanding, the phenomenal content of experiences can be reduced to representational content.[2] In short, the strategy is to try to show that experiences, and even sensations, are akin to the propositional attitudes in that they are type-individuated by way of their semantic or representational content. The arguments for content externalism would, therefore, apply to them on this basis.

The other source for externalist views of phenomenal consciousness derives from what is, in essence, a vehicle externalist approach.[3] Some have argued that phenomenal consciousness does not arise from the production of internal representations to which phenomenal properties, or qualia, attach. Rather, it arises from the active probing or exploration of environmental structures. In so far as consciousness has this sort of phenomenal character, this attaches to these worldly acts of exploration.

The first part of this chapter considers the arguments for externalism based on content externalism while the second half examines the arguments based on vehicle externalism.

Content externalism and representationism

The attack on the internality of consciousness that derives from content externalism is based on the following claims.

1. Conscious experiences are defined, or type-identified, by way of their phenomenal or qualitative properties.
2. The phenomenal properties of experiences reduce to the representational properties of those experiences.
3. Representational properties of experience are externally individuated.
4. Therefore, the phenomenal properties of experience are externally individuated and, since experiences are type-identified by way of their phenomenal properties, experiences are also externally individuated.

That is, both conscious experiences and the properties in virtue of which an item qualifies as a conscious experience are externally individuated. Hence, such items do not locally supervene on the internal states and processes of conscious subjects.

The claim that the phenomenal properties of experience reduce to the representational properties of that experience is known as *representationism*. According to this view, the phenomenal properties of any given experience are *constituted* by – are one and the same thing as – some, but not necessarily all, of the representational properties of that experience.

There are, however, two quite distinct ways of developing this general idea. The first, and by far the most common, way is what I shall call *object representationism*. When most people talk of representationism, I think this is what they have in mind.

Object representationism is the view that the phenomenal properties of any given experience are constituted by the property, possessed by that experience, of representing a particular object, event, process, situation, state of affairs and so on. The property of phenomenal redness, for example, thought to be possessed by some experience is identical with the property, possessed by that experience, of representing a red object or state of affairs. This is a property that an experience might have even in the absence of an environmental correlate, and so, it is argued, object representationism can account for the existence of illusory and hallucinatory experiences of redness. The hallucinatory or illusory character of an experience is, on this view, no more of a problem for representationism than the falsity of a belief is a problem for the idea that beliefs have semantic content. Just as a belief can represent a nonexistent state of affairs, so too can an experience.

Object representationism has been widely criticized, and most of these criticisms conform to a certain type. Essentially, the critical strategy involves trying to show the possibility, with respect to a set of experience tokens, of a variation in the representational properties of those tokens without a corresponding variation in their phenomenal properties. If this type of possibility is genuine, then, it is argued, the phenomenal properties of experiences cannot be constituted by their representational properties.

The most celebrated example of this type of strategy is Ned Block's inverted-earth thought-experiment: a variation on Putnam's twin-earth scenario.[4] We looked at this experiment in Chapter 7. On inverted earth, everything has a colour different from the colour it has on earth: the sky is yellow, grass is red, the sun is blue, Coca-Cola cans are green and so on. So, if you visited inverted earth, you would see the sky as yellow, the grass as red and so on. However, the vocabulary of the residents of inverted earth is also inverted. Thus, in talking of the colour of the sky, they use the term "blue"; and in talking of the colour of grass, they use the term "green" and so on. Furthermore, because of the differences between earth and inverted earth, the intentional or representational contents of the propositional attitudes and experiences of inverted earthlings are themselves inverted. Thus, when a resident of inverted earth wonders, as he would put it, "why the sky is blue", he is wondering not why the sky is blue but why the sky is yellow.

Suppose, now, you are taken to inverted earth. Under normal circumstances, the sky there would appear yellow and the sun would appear blue. However, suppose that during your transportation, a transportation in which you are rendered unconscious, scientists fit you with colour-altering lenses. These nullify the colour difference on inverted earth, so when you wake up on inverted earth, you notice no difference. The yellow sky looks blue to you, the blue sun looks yellow, and all the inverted earthlings around you describe the world in the way you would expect: they call the yellow sky "blue", the blue sun "yellow" and so on. From the point of view of the phenomenal character of your experiences, it seems, nothing is any different from the way it would have been had you stayed on earth.

Initially, Block argues, the representational contents of your experiences and propositional attitudes would also be the same. The causal rooting of your colour words is grounded, it seems, in your prior use on earth. So on your first day on inverted earth, for example, when you think that, for example, the sky is as blue as ever, you are expressing the same thought as you would have expressed on earth; it is just that in this case you are wrong. Moreover, your thought is not identical with the one a native of inverted earth would express with the same words. However, Block argues that after a suitable period of time the representational contents of your experiences and attitudes would change. After sufficient time had been spent on inverted earth, your use of colour terms would become tied to, or embedded in, your new physical and linguistic environment. This new embedding would, eventually, come to dominate, and your representational contents would, accordingly, shift so as to be the same as those of the natives.

Thus we seem to have a logically possible situation in which the representational properties of your experiences alter without any corresponding alteration in the phenomenal properties of those experiences. If this is correct, the phenomenal properties of experiences cannot be constituted by the representational properties of those experiences.

There are various ways of replying to the inverted-earth thought-experiment, and so attempting to avoid the conclusions it invites us to draw.[5] In my view, none of these replies work and the inverted-earth scenario does successfully establish that phenomenal properties cannot be constituted by representational ones, at least as the latter are understood by object representationism. To argue here for this claim would take us too far afield. What I do want to argue here, however, is that there is a way of understanding representationism that renders it immune to inverted-earth-type objections. I call this way of understanding the representationist thesis *mode representationism*.

Mode representationism is the view that the phenomenal character of any given experience is constituted by the *mode of presentation* of those objects revealed, or represented, by that experience. More precisely, phenomenal properties are identical with properties of representing objects under particular modes of presentation. The notion of a mode of presentation, of course, is here understood psychologically rather than, as Frege would have it, as an abstract entity.

It is important to realize that this is still a form of representationism. When an object, property, event, process, situation or state of affairs is represented in an experience, or, using my nomenclature, *revealed* in the having of the experience, then it is always so represented under some or other mode of presentation. An object of a certain sort of molecular configuration, thus, might be revealed as a red square. The combination of redness and squareness, thus, provides the mode of presentation of that particular object. However, no one would suppose that the redness and squareness are not represented features of the experience. On the contrary, the object is represented in the experience by way of the representation of redness and squareness. Slightly more precisely, the representation of the object in experience *consists in* the representation of redness and squareness. Thus, to view the phenomenal properties of an experience as identical with properties of representing objects under particular modes of representation is not to abandon representationism.

Mode representationism has notable advantages over its object representationist cousin. Most importantly, it seems immune to the type of inverted-earth experiment outlined above. To see this, remember that the inverted-earth scenario works by driving a wedge between phenomenal and representational properties of experiences. The moral of the scenario is that the representational properties of an experience type can vary (e.g. over time) while the phenomenal properties of the same experience type remain constant.

For example, with respect to the sky of inverted earth, my experience, representationally, is *of*, or about, something yellow; phenomenally, it is *as of* something blue. However, the mode representationist is able to accommodate this intuition. During my arrival on inverted earth, my experience represents the yellow sky under a blue mode of presentation. After a time sufficient for my becoming embedded in the new physical and linguistic environment, however, my experience of the sky still represents the sky under the same mode of presentation. Thus, the mode representationist can deny that the *relevant* representational properties of the experience change. If this is correct, the inverted-earth scenario does nothing to drive a wedge between phenomenal and representational properties.

This can be supported by the following qualification of the content of the general representationist thesis. It is not a logically necessary part of representationism, in either form, that the phenomenal properties of a particular experience be constituted by *all* the representational properties of that experience. Far more plausible is the claim that the former are constituted by, or identical with, *some* of the latter. The mode representationist can allow, then, that during my embedding in a new physical and linguistic environment some representational shift occurs but, at the same time, deny that this shift involves the representational properties that are constitutive of the phenomenal features of experience. Thus, my experiences, subsequent to my new embedding, are no longer *of* something blue. Nonetheless, they are still of something given under a blue mode of presentation. And it is these latter representational properties, the mode representationist can assert, that are constitutive of the phenomenal character of those experiences.

If either form of representationism turns out to be true, then the phenomenal properties of experiences reduce, in one way or another, to representational properties. However, if the arguments for content externalism are correct, such properties are externally individuated and any state that is type-individuated according to such properties is, thereby, externally individuated also. Thus, if, as representationism claims, the phenomenal properties of any given experience reduce to the representational properties of that experience, then the properties that type-individuate experiences are reducible to properties that are externally individuated in the sense introduced in Chapter 6. Therefore, experiences would also be externally individuated. In short, if the phenomenal properties of experience reduce to representational properties, then content externalism is as true of experiences as it is of propositional attitudes.[6]

Vehicle externalism and consciousness

The other attack on the internalist view of phenomenal consciousness – that is, on the claim that such consciousness is locally supervenient on states and processes occurring inside the skins of organisms – derives from the application of what is essentially a vehicle externalist account. First of all, recall the general vehicle externalist framework, as laid out in Chapter 9. The framework is constituted by the following claims.

1. The world is an external store of information relevant to cognitive processes such as perceiving, remembering, reasoning and so on.

It is such a store because, in all essentials, information is ubiquitous. It is in virtue of nomic dependencies (e.g. covariations) between items that one item can carry information about another. However, such relations can be externally instantiated just as much as they can be instantiated in the relation between an internal representation and its external correlate. In virtue of this, information exists in the environment and there are certain environmental structures that carry information relevant to cognition.

2. A process such as perceiving is essentially hybrid – it straddles both internal and external forms of information processing.
3. The external processes involve manipulation, exploitation and transformation of environmental structures that carry information relevant to the accomplishing of the perceptual task at hand.
4. At least some of the internal processes are ones concerned with supplying the cognizing organism with the ability to use appropriately relevant structures in its environment.

Suppose this schematic account is correct, at least in broad outline. How would we apply it to the case of visual experience? A useful place to begin is provided by Mackay.[7] Suppose you are a blind person holding a bottle.

You have the feeling of holding a bottle, but what tactile sensations do you actually have? Without slight rubbing of the skin, tactile information is considerably reduced, information pertaining to temperature will soon disappear through adaptation of receptors and so on. Nonetheless, despite the poverty of sensory stimulation, you actually have the feeling of having a bottle in your hand. Broadly speaking, there are two general approaches to explaining how this can be.

According to the first approach, the brain supplements, extends and embellishes the impoverished information contained in sensory stimulation with what are, essentially, various forms of inferential process. The result is the construction of an internal representation of the bottle. We can call this the *representational* approach.[8]

Mackay's answer, however, is quite different and provides a useful illustration of the *extended* approach. According to Mackay, information is present in the environment over and above that contained in sensory stimulation and this information is sufficient to specify that you are holding a bottle. In what does this information consist? Inspired by certain ideas in the phenomenological tradition – and in particular, Husserl's account of the way in which the content of a sensory experience is partly constituted by anticipations of the further sensory experience that would occur contingent upon certain eventualities obtaining, an idea we encountered in Chapter 3 – Mackay provides the following answer: your brain is tuned to certain *potentialities*. For example, it is tuned to the fact that if you were to slide your hand very slightly, a change would come about in the incoming sensory signals that is typical of the change associated with the smooth, cool surface of glass. Furthermore, your brain is tuned to the fact that if you were to move your hand upwards, the size of what you are encompassing with your hand would diminish (because you are moving to the bottle's neck) and so on.[9]

What does this talk of "tuning" mean? Basically, your brain has extracted various laws of what O'Regan and Noë call *sensorimotor contingency*.[10] Very roughly, your brain has extracted, and has now activated, certain laws pertaining to the way changes in motor action will be accompanied by changes in sensory input; it has, that is, extracted a certain mapping function from motor activity to sensory input. This provides the additional information lacking in sensory stimulation, information that specifies that you are holding a bottle.

According to Mackay, seeing a bottle is an analogous state of affairs. You have the impression of seeing a bottle if your brain has extracted knowledge concerning a certain web of contingencies. For example, you have knowledge of the fact that if you move your eyes upwards towards the neck of the bottle, the sensory stimulation will change in a way typical of what happens when a narrower region of the bottle comes into foveal vision. You have knowledge of the fact that if you move your eyes downwards, the sensory stimulation will change in a way typical of what happens when the white label is fixated by foveal vision.

As O'Regan and Noë have shown, visual perception, just like haptic perception, obeys its own laws of sensorimotor contingency. A fairly trivial example is the fact that in the contingency that the eyes close, the stimulation becomes uniform (i.e. blank). Here is a less trivial one. As the eyes rotate, the sensory stimulation on the retina shifts and distorts in a very particular way, determined by the extent of the eye movement. In particular, as the eye moves, contours shift and the curvature of lines change. For example, if you are looking at the midpoint of a horizontal line, the line will trace out an arc on the inside of your eyeball. If you now fixate upwards, the curvature of the line will change; represented on a flattened-out retina, the line would now be curved. In general, straight lines on the retina distort dramatically as the eyes move, somewhat like an image in a distorting mirror.

Each form of perception has its own contingency rules and, according to O'Regan and Noë, what differentiates visual perception from other forms is the structure of the rules governing the sensory changes produced by various motor actions. The sensorimotor contingencies within each sensory modality are subject to different invariance properties and so the structure of the rules that govern the perception in these modalities will be different in each case. To learn to perceive visually is to learn the rules of sensorimotor contingency, understood as a non-propositional form of *knowing how*, governing the relation between changes in the orientation of the visual apparatus and the resulting changes in the character of the perceived world.

If this vehicle externalist or *extended* account of perception is correct, there is little need to explain the haptic perception of the bottle in terms of the production or activation of an internal representation. The work of such a representation can be performed by the bottle itself. The bottle is an external structure that carries information over and above that present in any sensory stimulation the bottle is currently inducing in the hand. How does it carry such information? It provides a stable structure that can be probed or explored at will by the haptic modality. Mackay's suggestion is that the same is true of visual perception. The bottle also provides a stable structure that can be explored at will by the visual modality. Thus we arrive back at the general framework for vehicle externalism outlined earlier. Visual perception is essentially hybrid, made up of internal processes (extraction and activation of the laws of sensorimotor contingency) plus external processes (the probing or exploration of information-bearing structures in the environment). Visually perceiving is a process whereby the world – understood as an external store of information – is probed or explored by acts of perception, and the results of this exploration are mediated through the non-propositionally instantiated laws of sensorimotor contingency.

So we have two quite different general approaches to explaining visual perception, one representational and the other vehicle externalist or extended. How do we adjudicate between them? The case ultimately rests on empirical considerations and these, I think, strongly favour the extended approach.

Against visual representations

Consider, for example, the important experiments on *change blindness* performed by O'Regan and collaborators.[11] Observers are shown displays of natural scenes and are asked to detect cyclically repeated changes: a large object shifting, changing colour or appearing and disappearing. Under normal circumstances, changes of this magnitude would be noticed easily because such changes would create a transient signal in the visual apparatus that would be detected by low-level visual mechanisms. This transient automatically attracts attention to the location of the change and the change would therefore be immediately seen.

There are, however, ways of nullifying the role of the visual transient and this is precisely what is done in the change blindness experiments. One method involves superimposing a very brief global flicker over the whole visual field at the moment of the change. A similar effect can be achieved by making the change coincide with an eye saccade, an eye blink or a cut in a film sequence. In all these cases, a brief global disturbance swamps the local transient and thus prevents it from playing its normal attention-grabbing role. Another method involves creating a number of simultaneous local disturbances – which appear something like mud splashes on the scene – that act as decoys and so minimize the effect of the local transient.

The experiments show that under these sorts of conditions, observers have great difficulty seeing changes, even though they are very large and occur in full view. Indeed, measurements of the observers' eyes indicate that they could be looking directly at the change at the moment it occurs, and still not see it.[12]

The idea that visual perception consists in the activation of an internal representation of a portion of the visual world renders these results mysterious. On this representational model, all that would be required to notice a change in such a scene would be to compare one's current visual impressions with the activated representation; when and how the discrepancies between the former and the latter arose would be irrelevant. The change blindness results strongly support the claim that there is at least no complex and detailed internal representation. We do not notice even significant changes in a scene because we have no complex and detailed internal template against which to measure or compare them.[13] The detail and complexity of our experience is not duplicated internally.

What it is like to see

These results also provide us with a way of correctly locating the phenomenal character of visual experience. As we look at a complex and detailed scene, our visual experience seems to be complex and detailed. Complexity and detail are, we might say, part of what it is like to have this visual experience. The change blindness results, however, strongly suggest that the impression we have of seeing a complex, detailed world is not an impression grounded in any complex, detailed visual representation of that world. External complexity and detail is not internally reproduced.

How should we interpret this? Does this mean that our subjective impression of seeing everything is somehow mistaken? Worse, does it mean we can be mistaken about the way our experiences seem to us? Dennett seems to endorse this sort of interpretation, or did so at one time.[14] The interpretation is misguided. The claim that our subjective impressions are erroneous would follow only if we suppose that the subjective impression has to be grounded in an internal representation – that the accuracy of a subjective impression is to be measured by how closely it mirrors the structure of an internal representation – and this is precisely what the present account denies. We are aware of a complex and detailed world but this means only that we are aware of the world as being complex and detailed.

This mistaken interpretation is reinforced by a common confusion. The confusion consists in the idea that to claim that there is something that it is like to have or undergo an experience entails that this experience seems or feels a certain way. Once we accept that seeming or feeling are properties of experiences, it is but a small step to the claim that the way an experience must seem or feel has to be explained in terms of our awareness of those features of the experience in virtue of which it seems this. All this is erroneous. Experiences do not seem or feel a certain way. Rather, in the *having* of an experience, the *world* seems or feels a certain way.[15] Seeming or feeling, that is, are properties of the world: properties that it has *in virtue of* our having experiences.

So, the question is: why does the world seem this way – complex and detailed – when its seeming this way is not underwritten by an internal representation that represents it as being this way? There are two reasons.[16] First, the impression we have of seeing everything derives from the fact that the slightest flick of the eye allows any part of a visual scene to be processed at will. This gives us the impression that the whole scene is immediately available. Suppose you try to ascertain whether you are in fact seeing everything there is to see in a scene. How could you check this? Only, it seems, by casting your attention on each element of the scene and verifying that you have the impression of constantly seeing it. But, obviously, as soon as you do cast your attention on something, you see it. Therefore, you will always have the impression of constantly seeing everything.[17] Is this impression erroneous? Only if we think of seeing in terms of the production of an internal representation isomorphic with the part of the world seen. If, on the other hand, we accept that seeing consists in combining the results of environmental probing with knowledge of laws of sensorimotor contingency, we are indeed seeing the whole scene, for probing the world, and knowledge of these laws, is precisely what we do and have as we cast our attention from one aspect to the next.

Secondly, in addition to our ability to direct our attention at will to the visual world, the visual system is particularly sensitive to *visual transients*. When a visual transient occurs, a low-level "attention-grabbing" mechanism appears automatically to direct processing to the location of the transient. This means that should anything happen in the environment, we will generally see it consciously, since processing will be directed towards it. This gives us the impression of keeping tabs on everything that might change and so of consciously seeing everything. If we regard seeing as consisting in exploratory activity combined with knowledge of sensorimotor contingencies accompanying such exploration, then this impression is not erroneous. We do, indeed, see everything. The suspicion that we do not derives from a residual attachment to the idea that seeing consists in the production of an internal representation that maps onto the outside world.

Complexity and detail are genuine features of the phenomenal character of our experience. This is not because they attach to an internal representation of the perceived portion of the world. Rather, they exist in and attach to the act of probing or exploring a complex and detailed world as this act is combined with knowledge of the laws of sensorimotor contingency.

This general model can quite easily be extended to other types of visual experience. What it is like to see a uniform expanse of red, for example, arises from (but, I shall argue later, *pace* O'Regan and Noë, does not simply consist in) suitable exploration or probing of the red expanse in front of one combined with knowledge of the sensorimotor contingencies associated with such exploration. Thus, one has the ability to flick one's attention at will to any part of the red expanse in front of one and to have an appropriate sensitivity to any visual transients that may tarnish this expanse. In so doing, the sensory stimulation changes in a way consistent with the presence of a red expanse. We experience a uniform expanse of red not because of features of an accetivated internal representation but because we can explore, in this sense, a worldly uniform expanse of red.

In what sense is this a vehicle externalist account of phenomenal consciousness? On this view, the phenomenal features of experience do not attach to an internal state or process. The detail and complexity of an experience are partly constitutive of the way the having of that experience seems to its subject – they are partly constitutive, that is, of the phenomenal content of that experience. But these features are not, if O'Regan and Noë are correct, ones that attach to any state or process that occur inside the skin of that subject. Rather, they are features that exist in, and only in, the directing of awareness towards worldly objects and properties. Since this process of directing awareness is not an internal activity but one that essentially occurs in the world, the phenomenal properties that attach to this process are also, therefore, not internally constituted properties. They are properties that exist only in the relationship that an experiencing organism bears towards an external world. In other words, the vehicle of this sort of phenomenal content is, at least in part, an act of environmental probing or exploration. This vehicle of phenomenal content is, accordingly, an external one.

Imagery, dreams, hallucinations and so on

The fact that there is something that it is like to undergo non-perceptual experiences is going to provide the most obvious source of objections to this view. There is something that it is like, for example, to form a mental image of a scene; there is something that it is like to have dreams, hallucinations and the like.

The first point that should be made is that the traditional internalist view of consciousness consists in a universally quantified claim: *all* phenomenal character is internally constituted. Therefore, undermining this view requires only an existentially quantified counter-claim: *some* phenomenal character is not internally constituted. It is no part of vehicle externalism concerning phenomenal consciousness to claim that the phenomenal character of all experiences is externally constituted, just as it is no part of vehicle externalism, sensibly construed, to argue that all cognitive processes are externally constituted. The claim, rather, is only that the phenomenal character of some experiences is externally constituted. Therefore, to point to the existence of experiences – such as imaginings, dreams, hallucinations and the like – that have a phenomenal character that is, apparently, internally constituted is to miss the point.

This response, however, might itself be thought to miss the point. What underlies the appeal to imaginings, dreams and hallucinations, it might be argued, is the idea that the quasi-visual phenomenal character of these items is so close to the phenomenal character that exists in visually perceiving the world that both cry out for the same, unified explanation or, at least, a fundamentally similar explanation. Therefore, since we cannot give an extended account of quasi-visual phenomenal character, it might be thought, this casts significant doubt on the correctness of the extended account of visual phenomenal character.

This thought, of course, has a long and distinguished philosophical history and is what underwrites both sense-datum and representationalist accounts of perception. The account of what it is like to see developed here, employing so prominently the idea of exploration of environmental structures, should entail that this differs in fundamental ways from what it is like visually to imagine, dream or hallucinate – that the phenomenal character of seeing should diverge in significant ways from that of imagining, dreaming or hallucinating. Thus, it might be thought, the extended account cannot explain the logical possibility of imaginings, dreams and hallucinations being phenomenally indistinguishable from genuine visual perception.

If this is the basis of the appeal to quasi-visual phenomenal character, then we can turn the sense of dissatisfaction that underlies it on its head. Indeed, the appeal can actually be used to *support* the vehicle externalist account of what it is like to see. The existence of quasi-visual phenomenal character attaching to acts of imagining, dreaming and hallucinating would pose a threat to the vehicle externalist account of visual phenomenal character only if the former were indeed indistinguishable from, or at least very similar to, the latter. But suppose the converse were true. Suppose visual phenomenal character not only differed from its quasi-visual cousin but did so *in ways predicted or entailed by the vehicle externalist account* of the former. Then, this would not only undercut the force of the appeal to quasi-visual phenomenal character if this is used as an objection to the extended account of visual phenomenal character; it would mean that the appeal to the former would actually support the vehicle externalist account of the latter.

One entailment of the vehicle externalist model of visual phenomenal character is that the stability of the perceived visual field is a function of the stability of the visual world: the world towards which the exploratory perceptual activity is directed.[18] Without the stable world to hold our perceptual activity together, we should predict that any quasi-perceptual activity that is not directed towards a similarly stable world should lack the consistency, coherency and stability of genuine perception. This, of course, is precisely what we get in the case of dreams and hallucinations.

The vehicle externalist model of visual phenomenal character accords a central role to our ability to direct our attention at will to any part of the visual world. It is this that underlies the sense of complexity and detail that typically attends genuine visual phenomenology. We can direct our attention in this way only because the world provides a stable and enduring structure that supports such exploratory activity. Thus, another prediction that the vehicle externalist model makes is that it should be much more difficult, if not impossible, to direct one's attention in imaginings, dreams and hallucinations. The empirical work that has been done on this issue bears out this prediction.

Consider, for example, Chambers and Reisberg's study of perceptual versus imaginative flipping of ambiguous images.[19] Subjects were asked to observe and recall a drawing. The drawing would be ambiguous, of the duck/rabbit, faces/vase, old lady/young lady sort. The subjects, who did not know the duck/rabbit picture, were trained on related cases to ensure they were familiar with the phenomenon of ambiguity. Having been briefly shown the duck/rabbit picture, they were asked to form a mental image of it, attend to this image and seek an alternative interpretation of it. Despite the inclusion in the test group of several high vividness imagers (as measured by the Slee elaboration scale), none of the 15 subjects was able to find an alternative construal of their image. However, when subjects were later asked to draw the imaged duck/rabbit, all 15 were then able to find the alternative interpretation. The significance of this is that the ability to reinterpret the external drawing depends on slight changes in foveation; the external structure is subtly probed by the visual modality. The inability of subjects to discover the alternative construal of their image suggests that this sort of probing cannot be performed in the case of mental images. Directing of attention within mental images is, at the very least, much more difficult than within the perceived visual world. This is precisely what we should expect if the vehicle externalist model of visual phenomenal character were true.

Finally, visual phenomenology differs from that which attends acts of imagining, dreaming and hallucinating in one final way. The laws of sensorimotor contingency evident in visual perception simply do not operate in the latter sorts of experiential acts. To take just one example, even if it were possible to focus one's attention in, say, particularly vivid dreams or hallucinations – and the evidence for this is far from conclusive – such focusing is not attended by the sensorimotor contingencies that characterize visual perception. For example, in dreams, straight lines do not become curved as they move from the centre of foveation (or whatever passes for foveation in dreams).

In short, the appeal to quasi-visual phenomenal character provides the objector with a two-edged sword. Far from undermining the vehicle externalist account of visual phenomenal character, the most reasonable construal of the evidence, I think, suggests that it actually supports that account.

What it is like and the hard problem

O'Regan and Noë, who adopt essentially the same model of visual perception as defended here, claim that this model solves, or at least dissolves, the *hard problem* of consciousness: the problem of understanding how a pattern of neural activity, functional organization or the like could ever add up to phenomenology. Their argument runs as follows.

1. The phenomenal properties of experience are, supposedly, items that attach to internal representations, and the problem – the hard problem – of consciousness is one of seeing how the other features of these representations could ever constitute their phenomenal features.
2. The sensorimotor contingency model of perception obviates the need for representations.
3. But phenomenal properties, if they exist, are features of representations.
4. Therefore, phenomenal properties do not exist.
5. Therefore, there's nothing left to explain.

This, I think, is *not* a good argument. For a start, it is far from clear how we could apply the extended model to the case of non-perceptual qualia (including, as we have seen, quasi-visual phenomenal character). But without such application, we would not have solved the *generalized* hard

198

problem; at best we would have solved it for the case of perceptual phenomenal character. Yet even when restricted to the latter category, the argument is still not a good one.

Suppose you start off with a certain problem. Then you identify a common way this problem is theoretically glossed. You then show that the theoretical gloss is untenable and offer an alternative. You cannot legitimately conclude from this that you have solved the original problem. All you can conclude is that one way of understanding or glossing the original problem is inadequate. The problem is the hard problem. The gloss is that phenomenal properties are properties of internal representations. The alternative is the sensorimotor contingency model. But the hard problem is, I think, a deep problem, one that survives the loss of this or indeed a number of other theoretical glosses. Far from solving or dissolving the hard problem, O'Regan and Noë have, at best, merely managed to *relocate* it.

To see this, consider their account of what it is like to see colour, specifically a uniform expanse of red, in front of one. They write:

> Suppose you look at a red colored wall. The redness is on the wall, there to be appreciated. Because we have continuous access to the present redness, it is as if you are continuously in contact with it. This would explain the fact that the redness would seem to be continuously present in experience. This point can be sharpened. The "feeling of present redness" that would seem to accompany the seeing of something red is to be explained by the fact that we understand (in a practical sense) that at any moment we can direct our attention to the red wall.[20]

The way it seems or feels to undergo an experience of red consists, in all essentials, in the fact that we are able to direct our attention at will to the red expanse in front of us (and, presumably, that we exhibit an appropriate sensitivity to any visual transients blemishing this expanse). This ability is accompanied by an understanding of how such exploratory behaviour will be accompanied by changes in the character of sensory stimulation.

The problem with this account, however, is immediately obvious. Just what is it towards which we are directing our attention at will, and with respect to which certain predicted changes in sensory stimulation accompany this exploration? It is something with a certain molecular structure, hence a certain reflectance capacity: a surface that relates to the spectrum of visible light in a certain way, and which "changes the light when the surface is moved with respect to the observer or the light source".[21] What we are not directing our attention towards is something that is red in anything like the phenomenal sense. Of course, we can always define red simply as a type of reflectance capacity, or as a capacity to change light in various lawlike ways. But in the present context this would simply be a philosophical sleight of hand. That a surface with a certain reflectance capacity and that changes the ambient light when moved with respect to observer or light source should appear the way it appears to us – as red in the phenomenal sense – is just as much a problem as the original hard problem. Indeed, it is the *same* problem. The extended model of visual perception does not solve the hard problem for visual phenomenal character. It simply relocates it: it *externalizes* the hard problem.

Indeed, I have argued elsewhere that if we take seriously the idea that what it is like to undergo an experience attaches to acts of experiencing, rather than being found among the experience's objects, we should abandon the idea that what it is like can be reduced to anything else, even if our conceptual repertoire is godlike.[22] Roughly, very roughly, this is because reduction is a process whereby the contribution that the act of experience makes to an object is bracketed. What it is like to undergo an experience is, I believe, real and irreducible. It is just that it is not at all the sort of thing we have taken it to be.

Conclusion

The scope of externalism, which initially appeared quite narrow, has been progressively broadening over the course of Chapters 9 and 10. The application of externalist ideas to cognitive processes and the architectures that underwrite them was examined in Chapter 9, and this resulted in the view known as vehicle externalism. The extension of externalist ideas to phenomenal consciousness was examined here in Chapter 10. The extension was seen to have two distinct motivations, one based on the application of content externalism to consciousness and the other based on the application of vehicle externalism to consciousness.

The application of content externalism to consciousness takes the form of what is known as representationism: the claim that the phenomenal properties of experience reduce to representational properties. Two forms of representationism were distinguished: objects and mode representationism. Standard objections to object representationism – for example, Block's inverted-earth thought-experiment – do not apply to mode representationism. Mode representationism, therefore, seems to provide a more promising means for extending content externalism to consciousness.

The application of vehicle externalism to consciousness takes the form of the exploratory activity account of consciousness, an account developed most fully by O'Regan and Noë. According to this account, the vehicle of phenomenal content consists, at least in part, in an act of environmental probing or exploration. The vehicle of phenomenal content is, therefore, an external one. This does not, I think, add up to an *explanation* of phenomenal consciousness – contrary to some of the more optimistic claims of O'Regan and Noë. It does show us, however, the extent to which the vehicles of phenomenal consciousness – the structures and mechanisms that allow us to be the subjects of phenomenally conscious states – are externally located.

CHAPTER 11

Externalist axiology

The Cartesian tradition yields a very definite conception of what *value* – moral, aesthetic and so on – must be. Or, rather, it yields a specific framework of possibilities for the sort of thing value must be. The view of the mind as essentially an interiority – something located entirely inside the skins of mental subjects – presents us with a stark choice when trying to understand the nature of value. Either value must derive from the inside – from the activities of the mind – or it must exist on the outside, objectively present in the world independently of those activities. Broadly speaking, the former view is known as *subjectivism* and the latter as *objectivism*. This choice between subjectivist and objectivist models of value has pretty much defined moral debate since the time of Plato.

This debate has its problems. If we opt for the idea that value is ultimately a product of the mind, understood as something located exclusively inside the skins of mental subjects, then we are quickly led to the idea that value is not really in the world at all. That is, we are driven to the view that the world, and the things in it, do not really possess value in themselves. Should the activities of the mind that constitute value cease, there would be no value; the apparent value of worldly items would dissipate. Real value, on this subjectivist model, lies on the inside; it is possessed by the outside only to the extent that the inside is able to *project* it outwards. This projected value is thus secondary and derivative and this seems – or has seemed to many – to be a disguised way of denying that value exists in the world in any real sense.

The objectivist alternative, on the other hand, faces a different problem. It makes it completely mysterious how the world could have value. If we want to claim that things in the world – the *outside* – have value independently of the valuing activities occurring on the *inside*, then it seems we are forced into the extremely difficult job of explaining how, exactly, there can be value in the absence, or potential absence, of valuing.

How can something have value in the absence, or potential absence, of its being valued? What sort of thing is this value that it can exist in the absence of valuing? As we shall see, attempts to furnish these questions with convincing answers have, historically, been rather unsuccessful.

How would things change if we abandoned the Cartesian division between mind and world? If the mind were, as externalists of various stripes insist, thoroughly perforated and penetrated by the world, what implications would this have for our understanding of value? Axiology is the branch of philosophy concerned with the nature of value, in its various forms. This chapter will outline, in admittedly the broadest possible strokes, the prospects for developing an *externalist axiology*.

Axiological objectivism

Axiological objectivism, roughly speaking, is the view that value exists objectively in the world independently of the opinions, feelings, beliefs or attitudes of people or of any valuing consciousness in general. This characterization is complicated by two things. First, the notion of "in the world" is problematic, for some of the things that might have value – feelings of pleasure or happiness, for example – are things that are commonly supposed to exist in the head rather than the world. Secondly, and relatedly, value might be a property that attaches to things like opinions, feelings, beliefs or attitudes and so, in these cases at least, hardly be supposed to exist independently of these things, at least not in any straightforward sense.

For example, in some versions of objectivism value is, in fact, constituted by such things as feelings and attitudes. According to what is known as *hedonism*, for example, value is constituted by certain sorts of feelings, specifically feelings of pleasure or happiness. And according to the view known as *preference utilitarianism*, value is constituted by the satisfaction of certain sort of attitudes or preferences. Both of these qualify as forms of objectivism. This mandates a slight modification in the characterization of objectivism. What the formulation must rule out is not that value can be constituted by such things as feelings or attitudes but that this value can be constituted by our feelings and attitudes *towards* this value or to the things that have value – because this is the defining feature of subjectivism.

Take, for example, the case of hedonism. On many, if not all, views of the mental, the presence of happiness or unhappiness in a person is a perfectly objective fact about the world. It is not in any way dependent on our feelings or attitudes about that happiness. If happiness has value then, according to the objectivist, this is not because of our feelings or attitudes towards it. Therefore, there is nothing here that militates against value – even when understood objectively – being identical with happiness. Thus, a better formulation of the objectivist component of naturalism is this: value possessed by any given item is not in any way constituted or dependent upon the feelings or attitudes we have *about* that item. This is compatible with the claim that this value may itself be constituted by feelings and attitudes.

Within this general framework, objectivism can be divided into two forms. One form of objectivism identifies value with some group of natural features objectively present in the world; the other identifies it with a so-called non-natural feature. I shall refer to the former view as *naturalistic* objectivism and the latter as *non-naturalistic* objectivism.

Non-naturalistic objectivism

According to non-naturalistic objectivism, value is not to be identified with any natural feature of the world. Rather, value is a primitive and irreducible property that is objective but non-natural.[1] To say that this value is non-natural is to say that it is not empirically detectable, either through observation or inference on the basis of observation. And to say that this value is primitive and irreducible is to say that this value cannot be explained in any other terms. One cannot claim, for example, that value is to be identified, as the hedonist would have it, with pleasure. For this would be to explain value reductively in terms of pleasure. This, according to the non-naturalistic objectivist, is precisely what cannot be done for value. Value is simply what it is and nothing else. One cannot, therefore, give an account of the essence of this property, nor can one give an account of why some things have this property while others do not. Some things simply have the property and others do not and that is where explanation stops.

Problems with non-naturalistic objectivism turn on the epistemic status of, and our access to, any non-natural property. If such a property can be neither empirically detectable nor inferred on the basis of what is empirically detectable, then moral argument seems to reduce to a mystical form of intuitionism. Natural properties of objects may be recognized or discovered either empirically or by reasoning based on experience. We know, for example, that an object is circular by looking at it and that our fuel tank is empty by inference from other experiences (the gauge points to empty, the car won't start, etc.). The non-natural property of having value, however, cannot be empirically detected or inferred from other experiences that we have. This is the force of saying that it is non-natural. If it could be detected or inferred, then we could explain what it was in terms of the properties in virtue of which we detect or infer it and this would be to explain value in terms of those properties. According to non-naturalistic objectivism, this is precisely what we cannot do for value. Therefore, the non-natural property of intrinsic value can only be discovered through some sort of obscure faculty: through a faculty of *moral intuition*. On this view we can know moral truths not through our experience or our reason, but through our faculty of moral intuition.

However, such a faculty must clearly be unevenly distributed through-out the population. If a capacity for moral intuition were distributed equally and evenly in everyone, there would be as little controversy over which things have value as there would be about the colour of the sky (inverted-earth scenarios notwithstanding, of course). But, clearly, which things have value and which do not is not something generally agreed upon; this, after all, is why there are moral disagreements. Therefore, one must regard the faculty of moral intuition as being unevenly distributed between people. Perhaps it is vested in only a few gifted moral seers. Or perhaps, though more generally distributed, it varies wildly from one person to another. Either way, the possibility of moral persuasion based on rational discussion is aborted. One can only say things like: I "see" (i.e. intuit) the value of X and if you do not you are morally blind. The result is simple, undefended, entrenched opinions clothed, for the sake of respectability, in the guise of intuitions or primitive, irreducible, non-natural properties.

Naturalistic objectivism

Naturalistic objectivism avoids the mystery inherent in its non-naturalistic counterpart. A naturalistic theory of value is one that identifies intrinsic value with a natural feature of objects. To say that a feature is natural, roughly, is to say that it is capable of empirical detection, either through direct observation or through inference from what is directly observed. The objectivist component of this axiological view is, as we have seen, sometimes expressed by way of the requirement that the natural features constitutive of value be independent of the opinions, feelings, beliefs or attitudes of people, or of any valuing consciousness in general. More precisely, the value possessed by an item X (which may itself be a feeling or attitude of some sort) is not constituted by the feelings, attitudes and the like that a valuing consciousness bears towards X.

Hedonism counts as a form of naturalistic objectivism. Hedonism identifies value with pleasure, which, at least arguably, is an objective feature of the world, one whose existence is not constituted by the attitudes or feelings we bear towards it. Utilitarianism identifies value with an increase in the overall amount of happiness in the world, which can, similarly, be understood as an objective feature of the world. Other forms of naturalistic objectivism make value more independent of mental operations. In recent environmental philosophy, for example, it is common to see the value of nature identified with one or another natural feature of the environment: life, diversity, ecosystemic integrity and so on.

While avoiding the obscurity of its non-naturalistic counterpart, naturalistic objectivism has well-known problems of its own. Most importantly, any form of naturalistic objectivism is ultimately committed to the existence of a logical gap between *value* and *valuing*: the two are at least logically independent. And because of this, any form of naturalistic objectivism is, ultimately, subject to a charge of *arbitrariness*.

The problem is, perhaps, clearest for the versions of naturalistic objectivism implicated in recent environmental philosophy. Consider, for example, Kenneth Goodpaster's claim that life is intrinsically valuable and that, therefore, all living things have intrinsic value.[2] As Tom Regan points out, this seems to be an arbitrary claim.[3] The sceptic is entitled to ask: why is life crucial rather than some other feature such as consciousness or rationality? The problem is that one cannot simply assert that a certain property is what gives things intrinsic value and leave matters at that. Some sort of defence needs to be given of why this property is so important, of why this property in particular makes something intrinsically valuable. The problem, for naturalistic objectivists, is that they seem in principle incapable of providing such a defence. For naturalistic objectivists, the explanatory buck stops with the natural properties themselves. There is simply no explanation of why life, or richness, makes something intrinsically valuable; it just does. Explanation comes to an end with the connection between these sorts of natural properties and intrinsic value. There is, of course, no problem as such with the notion of explanation coming to an end. All explanation, as Wittgenstein has pointed out, must come to an end somewhere. The problem is that for anyone not already wedded to the naturalistic objectivist position, explanation seems to have been brought to a halt far too early. Thus it appears perfectly legitimate to ask for an explanation of why a particular property, such as life, should make something intrinsically valuable. It seems inadequate to say that it just does. The force of the arbitrariness charge, then, is that naturalistic objectivism brings the scheme of moral explanation and justification to an end at an implausibly early stage of the proceedings. Naturalistic objectivism thus seems to be irredeemably arbitrary.

The problem is almost as clear for more traditional cases of naturalistic objectivism. When Bentham, for example, says that pleasure is good, one way of understanding what he is doing is as offering a reductive explanation of goodness in terms of pleasure. However, the obvious response to this is that while it may well be that we regard pleasure as good – that is, we value it – it does not follow from this that pleasure *is* good. An obvious response to Bentham's position is, "What's so good about pleasure?" And we cannot avoid this by inferring that pleasure is valuable from the fact that we value pleasure without collapsing back into the subjectivist position that sees the value of any item X as deriving from our valuing of it. Similarly, when Kant claims that the capacity for (a certain type of) rationality confers on its bearer the status of an *end-in-itself*, and thus makes its bearer the possessor of a certain sort of value that it would not otherwise have, an obvious response is, "What's so good about rationality?" We may value this form of rationality but it does not follow from this that it is valuable in any objective sense. In short, traditional naturalistic forms of axiological objectivism suffer just as much from the charge of arbitrariness, and it is only the more self-serving nature of these traditional forms – with their focus on value-conferring features possessed by human beings – that obscures this fact.[4]

It might be thought that this problem could be avoided if only the naturalistic objectivist would desist from stopping the explanation and justification of their claims at such a ludicrously early stage. That is, instead of remaining content to assert that, for example, pleasure or life is intrinsically valuable, the naturalistically inclined objectivist should be prepared to go further, identifying the relevant features of pleasure or life that makes it intrinsically valuable. This strategy, however, would only push the problem back a stage. Suppose the naturalistic objectivist identifies a certain property of pleasure, call it property P, which on his view makes pleasure intrinsically valuable. Then he could make claims of the sort: "Pleasure is intrinsically valuable because of property P". But, then, the relevant property is not pleasure itself, but property P possessed by pleasure. This means that our objectivist is simply replacing one assertion with another. Instead of claiming that it is pleasure that is intrinsically valuable and leaving the process of explanation and justification at that, he is now claiming that it is property P that makes things intrinsically valuable and leaving the process of explanation and justification at that. Once again, this seems merely to invite the sceptical retort: "Why P? What makes P so important?"[5]

What the naturalistic objectivist seems to require is the identification of some property whose connection to intrinsic value is, as we might say, *transparent*. That is, he needs to identify a property whose relation to intrinsic value is so clear, obvious and necessary that it, by itself, explains why it makes things intrinsically valuable. He needs to identify a property whose explanatory relevance to intrinsic value is, so to speak, written on its face. This would be a very strange property indeed. No naturalistic theory of value has ever succeeded in identifying such a property. Even more worrying, it is doubtful that the idea of such a property makes any sense at all. It is doubtful, that is, that any coherent concept corresponds to this alleged property. The property would have to be one that in itself is capable of bridging what is known as the *is/ought* gap – one that, in virtue of its nature, is capable of magically underwriting and justifying the transition from a statement of fact to a statement of value. It is doubtful that such a concept is coherent. Thus, the naturalistic objectivist seems to find themself in a position that is quite common in philosophy: wanting something they cannot have.

Axiological subjectivism

The charge of arbitrariness that afflicts naturalistic forms of objectivism stems from the logical gap that objectivists are committed to inserting between value and valuing. The value of any item X is at least logically independent of X's being valued by any valuing consciousness. In virtue of this gap, it always makes sense to ask "Why X? What makes X so valuable?" The best way to avoid this problem, I think, is to deny the existence of this sort of logical gap. Value is intrinsically bound up with valuing; we cannot even logically separate the two. This, in all essentials, is the strategy of axiological subjectivism.

A subjectivist account of value tries to ground value in the valuing activities of the human, or other, mind. Different forms of subjectivism will have different accounts of what these valuing activities are, but all of these are united by the idea that ethical judgements reflect our own feelings only and not facts about the external world. Hume provides a classic statement of the subjectivist position.[6]

According to Hume, a moral judgement such as, for example, that a certain action is good or that it is evil, is founded neither upon reason nor upon correspondence to the world. Rather, the foundation is provided by *sentiment*. Good and evil – consequently value and disvalue – are not objective qualities of things in the world but, rather, derive from us. In particular, what we call good and evil are, in fact, feelings of approval or disapproval, sympathy or repugnance, that actions and events elicit in us. Hume illustrates his account with a now famous example, which we looked at in Chapter 2. Suppose we come across the scene of a murder. Upon inspecting the body, we might be able to discover how long the person has been dead, the cause of their death, what the murder weapon was and so on. We might even be able to identify the murderer and his or her motive for the crime. These are all what Hume would call *matters of fact*. However, that the murder is morally wrong is something we can never discover by looking at the world. The wrongness of murder is not a matter of fact; it is not a fact or feature objectively contained in the murder. Rather, it is something we bring to the murder; something that we *project* on to the murder. When we come across the murder scene, we feel, perhaps, horror, dread, aversion, panic and alarm, and we project these feelings on to the murder. The feelings cause us to judge that murder is wrong and the content of our judgement is, accordingly, constituted by these feelings. However, our projection of these feelings on to the murder itself causes us to think of this wrongness as a fact objectively contained in the murder as such. Moral judgements are the result of feelings or sentiments that we project on to external events, and, as such, the content of these judgements is constituted by these feelings. Our projection of these feelings, however, causes us to think of the moral judgement as representing a feature of these external events.

It might be thought that axiological subjectivism of this sort leads to a chaotic form of moral relativism. If value depends on feelings or sentiment, and if such feelings can vary wildly from one person to another, then what has value will fluctuate accordingly. Hume, however, was quick to deny this possibility on the grounds that the moral sentiments – sympathy, empathy, fellow-feeling, affection and the like – are natural and universal features of humanity, possessed by all *normal* (i.e. non-sociopathic) individuals. If, for example, I did not feel horror and revulsion when I came across the scene of the murder, I would very definitely not be normal and would probably be classified as a sociopath. Thus, moral judgements need not vary wildly from one person to another because the moral sentiments that ground such judgements are distributed uniformly – more or less – across different individuals.

There are various ways of attempting to explain why the moral sentiments should be uniformly distributed in this way. One way, for example, appeals to evolutionary theory and this account was anticipated, in all essentials, by Darwin when he wrote *The Descent of Man*.[7] According to this account, in broad outline, bonds of affection between parents and offspring have a respectable evolutionary explanation in that they can promote the survival of genes passed on from one to the other. Such bonds permit the formation of small social groups based on kinship (i.e. sharing of genetic profile). However, suppose a random mutation, occurring in certain individuals but not others, resulted in the extension of the natural parental and filial affections to less closely related individuals. This would permit the enlargement of the family group. Should the newly extended community be better at surviving than smaller groups, for example by being more adept at defending itself or more adept at provisioning for itself, then the fitness of its individual members would also be increased. Hence this mutation would be passed on at a differentially greater rate. And, in this way, these more diffuse parental and filial affections, which Darwin, echoing Hume, calls the *social sentiments*, would spread throughout a population. In this way, Darwin argued, the moral sentiments could have co-evolved with the evolution of proto-human societies. The moral sentiments were necessary to the continuing survival of such societies and the societies, in turn, conferred differential inclusive fitness on their members.

It is, in fact, highly unlikely that the Darwinian explanation of the uniformity of the distribution of the moral sentiments will work. In particular, Darwin's explanation is committed to what is known as *group selectionism*: the view that we can explain the existence of a group in terms of the claim that the fitness of an individual can be increased by adopting behaviour that contributes to the survival of the group. The problem with group selectionism, in this sense, is that it is almost certainly false. The problem with an individual adopting behaviour that is selected because it contributes to the survival of a group is that it does not constitute what is known as an *evolutionary stable strategy*. In any such community of self-sacrificing individuals, a mutant gene that promoted selfish behaviour would spread like wildfire. Thus what evolutionary theory, in fact, predicts is a more or less stable ratio of egoistic to altruistic characteristics – both within and between individuals – distributed throughout this community. Thus, Darwin's explanation of the universality, or near universality, of the social sentiments is incorrect and Hume's reliance on such sentiments in his axiology is, accordingly, problematic.[8]

I shall not, however, dwell on this problem. Instead, what I want to focus on is a widespread intuition that subjectivism leads, in effect, to another kind of arbitrariness. The arbitrariness charge levelled at axiological objectivism derived from the thought that this view inappropriately divorces value from valuing; value exists logically, if not psychologically, independently of valuing. The problems, that is, derive from the thought that objectivism makes the gap between value and valuing too great. Axiological subjectivism, on the other hand, faces the opposite problem: it makes the gap between value and valuing too small. Indeed, for axiological subjectivism, there is no gap at all between value and valuing.

Even if it were possible to develop an account of the uniformity of the social sentiments – the acts of valuing from which value supposedly derives – it would still be true that any given item that had value would do so only because it was valued by someone or something. Whether this valuing was distributed uniformly throughout a given population or species or not, the fact remains that the order of ontological dependence runs from valuing to value. Value is to be explained in terms of valuing and value exists only because there is valuing.

This, according to many, seems to provide a problem for subjectivist accounts, for they fail to do justice to the intuition that we value things because they have value, and not conversely. They do not have value simply because we value them; the order of explanation runs in the opposite direction. This, of course, is scarcely an objection to axiological subjectivism. Our intuitions do not necessarily conform to reality. Perhaps it seems to us as if we value things because they are valuable and not vice versa. But the way things seem and the way things are do not, of course, necessarily coincide.

Nevertheless, there is a point behind the intuition. If value is a product of valuing, and valuing is a mental process, then value ultimately derives from mental processes. It seems difficult to reconcile this with the intuition we all have that value is not simply a construction of the mind but a denizen of the world as much as the mind. If value is a product of mental processes, then there is, in effect, no value in the world. The value that appears to be there is not really there at all.

In this way, subjectivism clashes with our intuitions about the nature of value. One common subjectivist strategy is to try – so far as this is possible – to mitigate the nature of this clash. Subjectivists attempt to show that subjectivism can, appearances to the contrary, account for our intuitions about the nature of value, or at least those intuitions that are worth saving.[9] Without in any way prejudging the success or otherwise of the often ingenious work produced by axiological subjectivists on behalf of our moral intuitions, it is sufficient for our purposes to point out that externalism might provide us with another option. To see precisely what this option amounts to, however, we first need to look more closely at why subjectivism clashes with our intuitions.

The general problem, as we have seen, is that subjectivism seems insufficient to ground the idea that things independent of the mind are literal possessors of value. Value is ultimately a denizen of the mind and our locating it in the world outside the mind is the result of an unrecognized or insufficiently acknowledged projection on our part. That is, the problem for subjectivism, is the problem of explaining how value can be anywhere other than inside the human mind.

However, this general point can be broken down into two distinct claims, one about the *ontological status* of value, and the other about its *location*. Suppose, as presumably we have to if externalism is true, we eschew talk of what is inside and outside the mind. If externalism – in any of its forms – is correct, then there may well not exist the requisite separation of mind and world to allow for the question of whether value exists inside the mind or in the world. Therefore, equally, it would not allow for the possibility of one way of phrasing the clash with intuition engendered by the subjectivist account: that it cannot explain how value can exist outside the mind. The question of whether value lies inside or outside the mind is predicated on the assumption that the mind is the sort of thing that has an inside and an outside; this is precisely the assumption that externalism calls into question. Therefore, how can it be an objection to subjectivism that it entails that value really exists only inside the mind, and not in the world, when externalism – in many of its forms – entails that the mind is not the sort of thing that has an inside, hence not the sort of thing that has an outside? Thus, externalism seems to undermine one way of explaining the subjectivist clash with intuition.

This leaves, however, the alternative: subjectivism entails that value is ontologically dependent on acts of valuing. Let us replace talk of the mind with talk of mental activity. Then, the subjectivist thesis can be formulated without recourse to the inadvisable metaphors of inside and outside. The thesis, then, is simply that value is dependent for its existence on mental – specifically valuing – activity. Objectivism denies this. Thus, we can formulate the positions with recourse to these disingenuous metaphors and so can also formulate the problems without such recourse. The problem with subjectivism, in particular, is that it makes value wholly dependent on valuing activities and cannot allow for the existence of value independent of such activities.

However, the problem with this response is that it is now unclear why this is an *objection* to subjectivism. Why should the existence dependence of value on valuing activities be regarded as a *problem*? Most cases of existence dependence do not cast into doubt the existence of the item that is thus dependent. Human beings, and all macro-objects, are existence-dependent on atoms and molecules but this in no way impugns the reality of human beings or other macro-objects. Existence dependence, by itself, carries with it no ontological disquietude. What motivates the anxiety in the case of value is, I think, the unexorcized temptation to suppose that the existence dependence of value on mental activity entails that value does not really exist in the world. This temptation derives from an unexorcized

Cartesian assumption that the mental is the sort of thing that can have an inside and, hence, an outside. In other words, while the clash with intuition engendered by axiological subjectivism can be developed in two ways, only one of these has any real bite. It is only if we run these two ways together– run the question of derivative ontological status together with the unexorcized Cartesian talk of inside and outside – that we think there is any real problem here. Externalism – in its various stripes – might go a considerable way to lessening the perceived gap between subjectivism and moral intuition.

Axiological subjectivism, reinterpreted in externalist terms, is the view that value is ontologically dependent on valuing. It is not the view that value truly resides only in the mind and is then somehow projected outwards to give the subjective impression of worldly residence. The mental activities that, on the subjectivist view, constitute value are themselves activities that occur, partly but often essentially, in the world. And one cannot project something out into the world when it is already out in the world in the first place.

The structure of value judgements

Given this general framework for combining axiological subjectivism with externalism, it might be worth looking at the nature of value judgements. When we claim something like "X has value", what exactly are we doing? I want to suggest that there are three things going on in any such judgement: the judgement can be broken down into what we can call *origin*, *content* and *character*.

Consider, first, the notion of judgemental *origin*. Callicott has pointed out that to make a claim about the origin of value is not, at least not directly, to say anything about which objects possess value. In particular, the claim that the origin of value lies in various subjective feelings or sentiments does not entail that the only things that possess value are those feelings or sentiments. A claim can have an origin in subjective feelings without being about or directed towards those feelings. To suppose that there is a straightforward inference from claims concerning the *origin* of value claims to claims concerning the *content* of those claims – roughly, what those claims are about – is to commit one version of the *genetic fallacy*.

In terms of this distinction between origin and content, then, we might formulate subjectivism as the claim that value judgements have a subjective origin – their origin lies in various feelings, attitudes, opinions and so on

213

possessed by valuing subjects. This does not, however, entail that they have a subjective content: that they are about those feelings, opinions and attitudes. Nor, if the arguments of the preceding section are correct, does it entail that the origin of value is located inside the heads of subjects; the acts of valuing that constitute the basis of value judgements are themselves distributed on to the world. So subjectivism, reinterpreted externalistically, entails neither that the content of value judgements is internal to the valuing subject nor even that the origin of such judgements is internal to the valuing subject.

Externalism – specifically, content externalism – provides us with another distinction that is, I think, important in understanding the nature of value judgements. The distinction is that between the *content* and the *character* of a judgement.[10] The sentence "Today is fine", while expressing the same character on each occasion of use, differs in truth-conditions on each day on which it is used. The character of the statement is thus the same on each occasion but the content differs on each occasion of use. Similarly, the utterance "I am tired" possesses the same character on each occasion of use but differs in content depending on the utterer and time of utterance.

The distinction is, roughly, that between *what* is presented in a judgement (content) and the *way in which* it is presented (character). If we both judge that we are about to be attacked by a bear, the judgement, so the idea goes, presents the world to us in a certain way. But my judgement is about me – *I* am about to be attacked by a bear – while your judgement is about you – *you* are about to be attacked by a bear. The judgements differ in content, since they are about different things, but share the same character; they present the world to the subject in the same way.

In the case of the judgement "X has value" we can make essentially the same distinction. We distinguish, that is, what the judgement is about from the way in which the judgement presents the world to the judger. Take Hume's example of the murder discussed earlier. We come across a murder and we judge that it is wrong. This is a judgement of disvalue, as we might say. The origin of this judgement, if subjectivism is true, lies in various feelings of disapproval we have pertaining to this situation (and to murders in general). The character of the judgements might vary from person to person, but, typically, it will consist in the world being presented as shocking, deplorable and revolting. The content of the judgement will be the murder itself, and the claim is that the murder is wrong.

In this case, of course, the origin and the character of the judgement are not entirely separable. But this is not always the case. The character of the judgement can vary quite considerably depending on the type of value judgement involved. Consider, for example, judgements of environmental value – judgements that the environment is valuable.[11] The character of such judgements can often be essentially aesthetic. Various studies have shown, for example, that a cross-cultural selection of individuals, when presented with photographs of a variety of environments, consistently expressed a preference for savannah-type environments over others. The evolutionary explanation for this turns on the role played by savannahs in human evolution. The savannahs of tropical Africa, the presumed ground of human origins, afford high resource potential for large ground-based primates such as ourselves. In tropical forests, for example, nourishment is primarily afforded in and by the canopy; a ground-based omnivore, in these environments, functions largely as a scavenger, gathering up bits of food that fall from the more productive canopy. In savannahs, however, trees are scattered and much of the productivity is found within two metres of the ground where it is directly accessible to a ground-based omnivorous ape. Biomass and production of protein are also much higher in savannahs than in forests. The savannahs also afford distant views and the low groundcover favourable to a nomadic lifestyle. The savannah is, thus, an environment that affords what we need: nutritious food that is relatively easy to obtain; trees that afford protection from the sun and escape from predators; long unobstructed views; and frequent changes in elevation that allow us to orient in space. Evolution, it is assumed, should have equipped us with mechanisms that aid adaptive responses to the environment, and thus we should prefer savannah-type environments to other types of biome.

When presented with this type of environment, either in the flesh or in the form of a photograph, our judgement that this type of environment is valuable can be divided, in the same sort of way, into origin, content and character. The content of the judgement might be, for example, that the environment is a good one. This is a claim about the environment, not a claim about us or our feelings. The origin of the judgement in this sort of case is an instrumental one, turning on the role this sort of environment can play in our survival and our general background attitudes towards this survival. The character of the judgement, in this case, is aesthetic – the environment presents itself to us as aesthetically pleasing, more so than other types of environment, at least statistically speaking.

Notice that no component of this judgement – origin, content or character – is ever purely internal to the valuing subject. The content concerns the world itself. The sorts of mental states that go into the origin and character of the judgement need not, if externalism is correct, ever be purely internal states. Value may be dependent on valuing but this does not mean that value exists only in the head.

Conclusion

The Cartesian conception of the mind has bequeathed us a stark framework for thinking about the nature of value. Either, as the objectivist claims, value exists in the world independently of the activities of the mind, or, as the subjectivist claims, value is a construction of the mind that is somehow projected outwards on to the world. Both views have serious problems. Objectivism opens up too wide a gap between value and valuing, and thus seems to render value judgements as arbitrary or lacking in justification. Subjectivism, in the eyes of many, makes the connection between value and valuing too close and thus allegedly fails to account for our moral intuitions.

One way of employing externalist insights in the understanding of value (the way outlined in this chapter), is to mitigate some of the more serious drawbacks to subjectivist accounts. First, if externalism, in one or another of its forms, is correct, then the choice between thinking of value as either internal or external makes no sense. Such a dichotomy requires that we regard mental phenomena in Cartesian fashion: as essentially internal items contraposed with a world regarded as an essentially external one. However, if externalism is correct, the activities of the mind, including those activities that, on the subjectivist view, constitute value are already out in the world. Secondly, and consequently, subjectivism, reconstrued along externalist lines, does not involve the claim that value is located in the head but only the anodyne claim that value is ontologically dependent upon valuing. If value were located in the head, then we would have genuine problems understanding how value could actually be possessed by things in the world. But if the content of subjectivism is simply that value is ontologically dependent on valuing, then no such problems exist. Many things are ontologically dependent on other things, but this in no way undermines their ontological status.

This, then, is what externalism lends subjectivism. It allows axiological subjectivism the claim that things in the world can be genuine bearers of value. Value may be ontologically dependent on valuing, but value is no more in the head than is valuing. And valuing, like other mental processes, need not be in the head at all. Not if externalism is true.

CHAPTER 12

Conclusion: externalism, internalism, and idealism

Chapter 1 characterized the concept of Cartesian internalism in terms of two claims, one concerning the location of mental phenomena and the other concerning the possession of such phenomena by a subject.

Cartesian internalism

The Location Claim: any mental phenomenon is spatially located inside the boundaries of the subject, *S*, that has or undergoes it.

The Possession Claim: the possession of any mental phenomenon by a subject *S* does not depend on any feature that is external to the boundaries of *S*.

The notion of a boundary, here, is understood as a physical boundary between organism and environment, in this case, the skin. The two claims, it was argued, are not equivalent. The former claim applies to mental particulars – concrete, non-repeatable event-, state- or process-tokens; the latter to mental properties – abstract, multiply-exemplifiable, event-, state-, and process-*types*. A claim about the *location* of a mental particular is logically quite distinct from a claim about the *possession* of a mental property. Sunburn, to take Davidson's example, is a relational property, individuated in part by its relation to the external factors that cause it. Thus, it does not conform to the Possession Claim: possession of the property of being sunburnt does depend on features external to the skin of whoever it is that is sunburnt. However, particular instances of sunburn do satisfy the Location Claim. Particular instances of sunburn, that is, do not extend beyond the skin of the person who is sunburnt.

The two claims, therefore, are not equivalent, and the precise relation between them is going to depend on how key concepts – most obviously, the concepts of "particular" and "property" – are interpreted. For example, if we understand particulars as concrete particulars (as is orthodox) then we are going to regard the two claims as having a degree of logical independence that they would not have if we understood particulars as abstract particulars or tropes. However, whatever the precise nature of the relation between the Location Claim and the Possession Claim turns out to be, we can use the Location Claim and Possession Claim that define Cartesian internalism as a way of characterizing externalism and this characterization would provide, to a considerable extent, a common thread that allows us to unify many of those strands identified in previous chapters. The characterization of externalism is provided, essentially, by a transposition of the Location and Possession Claims as they are used to define Cartesian internalism. That is:

Externalism

The Location Claim (LOC): at least some mental phenomena are not spatially located inside the boundaries of the subject, *S*, that has or undergoes them.

The Possession Claim (POS): the possession of at least some mental phenomena by a subject *S* depends on features that are external to the boundaries of *S*.

A position is externalist, then, if it is committed to one, or both, of these claims; a position is internalist if it denies both of them. This, in itself, is logically interesting. In order to be internalist, a position is committed to denying both LOC and POS. However, I have claimed, in order to be externalist, a position need only be committed to one, and not both, of these claims. This failure of parallax would seem to indicate that externalism cannot be taken as simply the logical opposite of internalism. This point, I think, is important. If internalism is taken to involve the denial of both LOC and POS, then externalism cannot, logically, be taken as the opposite of externalism unless it involves commitment to both. So if an externalist position only involves commitment to one – say POS – it cannot be taken as the logical opposite of internalism. If this is correct, to what is our watered-down variety of externalism to be considered in opposition? The short, but I think nonetheless correct, answer is: *idealism*. There are two ways of understanding externalist positions, depending on whether such positions involve commitment to one of or both LOC and POS. Commitment to both makes such a position the logical opposite of internalism. Commitment to POS alone makes the position the opposite of idealism.[1]

To see what is at issue here, recall the logical position occupied by idealism, as explained in Chapter 3. Cartesian internalism, we are supposing, involves a straightforward denial of both LOC and POS.

Idealism, then, is predicated on the separation of mind and world licensed by this denial. That is, the view of the mind as an interiority, licensed by the denial of LOC and POS, generates what I referred to as the *matching problem*. If mind and world are separate entities in the manner entailed by the denial of LOC and POS, that is, if the mind is something inner as opposed to the something outer that is the world, then we have the *matching problem* described in Chapter 3. How is it that the mind, as interiority, is able to latch on to the world in the way it seems required to if we are able to know, or even believe, anything about the world? The idealist solution to the matching problem involves, in effect, a transposition of the possession claim, POS. Instead of the possession of mental properties by a subject being dependent on what is present in the world, idealism claims, in effect, that possession of worldly properties by an object in the world (including, on many versions of idealism, the property of being an object) is dependent on what is present in the mind.

In this way, then, idealism is predicated on the sort of Cartesian split between the mind as interiority and the world as exteriority that is licensed by the negation of LOC (or, equivalently, by the affirmation of the Cartesian version of the Location Claim). Idealism results from the tacit acceptance of the internal location of mental particulars and the resulting attempt to put mind and world together in a way that is thought necessary to solve the matching problem, by way of a transposition of POS. Once we separate mind and world by way of the claim that mental particulars are internally located (i.e. by the negation of LOC), then we are going to have some work to do in putting them back together again. This work, in the idealist scheme of things, is carried out by the transposition of POS described above.

This means that any externalist position that is characterized by a commitment to POS but coupled with the claim that mental particulars are internally located (i.e. a denial of LOC) is logically opposed not to internalism but to idealism. An externalist position that involves commitment to POS, but a denial of, or remaining neutral on, LOC is an attempt to solve the matching problem in a way that mirrors the idealist attempt. The idealist tries to solve the matching problem by way of the idea that possession of worldly properties by an object in the world is dependent on what is present in the mind. Externalism, however, in its commitment to POS, turns on the claim that possession of mental properties by a subject logically depends on what is present in the world.

So the logical status of externalism, and in particular whether it is conceived of as logically opposed to internalism or idealism, depends on how far one is willing to push it. An externalism that endorses only POS is the logical opposite of idealism. It is only if externalism endorses both POS and LOC that it can be legitimately thought of as the logical opposite of internalism. At issue is the status and role of externalism itself. If we regard externalism as committed only to POS, with LOC as something it can deny, or towards which it can afford to remain neutral, then we are in effect going to regard externalism as a kind of damage limitation exercise: an attempt to mitigate the damage produced by the dichotomizing of mind and world introduced by the idea that mental particulars are internally located. But behind this attempt, the fundamental idea – or at least *one* fundamental idea – of the mind as an interiority remains intact. If, on the other hand, we regard externalism as committed to both POS and LOC, then we will regard it as an attempt to undermine the distinction that produced the damage in the first place.

Some forms of externalism, quite clearly, only endorse POS, or, at least, that is all they can legitimately endorse. This is most obviously true for *content* externalism: the view that most people have in mind when they talk about externalism. It is certainly true that many people have presented content externalism as committed to both POS and LOC. However, as was argued in Chapter 6, the arguments for content externalism establish only POS: they do not, *by themselves*, give us any reason for endorsing LOC. The external individuation of mental content is perfectly compatible with the internal location of the vehicles of this content, these vehicles being, for example, mental representations of one or another stripe. If, as orthodoxy has it, mental states are relations to representations, the external individuation of mental content is compatible with the internal location of mental states. Thus, we have an externalism developed in terms of POS, but not LOC. It might, of course, be possible to argue for the external location of mental particulars based on considerations of content. But the point is that such arguments would have to be ones *in addition* to the traditional arguments for externalism. Those arguments by themselves do not establish LOC.[2]

The position of Sartre is more difficult to gauge. I think the most reasonable construal of the evidence is that Sartre is indeed committed to both POS and LOC, but is committed to the latter essentially by a form of default and for reasons quite distinct from those advanced by other forms of externalism (for example, the vehicle externalism discussed in Chapter 9).

The issue is clouded by the possibility of adopting two distinct stances with respect to LOC. According to LOC, at least some mental phenomena are not spatially located inside the boundaries of the subject, S, that has or undergoes them. To affirm this claim, however, is not necessarily to claim that they are located, even in part, *outside* the subject. To deny internal location is not to affirm external location.

For Sartre, of course, the idea that mental states are located anywhere at all is a problematic one. Consciousness, for Sartre, is literally a nothingness. It is nothing but a directedness towards transcendent objects. Consciousness is that in virtue of which a given transcendent object can be revealed in one way or another, as being this way or that way. But that is all that it is. Consciousness has no contents; it is an empty directedness towards transcendent objects, which it is not. As such, consciousness is not an item in the world. No matter how hard you look around at the world, consciousness will never be among the items you discover; it exists only, so to speak, in the looking and not as one of the items looked at. So consciousness, for Sartre, is nowhere at all.

Thus, Sartre would certainly deny the internalist claim that mental phenomena are located inside the boundaries of mental subjects. Thus, in one sense, he endorses LOC. To the extent consciousness is, it is nowhere at all. And if it is nowhere at all, it cannot be located specifically inside the skins of conscious creatures. However, his endorsement of LOC, therefore, does not depend on any specifically externalist considerations. He endorses LOC not because he thinks mental phenomena are, in some way, external, but because he thinks they are nowhere at all.

It is in his endorsement of POS that we find the specifically externalist character of Sartre's position: "Consciousness is born supported by a being which is not itself. This is what we call the ontological proof."[3] All consciousness is, essentially, consciousness of something – there is no consciousness that is not a *positing* of a transcendent object. Transcendent objects, for Sartre, are precisely not parts or components of consciousness. Thus, given that many of these transcendent objects will be objects that exist outside the skins of mental subjects, which for Sartre are identified with active bodily subjects, this entails that the possession of at least some mental phenomena by a mental subject S depends on features that are external to the boundaries of S. That is, Sartre is committed to POS. And it is in this commitment that we find the specifically externalist component of Sartre's thought. In his endorsement of LOC, we find arguments that are anti-internalist but not specifically externalist. In his endorsement of POS, however, we find arguments that are, pronouncedly, externalist.

The extent to which Wittgenstein was an externalist presents similar problems of interpretation. The specifically externalist aspect of Wittgenstein's thought is, I think, captured in his endorsement of POS. Wittgenstein is clearly committed to POS. The precise nature of these structures, of course, depends on what interpretation of the notion of a custom one is willing to endorse. On the community interpretation, the structures in question will be patterns of linguistic usage that are, necessarily, distributed across more than one person. According to the individual interpretation, on the other hand, the external structures will be patterns of usage that may, but need not, be distributed across more than one person but must be extended through time. Mental states or processes such as meaning, intending and understanding are, according to Wittgenstein, simply not possible in the absence of such structures. Therefore, the instantiation in a subject of states or processes such as meaning, intending and understanding depends on the existence of structures that are external to – outside the skin of – that subject. This is a statement of POS.

Wittgenstein also, I think, rejects LOC, and for reasons in many ways similar to those of Sartre. He rejects LOC not because he thinks mental states or processes such as meaning, intending and understanding something by a sign are located, in whole or in part, outside the skins of their subjects, but because he thinks they are not the sort of thing to be located anywhere in particular at all. Consider, for example, the following passage from the *Investigations*.

> "Understanding a word": a state. But a *mental* state? – Depression, excitement, pain are called mental states. Carry out a grammatical investigation as follows: we say
> "He was depressed the whole day"
> "He was in great excitement the whole day"
> "He has been in continuous pain since yesterday"
> We also say "Since yesterday I have understood this word". "Continuously" though? – To be sure, one can speak of an interruption of understanding. But in what cases? Compare: "When did your pains get less?" and "When did you stop understanding that word?"[4]

Understanding is simply not the sort of thing to have spatial and temporal boundaries. The same is true of meaning and intending. As capacities to adjust one's use of a sign to bring it into line with what is customary, or is in practice, they no more have a determinate spatial and temporal location than, for example, the capacity to drive one's car on the correct side of the road or to play Chopin's *Fantasie Impromptu in C Sharp Minor*.[5]

Thus Wittgenstein, like Sartre before him, would reject LOC, but not for specifically externalist reasons. What lies at the heart of his rejection of LOC is his hostility to the idea that items such as meaning, intending and understanding are the sort of things that have a determinate location at all, and not the suspicion that they do have a location and this is partly external. Thus, while Wittgenstein does reject LOC, the specifically externalist aspect of his thought is, I think, to be found in his rejection of POS rather than LOC.

With vehicle externalism (active externalism, architectural externalism, environmentalism or whatever we want to call it) matters take a distinctively more radical turn. And "radical", here, is employed in the same way as in Chapter 7. Radical externalism, in this sense, is opposed to reactionary externalism. The latter understands externalism as involving simply commitment to POS. The former, however, understands it as involving commitment to LOC and, therefore, also POS. Given the foregoing analysis of Sartre and Wittgenstein, however, it seems that we need a threefold distinction. This would be between *reactionary, radical* and *very radical* externalism.

A form of externalism is reactionary if it involves commitment to POS but remains neutral on LOC. Standard content externalism falls into this category. A form of externalism is radical if it involves commitment to both POS and LOC, but endorses LOC not necessarily because it thinks mental particulars are externally located but for some other reason, for example, because it thinks mental particulars are not the sort of thing to have location. The views of Sartre and, possibly, Wittgenstein fall into this category. Finally, very radical externalism involves endorsement of both POS and LOC, but, in addition, it endorses LOC for the specific reason that it thinks mental particulars are, in part, *externally* located.

What is characteristic of vehicle externalism is the idea that both POS and LOC should be endorsed *for specifically externalist reasons*. Thus, with vehicle externalism we have the endorsement of POS for the familiar reasons identified by both Sartre and Wittgenstein; namely, that possession of many mental phenomena is simply not possible in the absence of features that are external to the skins of the subjects of those phenomena. But, crucially, we also have an endorsement of LOC and this time the endorsement has a specifically externalist rationale. That is, the claim that not all mental particulars are located inside the skins of their subjects is endorsed precisely because at least some mental particulars are located, in part, *outside* the skins of their subjects. That is, the denial of the internality of mental particulars is combined with a claim of their, at least partial, externality.

A vehicle externalist typically argues for this by way of the idea that the vehicles of mental states and processes – the architectural devices or mechanisms in virtue of which a mental subject has mental states in the first place – are located, in part, outside the skins of mental subjects. This is the strategy endorsed by at least some of the versions of vehicle externalism that we examined in Chapter 9 and also by the approach to understanding consciousness based on vehicle externalist considerations that we looked at in Chapter 10. The sub-personal mechanisms in virtue of which we can be mental subjects – for example, the information-processing operations in virtue of which we can be the subjects of cognitive processes – are ones that extend beyond the boundaries of the subject's skin. Therefore, according to vehicle externalism, so too do cognitive processes.

This type of argument, of course, does not necessarily involve a vehicle-content confusion, as long as the vehicle externalist is careful in the way they express their argument. The best way of doing this is, I think, a *burden of proof* argument. Once we allow that the mechanisms and architectures that allow us to be mental subjects extend beyond our skins, there is little principled reason for supposing that the products of such mechanisms – mental states and processes – are confined within the skin. Therefore, the burden of proof is on the defender of the idea that mental particulars have a purely internal location, a burden of proof they will, I think, have difficulty discharging.[6] In any event, in endorsing both POS and LOC, and in doing so for specifically externalist reasons, vehicle externalism can justifiably claim to be the most radical form of externalism on the block.

Notes

Chapter 2: Cartesianism

1. R. Descartes, *The Philosophical Writings of Descartes* [3 vols], J. Cottingham, R. Stoothoff, D. Murdoch and [vol. 3 only] A. Kenny (trans.) (Cambridge: Cambridge University Press, 1984–91), vol. 1, 208.
2. Descartes, *The Philosophical Writings of Descartes*, vol. 1, 140.
3. G. Ryle, *The Concept of Mind* (London: Hutchinson, 1949), 17ff.
4. Descartes, *The Philosophical Writings of Descartes*, vol. 1, 140.
5. The influence of Ruth Millikan is, of course, all over this characterization. See her *Language, Thought, and other Biological Categories* (Cambridge, MA: MIT Press, 1984). See also her *White Queen Psychology, and other Essays for Alice* (Cambridge, MA: MIT Press, 1993). The characterization corresponds to what many call an *etiological* conception of function.
6. This is, of course, only one way of characterizing this elusive concept and a way peculiarly gerrymandered to suit our purposes at that.
7. My attitude towards tropes actually tends to fluctuate wildly. For a good systematic defence of tropes, see K. Campbell, *Abstract Particulars* (Oxford: Basil Blackwell, 1990).
8. J. Kim, "Concepts of Supervenience", *Philosophy and Phenomenological Research* 65 (1984), 153–76. This formulation corresponds to what Kim calls "strong" supervenience, as opposed to a weaker, and less satisfactory, alternative. In the weaker alternative, the second modal operator is omitted.
9. I have argued elsewhere that claim 3 is, in fact, entailed by claim 1, although this does rest on an interpretation of property-instances as abstract particulars. This being controversial, it is perhaps best to distinguish the interpretations here. See my *Supervenience and Materialism* (Aldershot: Avebury, 1995), Chapter 2.
10. For further discussion, see my *The Philosopher at the End of the Universe* (London: Ebury, 2003), Chapter 2.
11. This characterization leans heavily on the work of Peter F. Strawson. Indeed, it is essentially a transposition of his account of individuation dependence (minus his "linguistic condition"). See his *Individuals: An Essay in Descriptive Metaphysics* (London: Methuen, 1959).
12. The expression, and indeed the idea associated with it, is due to J. Baird Callicott. See his *In Defense of the Land Ethic* (New York: SUNY Press, 1989).
13. The question of whether each theory also satisfies the other requirement is more complex. Pretty clearly, the type-identity theory also satisfies the Location Claim, since it entails that

every mental event- or state-token is an instance of a property that is individuation independent of anything occurring outside the skin of the individual that exemplifies that property. It is, then, difficult to see how such an event- or state-token could fail to satisfy the Location Claim. Whether the token-identity theory satisfies the Possession Claim is a far more complex question. It would certainly do so if the Location Claim entailed the Possession Claim, so that internal location of a mental event-token entailed the environmental individuation independence of the type of which this token is an instance. I have, in essence, defended such an inference elsewhere (*Materialism and Supervenience*, Ch. 2), but the issue is far too abstruse to go into here.

14. In this context, it is common to distinguish what are known as *causal role identity theories* from *functional state identity theories*. Both views accept that mental state types are defined by their causal or functional roles. The causal role identity theory goes on to make the further claim that mental state types are identical with the physical (usually neurophysiological) state types that fill the roles that define them. The functional state identity theory, on the other hand, identifies mental state types with the functional roles themselves, but allows that the physical state types that fill these roles realize the mental state types in question.

15. Notions of spatial containment always seem to sit rather uneasily with Descartes's claim that the mind is essentially non-spatial. The distinction between spatial location and spatial extension, I think, only partially alleviates this sense of unease.

16. R. Chisholm, *Theory of Knowledge* (New York: Prentice Hall, 1966).

Chapter 3: Idealism

1. Immanuel Kant, *Critique of Pure Reason*, (Riga, 1781/1787) N. Kemp Smith (trans.) (London: Macmillan, 1929). I shall follow convention in referring to the first edition of the *Critique* by way of the letter "A", and the second edition by way of the letter "B".

2. Kant, *Critique of Pure Reason*, A42/B59.

3. *Ibid.*, A268.

4. *Ibid.*, A268.

5. J. G. Fichte, *The Science of Knowledge* (1794), P. Heath & J. Lachs (trans.) (Cambridge: Cambridge University Press, 1982).

6. A. Riehl, *Der Philosophie Kritizismus und seine Bedeutung für die positive Wissenschaft* (Leipzig: Engelmann, 1887).

7. Kant, *Critique of Pure Reason*, A225–445/B454–473.

8. *Ibid.*, A42/B59. See earlier.

9. Let it be clear that I am here referring to the arguments of contemporary anaemic imitators of Kant, not to the arguments of Kant himself.

10. E. Sapir, "Conceptual Categories in Primitive Languages", *Science* **74** (1931), 578. Reprinted in D. Hymes (ed.), *Language in Culture and Society: A Reader in Linguistics and Anthropology* (New York: Harper & Row, 1964) (page references are to the latter). B. L. Whorf, *Language, Thought, and Reality* (Cambridge, MA: MIT Press, 1956).

11. Whorf, *Language, Thought, and Reality*, 57.

12. *Ibid.*, 145.

13. Actually, it may well not turn out to be correct. There are two difficulties. First, Whorf's gloss on the character of Hopi is, at best, controversial, at worse misguided. See, for example, E. H. Lenneberg, "Cognition in Ethnolinguistics", *Language* **29** (1953), 463–71. Secondly, it is not at clear that we can even legitimately speak of *our* concept of time. It is not clear that we even have a coherent concept of time ourselves. And if so, how can we meaningfully talk of this differing from that of the Hopi?

14. Whorf, *Language, Thought, and Reality*, 213.

15. *Ibid.*, 162.
16. For example, between /cot/ and /caught/. Or, to take another example, I once gave a talk in a university in Georgia, where, subsequent to the talk, a young woman came up to me and told me how much she had enjoyed the talk. At least, that's what I think she said. There were, in fact, two possibilities. Either she was indeed saying how much she had enjoyed the talk (i.e. "I enjoyed ya"), or she was making a locative claim concerning her present position (i.e. "I in Georgia"). The round lips that accompany pronunciation of /Georgia/ in standard English are not present in southern US dialects.
17. F. de Saussure, *Course in General Linguistics*, C. Bally & A. Sechehaye (eds), W. Baskin (trans.) (New York: McGraw-Hill, 1966), 88.
18. *Ibid.*, 20.
19. *Ibid.*, 107.
20. T. Hawkes, *Structuralism and Semiotics* (London: Methuen, 1977), 17.
21. F. Jameson, *The Prison-House of Language* (Princeton, NJ: Princeton University Press, 1972), 30.
22. J. Culler, *Saussure* (London: Fontana, 1976), 36.
23. Hawkes, *Structuralism and Semiotics*, 25.
24. *Ibid.*, 26.
25. *Ibid.*, 149 (his emphasis).
26. *Ibid.*, 28.
27. Jameson, *The Prison-House of Language*, 109–10.
28. *Ibid.*, 33.
29. Kuhn's principal work is *The Structure of Scientific Revolutions* (Chicago, IL: University of Chicago Press, 1962). This work is usefully contrasted with his far less popular but, in my view, far more sensible, *The Essential Tension* (Chicago, IL: University of Chicago Press, 1977). Feyerabend's most famous work is *Against Method* (London: New Left Books, 1975).
30. See, for example, W. H. Newton-Smith, *The Rationality of Science* (London: Routledge, 1981), Chapter 7.
31. Kuhn, *The Structure of Scientific Revolutions*, 117.
32. This was first pointed out by M. Devitt & K. Sterelny, *Language and Reality* (Oxford: Basil Blackwell, 1987), 204.
33. A particularly clear statement of his approach can be found in the introduction to M. Dummett's *The Logical Basis of Metaphysics* (Cambridge, MA: Harvard University Press, 1991).
34. Dummett, *The Logical Basis of Metaphysics*, 12.
35. *Ibid.*
36. M. Dummett, *Elements of Intuitionism* (Oxford: Oxford University Press, 1977), 383.
37. Dummett, *The Logical Basis of Metaphysics*, 8.
38. *Ibid.*, 12.
39. This general idea is also what underwrites structuralism and Sapir–Whorf linguistic anthropology. However, in these latter cases, claim 2 would be converted to the stronger form:
    2*. The structure of language *determines* the structure of thought.
    The end result is the same: examination of reality by way of the examination of language.
40. Dummett, *The Logical Basis of Metaphysics*, 3. Dummett also adds:
    [I]t is that syntactic analysis in terms of which we may explain the sentence's having the meaning that constitutes it as an expression of a certain thought. This is why Frege was able to claim that the structure of a sentence reflects the structure of the thought.
41. F. Nietzsche, *Twilight of the Idols*, R. J. Hollingdale (trans.) (London: Penguin, 1968), 40.

Chapter 4: The "radical reversal" of idealism

1. E. Husserl, *Cartesian Meditations*, D. Cairns (trans.) (The Hague: Martinus Nijhoff, 1960), §19.
2. See, for example, A. Gurwitsch, "The Phenomenology of Perception: Perceptual Implications", in *An Invitation to Phenomenology*, J. M. Edie (ed.) (Chicago, IL: Quadrangle Books, 1965).
3. E. Husserl, *Ideas Pertaining to a Pure Phenomenology and to a Phenomenological Philosophy*, F. Kersten (trans.) (The Hague: Martinus Nijhoff, 1983), 416–18. Henceforth referred to as *Ideas*.
4. Husserl, *Ideas* §150; see also *Cartesian Meditations* §21.
5. See Gurwitsch, "Some Fundamental Principles of Constitutive Phenomenology", in *An Invitation to Phenomenology*, J. M. Edie (ed.).
6. Whether Berkeley thought it was *possible* for things to be any other way is an interesting question, both textually and in terms of the logical implications of his view. Thankfully, however, it is not a question that need detain us.
7. Husserl, *Ideas*, §47.
8. *Ibid.*, §97.
9. *Ibid.*, §49.
10. J.-P. Sartre, *Being and Nothingness*, H. Barnes (trans.) (London: Methuen, 1958), xxxvi. First published as *L'Etre et le Neant* (Paris: Gallimard, 1943).
11. Sartre, *Being and Nothingness*, 171.
12. *Ibid.*, xxvii.
13. J.-P. Sartre, *The Psychology of Imagination* (trans., anon.), 2–3. First published as *L'Imaginaire* (Paris: Gallimard, 1940).
14. Sartre, *Being and Nothingness*, xxxvii.
15. Sartre, *The Psychology of Imagination*, 3–4.
16. Sartre, *Being and Nothingness*, 74–5.
17. *Ibid.*, 78.
18. *Ibid.*, 123.
19. *Ibid.*, 187.
20. *Ibid.*, liii.
21. *Ibid.*, xxxvii.
22. *Ibid.*, xxx.
23. Sartre, *The Transcendence of the Ego*, F. Williams & R. Kirkpatrick (trans.) (New York: Farrar, Strauss and Giroux, 1962), 83.
24. Sartre, *Being and Nothingness*, xxx.
25. *Ibid.*, xxviii.
26. *Ibid.*, xxix.
27. *Ibid.*, xxx.
28. *Ibid.*, xxxvii.
29. *Ibid.*, 176–7.

Chapter 5: The attack on the inner

1. Wittgenstein's primary relevant work is the posthumously published, *Philosophical Investigations*, G. E. M. Anscombe, R. Rhees, & G. H. von Wright (eds), G. E. M. Anscombe (trans.) (Oxford: Blackwell, 1953).
2. See, for example, Wittgenstein, *Philosophical Investigations*, §201.
3. See Wittgenstein, *Philosophical Investigations*, §201 for this view of interpretation.
4. Wittgenstein, *Philosophical Investigations*, §239.

5. *Ibid.*, §140. The emphasis is his.
6. *Ibid.*, §201.
7. *Ibid.*, §191 (his emphases).
8. *Ibid.*, §201.
9. *Ibid.*
10. *Ibid.*, §243.
11. *Ibid.*, §258.
12. *Ibid.*, §202.
13. *Ibid.*, §199; cf. §150.
14. *Ibid.*, §198.
15. *Ibid.*, §199.
16. *Ibid.*, §211.
17. *Ibid.*, §219.
18. Wittgenstein, *Remarks on the Foundations of Mathematics*, G. H. von Wright, R. Rhees & G. E. M. Anscombe (eds) (Cambridge, MA: MIT Press, 1983), 349.

Chapter 6: Content externalism

1. H. Putnam, "The Meaning of 'Meaning'", in *Language, Mind and Knowledge: Minnesota Studies in the Philosophy of Science*, vol. 7, K. Gunderson (ed.) (Minneapolis, MN: University of Minnesota Press, 1975). Reprinted in Putnam, *Philosophical Papers*, vol. 2, *Mind, Language and Reality* (Cambridge: Cambridge University Press, 1975).
2. T. Burge, "Individualism and the Mental", in *Midwest Studies in Philosophy*, vol. 4, P. French, T. Uehling & H. Wettstein (eds) (Minneapolis, MN: University of Minnesota Press, 1979), 73–121. See also his "Other Bodies" in *Thought and Object*, A. Woodfield (ed.) (Oxford: Oxford University Press, 1982), 97–120; "Two Thought Experiments Reviewed", *Notre Dame Journal of Formal Logic* 22 (1982), 284–93; "Individualism and Psychology", *The Philosophical Review* 95 (1986), 3–45; "Cartesian Error and the Objectivity of Perception", in *Subject, Thought, and Context*, P. Pettit & J. McDowell (eds) (Oxford: Oxford University Press, 1986), 117–36.
3. Burge, "Individualism and Psychology", 6.
4. The relevant account of indexicals can be found in D. Kaplan, "Demonstratives", in *Themes from Kaplan*, I. Almog, J. Perry & H. Wettstein (eds) (Oxford: Oxford University Press, 1989). Also, J. Perry, *The Problem of the Essential Indexical* (Oxford: Oxford University Press, 1993).
5. C. McGinn, *Mental Content* (Oxford: Blackwell, 1989), 4–9.
6. P. F. Strawson, *Individuals*, 30ff. The notion of *individuation independence* that was used in characterizing the Possession Claim in Chapter 1 was based on the the negation of claims (ii)–(iv).
7. For reasons that will become clear in "Narrow content", p. 110, I have modified McGinn's version of (iii): "the essence of Fs is (partly) constituted by that of Gs". Essentially, I think, McGinn's version of (iii) is ambiguous and potentially slides over two importantly different claims. The difference between these will also surface in the next chapter.
8. C. McGinn, "The Structure of Content", in *Thought and Object*, A. Woodfield (ed.) (Oxford: Oxford University Press, 1982), 207–8, 210.
9. McGinn, *Mental Content*, 7ff.
10. This thought-experiment is inspired by Wittgenstein's discussion of a linguistic community that runs red and green together as the colour "Patrician" and blue and yellow together as the colour "Plebeian". See Wittgenstein, *The Blue and Brown Books* (Oxford: Basil Blackwell, 1960). It is also of a piece with N. Goodman's later discus-

sion of non-projectible predicates such as "grue". See his *Fact, Fiction and Forecast* (London: Methuen, 1954).

11. J. Searle, *Intentionality* (Cambridge: Cambridge University Press, 1983).
12. J. Fodor, *Psychosemantics* (Cambridge, MA: MIT Press, 1986), 50.
13. *Ibid.*
14. *Ibid.*
15. *Ibid.*, 48.
16. This is not a criticism of Fodor. His concerns were quite different: to safeguard the legitimacy of psychological explanations that employed or invoked content-based states such as beliefs, desires and the like.
17. The example is taken from Fodor, *Psychosemantics*, 19.
18. The problems here are well illustrated by J. Hornsby, "Physicalist Thinking and Conceptions of Behaviour", in *Subject, Thought, and Context*, Pettit & McDowell (eds), 95–115.

Chapter 7: The scope and limits of content externalism

1. This passage is taken from the end of Conan Doyle's Sherlock Holmes story, "The Speckled Band". The passage is cited in Fodor, *Psychosemantics*, 13–14.
2. D. Marr, *Vision* (San Francisco, CA: W. H. Freeman, 1979).
3. See D. Dennett, *Brainstorms* (Cambridge, MA: MIT Press, 1981); and *The Intentional Stance* (Cambridge, MA: MIT Press, 1987).
4. This orthodoxy, however, is increasingly being challenged. The challenge stems from proponents of one or another form of *representationalism* about consciousness. Michael Tye, for example, has argued that pain does, in fact, have a representational function – the function of representing whatever bodily damage brings it about. See his *Ten Problems of Consciousness* (Cambridge, MA: MIT Press, 1995), and also "A Representational Theory of Pains and their Phenomenal Character", in *The Nature of Consciousness*, N. Block, O. Flanagan & G. Guzeldere (eds) (Cambridge, MA: MIT Press, 1997).
5. See, again, Tye, *Ten Problems of Consciousness* and "A Representational Theory of Pains".
6. N. Block, "Inverted Earth", in *The Nature of Consciousness*, Block *et al.* (eds), 677–93.
7. See, for example, Tye, *Ten Problems of Consciousness*; W. Lycan, *Consciousness and Experience* (Cambridge, MA: MIT Press, 1996). In *The Nature of Consciousness* (Cambridge: Cambridge University Press, 2001), I argue that another form of representationism – which I call *mode representationism* – can accommodate the inverted-earth thought-experiment, and still leave room for the idea that phenomenal content reduces to representational content (although I reject this reduction on other grounds).
8. This claim is defended by McGinn in *Mental Content*, 47ff.
9. This argument has been developed by C. Macdonald, "Weak Externalism and Mind–Body Identity", *Mind* 99 (1990), 387–404. A similar point was developed by D. Davidson, "Knowing One's Own Mind", *Proceedings of the American Philosophical Association*, 1987.

Chapter 8: Externalism and first-person authority

1. R. Descartes, *Rules for the Direction of the Understanding*, in *The Philosophical Writings of Descartes*, E. S. Haldane & G. R. T. Ross (eds & trans.) (Cambridge: Cambridge University Press, 1911).

2. R. Descartes, *Principles of Philosophy*, in *The Philosophical Writings of Descartes*, E. S. Haldane & G. R. T. Ross (eds & trans.).

3. This way of developing the problem is due to M. McKinsey, "Anti-individualism and Privileged Access", *Analysis* 51 (1991), 9–16. See also J. Brown, "The Incompatibility of Anti-individualism and Privileged Access", *Analysis* 55 (1995), 149–56.

4. There are actually two different problems here, an "achievement problem" and a "consequence problem". The former concerns how Emma can know a priori that she's thinking a water thought and a retaw thought if she can only tell the difference between water and retaw empirically. The latter is that if Emma has first-person authority over her thoughts, then it seems she should be able to know a priori what the environment contains. In some contexts, this difference can be quite important. For the purposes of simply identifying the general terrain of the clash between externalism and first-person authority, however, I shall treat them simply as differences of emphasis.

5. The idea of slow-switching was introduced by T. Burge in "Individualism and Self-knowledge", *The Journal of Philosophy* 85 (1988), 649–63. Discussion of its pertinence can be found in T. Warfield, "Externalism, Self-knowledge, and the Irrelevance of Slow-switching", *Analysis* 57 (1997); and also P. Ludlow, "On the Relevance of Slow-switching', *Analysis* 57 (1997), 285–6.

6. Influential compatibilist arguments have been provided by Davidson, "Knowing One's Own Mind"; Burge, "Individualism and Self-knowledge"; J. Heil, "Privileged Access", *Mind* 97 (1988), 238–51. All are reprinted in *Externalism and Self-Knowledge*, P. Ludlow & N. Martin (eds) (Stanford, CA: CSLI Publications, 1998). All page references are to the last.

7. Influential incompatibilist arguments have been developed by P. Boghossian, "Content and Self-knowledge", *Philosophical Topics* 17 (1989), 5–26; McKinsey, "Anti-individualism and Privileged Access"; Brown, "The Incompatibility of Anti-individualism". All are reprinted in *Externalism and Self-Knowledge*, P. Ludlow & N. Martin (eds). All page references are to the latter.

8. M. McKinsey seems to fall into this camp. See his "Apriorism in the Philosophy of Language", *Philosophical Studies* 52 (1987), 1–52.

9. Davidson and Burge fall into this camp.

10. Davidson, "Knowing One's Own Mind".

11. *Ibid.*, 102.

12. Equivalently, we reject the internalist's Possession Claim, but do not similarly reject his Location Claim.

13. McKinsey, "Anti-individualism and Privileged Access", 177.

14. Davidson, "Knowing One's Own Mind", 108.

15. See, for example, F. Dretske, *Naturalizing the Mind* (Cambridge, MA: MIT Press, 1995).

16. I emphasize that this is a caricatural version of the view. Dretske's development of the idea is much more plausible.

17. Considerations of space force me to omit Davidson's fascinating positive account of first-person authority, one which turns on the different role played by interpretation in accounting for one's knowledge of the mental states of others on the one hand and of one's own mental states on the other. It should be noted that nothing said in this section in any way counts against his positive proposal.

18. Burge, "Individualism and Self-knowledge".

19. S. Kripke, *Naming and Necessity* (Cambridge, MA: Harvard University Press, 1980).

20. McKinsey, "Anti-individualism and Privileged Access", 180–82.

21. This is an application of McGinn's distinction between weak and strong externalism. A thought about diamonds is compatible with the absence of diamonds in her environment, as long as diamonds exist in the same possible world.

Chapter 9: Vehicle externalism

1. The label "vehicle externalism" derives from S. Hurley, *Consciousness in Action* (Cambridge, MA: Harvard University Press, 1998). A. Clark & D. Chalmers, on the other hand, refer to essentially the same position as "active externalism": see "The Extended Mind", *Analysis* **58** (1998), 7–19. I have called the position "environmentalism". See my *The Body in Mind: Understanding Cognitive Processes* (Cambridge: Cambridge University Press, 1999).
2. Clark & Chalmers, "The Extended Mind".
3. R. Dawkins, *The Extended Phenotype* (Oxford: Oxford University Press, 1982), 200. I discuss this example, and its implications for cognition, in *The Body in Mind*, 74–9.
4. As the neuroscientist Rodolfo Llinas observes, the process is much like what goes on when a university lecturer acquires tenure.
5. See, for example, J. C. Holmes & W. M. Bethel, "Modifications of Intermediate Host Behaviour by Parasites", in *Behavioural Aspects of Parasite Transmission*, E. U. Canning & C. A. Wright (eds) (London: Academic Press, 1972), 123–49.
6. A. Clark, *Microcognition: Philosophy, Cognitive Science and Parallel Distributed Processing* (Cambridge, MA: MIT Press, 1989), 64.
7. See Rowlands, *The Body in Mind*, 80.
8. S. J. Gould & E. S. Vrba, "Exaptation: A Missing Term in the Science of Form", *Paleobiology* **8**(1) (1982), 4–15.
9. J. J. Gibson, *The Senses Considered as Perceptual Systems* (Boston, MA: Houghton-Mifflin, 1966); *The Ecological Approach to Visual Perception* (Boston, MA: Houghton-Mifflin, 1979). I discuss Gibson at more length in *The Body in Mind*, Chapter 5.
10. I defend what is in essence a vehicle externalist account of remembering in *The Body in Mind*, Chapter 6.
11. M. Cole, L. Hood & R. McDermott, "Ecological Niche Picking", in *Memory Observed*, U. Neisser (ed.) (San Francisco, CA: W. H. Freeman, 1982).
12. I discuss this case in *The Body in Mind*, Chapter 6. The example derives from the seminal work of A. R. Luria & L. S. Vygotsky: see their *Ape, Primitive Man, and Child* (Cambridge, MA: MIT Press, 1992).
13. I defend this, at much greater length, in *The Body in Mind*, Chapter 6.
14. D. E. Rumelhart, J. L. McClelland & the PDP Research Group, *Parallel Distributed Processing: Explorations in the Microstructure of Cognition 1, Foundations* (Cambridge, MA: MIT Press, 1986).
15. See A. Clark, *Being There: Putting Brain, Body and World Together Again* (Cambridge, MA: MIT Press, 1997), 36.
16. D. Kirsh & P. Maglio, "On Distinguishing Epistemic from Pragmatic Action", *Cognitive Science* **18** (1994), 513–49.
17. Clark & Chalmers, "The Extended Mind", 8.
18. *Ibid*.
19. *Ibid.*, 13.
20. *Ibid*.
21. *Ibid.*, 15.

Chapter 10: Externalism and consciousness

1. T. Nagel, "What is it Like to be a Bat?", *Philosophical Review* **83** (1974), 435–50. F. Jackson, "Epiphenomenal Qualia", *Philosophical Quarterly* **32** (1982), 127–32 and "What Mary Didn't Know", *Journal of Philosophy* **83** (1986), 291–5. J. Levine, "Materialism and Qualia: The Explanatory Gap", *Pacific Philosophical Quarterly* **64**

(1983), 354–61. C. McGinn, "Can We Solve the Mind–Body Problem?" *Mind* **98** (1989), 349–66 and *The Problem of Consciousness* (Oxford: Basil Blackwell, 1991). David Chalmers, *The Conscious Mind: In Search of a Fundamental Theory* (Oxford: Oxford University Press, 1996).

2. This position has been defended by Tye, *Ten Problems of Consciousness*. Also Lycan, *Consciousness and Experience*.

3. This sort of approach has been recently championed by K. O'Regan and A. Noë. See their "A Sensorimotor Account of Vision and Visual Consciousness", *Behavioral and Brain Sciences* **23** (5) (2001). See also their "What is it Like to See: A Sensorimotor Theory of Perceptual Experience", *Synthese* **79** (2001), 79–103. For a more general development of this idea, see A. Noë, 'On What We See', *Pacific Philosophical Quarterly* **83** (2002), 57–80.

4. Block, "Inverted Earth".

5. See, for example, Tye, *Ten Problems of Consciousness*, and Lycan, *Consciousness and Experience*.

6. I have argued elsewhere, however, that phenomenal properties do not reduce to representational ones. See my *The Nature of Consciousness*. My externalism about consciousness derives from vehicle, rather than content, externalist principles.

7. D. M. Mackay, "Theoretical Models of Space Perception", in *Aspects of the Theory of Artificial Intelligence*, C. A. Muses (ed.) (New York: Plenum, 1962), 83–104; "Ways of Looking at Perception", in *Models for the Perception of Speech and Visual Form*, W. Wathen-Dunn (ed.) (Cambridge, MA: MIT Press, 1967), 25–43; "Visual Stability and Voluntary Eye Movements', in *Handbook of Sensory Physiology* vol. 7, R. Jung (ed.) (Berlin: Springer, 1973), 307–31.

8. With regard to visual perception, the work of David Marr provides a paradigm example of this type of approach. See especially his *Vision*.

9. The affinities between this sort of approach and that championed by Gibson are perhaps too obvious to mention. Indeed, I might have referred to this as the *ecological* approach but for the fact that this carries some unfortunate connotations deriving from Gibson's proclivity for overstating his case.

10. O'Regan & Noë, "A Sensorimotor Account of Vision". See also their "What is it Like to See".

11. K. O'Regan "Solving the 'Real' Mysteries of Visual Perception: The World as an Outside Memory", *Canadian Journal of Psychology* **46**(3) (1992), 461–88; K. O'Regan, R. A. Rensink & J. J. Clark, "'Mud Splashes' Render Picture Changes Invisible", *Investigative Ophthalmology and Visual Science* **37** (1996), §213; K. O'Regan, R. A. Rensink & J. J. Clark, "Change Blindness as a Result of Mudsplashes", *Nature* **398** (1999), 34. K. O'Regan *et al.* "Picture Changes During Blinks: Looking Without Seeing and Seeing Without Looking", *Visual Cognition* **7** (2000), 191–212.

12. See O'Regan *et al.* "Picture Changes During Blinks".

13. For a wealth of further empirical support, see O'Regan and Noë, "A Sensorimotor Account of Vision".

14. D. Dennett, *Consciousness Explained* (Boston, MA: Little Brown, 1991).

15. Peter Carruthers is commendably explicit in making the claim that one of the principal motivations – perhaps even *the* principal motivation – for higher-order representation models of consciousness consists in the necessity of accounting for the way experiences seem or feel. And he is quite clear that this is distinct from the way the world seems or feels in the having of an experience. Whereas "horizontal" accounts of consciousness might be able to account for the latter, he claims, only a higher-order account can account for the former. See his "Natural Theories of Consciousness", *European Journal of Philosophy* **6** (1998), 53–78. This is an excellent reason – one of many I think – to reject higher-order representation accounts of consciousness. It might be thought that in introspection, experiences – as opposed to the world – can seem or feel

a certain way. But given the transparency of experience what would this mean? When I introspectively focus on a visual experience, for example, my introspective experience passes all the way through to the public objects and properties of my experience. The phenomenal character of my introspective experience consists in the directing of this experience to these objects. If this is correct, then it is only the world – construed broadly enough to include human bodies – that can feel or seem a certain way, never experiences. See my *The Nature of Consciousness*.

16. See O'Regan "Solving the 'Real' Mysteries".
17. O'Regan & Noë, "A Sensorimotor Account of Vision".
18. O'Regan and Noë argue, correctly in my view, that this is an entailment of enormous significance. Broadly speaking, it renders superfluous an entire tradition of appeals to mechanisms – extra-retinal signals, saccadic suppression devices and so on – whose function is somehow to construct stability out of the unstable, disjointed information present in sensory stimulation. See "A Sensorimotor Account of Vision".
19. D. Chambers & D. Reisberg, "Can Mental Images be Ambiguous?", *Journal of Experimental Psychology: Human Perception and Performance* 2 (1985), 317–28.
20. O'Regan & Noë, "What it is Like to See". This account is developed in more sophisticated form in "A Sensorimotor Account of Vision".
21. O'Regan & Noë, "A Sensorimotor Account of Vision".
22. M. Rowlands, *The Nature of Consciousness* (Cambridge: Cambridge University Press, 2001), Chapter 10.

Chapter 11: Externalist axiology

1. A non-naturalistic form of objectivism has, famously, been defended by G. E. Moore. See his *Principia Ethica* (Cambridge: Cambridge University Press, 1903).
2. K. Goodpaster, "On Being Morally Considerable", *Journal of Philosophy* 78 (1978), 308–25.
3. T. Regan, "The Nature and Possibility of an Environmental Ethic", *Environmental Ethics* 3 (1981), 19–34.
4. This point is made by Callicott, "Intrinsic Value, Quantum Theory, and Environmental Ethics" in his *In Defense of the Land Ethic*, 159. See also my *The Environmental Crisis: Understanding the Value of Nature* (Basingstoke: Macmillan, 2000), 40.
5. See my *The Environmental Crisis*, 40–41.
6. The classic statement of Hume's meta-ethical position is to be found in Book III of his *Treatise of Human Nature*, P. S. Ardal (ed.) (London: Fontana, 1962). See also his *An Enquiry Concerning the Principles of Morals*, P. H. Nidditch (ed.) (Oxford: Oxford University Press, 1975).
7. C. Darwin, *The Descent of Man* (London: John Murray, 1871).
8. I discuss this issue at much greater length in my *The Environmental Crisis*, 67–73.
9. Much of the work of Simon Blackburn provides a good example of this sort of strategy. See, in particular, his *Ruling Passions* (Oxford: Oxford University Press, 2000).
10. The distinction derives from the work on indexicals of David Kaplan. See his "Demonstratives".
11. I discuss this sort of case in much more depth in my *The Environmental Crisis*.

Chapter 12: Conclusion: externalism, internalism and idealism

1. It might be thought that I have omitted the possibility of an externalist position that is committed to LOC but not POS. However, on any reasonable understanding of LOC, commitment to this without commitment to POS is not a genuine logical possibility. If

mental particulars are located outside the skins of mental subjects, then it simply is not possible to deny that the possession of some mental phenomena by a subject is independent of features that are external to that subject, at least under some description of that phenomenon. LOC, in other words, entails POS.

2. The work of John McDowell is relevant here. See, particularly, his "Singular Thought and the Extent of Inner Space", in *Subject, Thought and Context*, Pettit & McDowell (eds), 136–69.

3. Sartre, *Being and Nothingness*, xxxvii.

4. Wittgenstein, *Philosophical Investigations*, 59. This is a footnote pertaining to the discussion of sections 145ff. For example, #150: "The grammar of the word 'knows' is evidently closely related to that of 'can', 'is able to' . . .".

5. As I mentioned in Chapter 5, there is a way of understanding dispositions and capacities as internal structural states of individuals. This understanding, however, is not endorsed by Wittgenstein.

6. I defend this general strategy in *The Body in Mind*. See especially Chapter 1 for a discussion of these sorts of tactical nuances.

Bibliography

Allison, H. 1983. *Kant's Transcendental Idealism*. New Haven, CT: Yale University Press.
Armstrong, D. 1968. *A Materialist Theory of the Mind*. London: Routledge.
Bird, G. 1962. *Kant's Theory of Knowledge*. London: Routledge.
Blackburn, S. 1984. "The Individual Strikes Back", *Synthese* 58: 281–301.
Blackburn, S. 2000. *Ruling Passions*. Oxford: Oxford University Press.
Block, N. 1981. "Troubles with Functionalism". In *Readings in the Philosophy of Psychology*, vol. 1, N. Block (ed.), 268–306. Cambridge, MA: MIT Press.
Block, N. 1990. "Inverted Earth". In *Philosophical Perspectives*, 4, J. Tomberlin (ed.), 53–79. Atacadero, CA: Ridgeview Publishing. [Reprinted in *The Nature of Consciousness*, N. Block, O. Flanagan & G. Guzeldere (eds) (Cambridge, MA: MIT Press, 1997), 677–93.]
Boghossian, P. 1989. "Content and Self-knowledge", *Philosophical Topics* 17: 5–26.
Brown, J. 1995. "The Incompatibility of Anti-individualism and Privileged Access", *Analysis* 55: 149–56.
Burge, T. 1979. "Individualism and the Mental". In *Midwest Studies in Philosophy*, vol. 4, P. French, T. Uehling & H. Wettstein (eds), 73–121. Minneapolis, MN: University of Minnesota Press.
Burge, T. 1982. "Other Bodies". In *Thought and Object*, A. Woodfield (ed.), 97–120. Oxford: Oxford University Press.
Burge, T. 1982. "Two Thought Experiments Reviewed", *Notre Dame Journal of Formal Logic* 22: 284–93.
Burge, T. 1986. "Cartesian Error and the Objectivity of Perception". In *Subject, Thought, and Context*, P. Pettit & J. McDowell (eds), 117–36. Oxford: Oxford University Press.
Burge, T. 1986. "Individualism and Psychology", *The Philosophical Review* 95: 3–45.
Burge, T. 1988. "Individualism and Self-knowledge", *The Journal of Philosophy* 85: 649–63.
Callicott, J. Baird 1989. *In Defense of the Land Ethic*. New York: SUNY Press.
Campbell, K. 1990. *Abstract Particulars*. Oxford: Basil Blackwell.
Carruthers, P. 1998. "Natural Theories of Consciousness", *European Journal of Philosophy* 6: 53–78.
Chalmers, D. 1996. *The Conscious Mind: In Search of a Fundamental Theory*. Oxford: Oxford University Press.
Chambers, D. & D. Reisberg 1985. "Can Mental Images be Ambiguous?" *Journal of Experimental Psychology: Human Perception and Performance* 2: 317–28.
Chisholm, R. 1966. *Theory of Knowledge*. New York: Prentice Hall.
Churchland, P. 1984. *Matter and Consciousness*. Cambridge, MA: MIT Press.
Clark, A. 1989. *Microcognition: Philosophy, Cognitive Science and Parallel Distributed Processing*. Cambridge, MA: MIT Press.

Clark, A. 1997. *Being There: Putting Brain, Body and World Back Together Again*. Cambridge, MA: MIT Press.

Clark, A. & D. Chalmers 1998. "The Extended Mind", *Analysis* 58, 7–19.

Cole, M., L. Hood & R. McDermott 1982. "Ecological Niche Picking". In *Memory Observed*, U. Neisser (ed.), 72–85. San Francisco, CA: W. H. Freeman.

Culler, J. 1976. *Saussure*. London: Fontana.

Darwin, C. 1871. *The Descent of Man*. London: Murray.

Davidson, D. 1970. "Mental Events". In *Experience and Theory*, L. Foster & J. W. Swanson (eds), **78–88**. London: Duckworth. [Reprinted in D. Davidson (ed.), *Essays on Actions and Events* (Oxford: Oxford University Press, 1980).]

Davidson, D. 1987. "Knowing One's Own Mind", *Proceedings of the American Philosophical Association* 60: 441–58.

Dawkins, R. 1982. *The Extended Phenotype*. Oxford: Oxford University Press.

Dennett, D. 1981. *Brainstorms*. Cambridge, MA: MIT Press.

Dennett, D. 1987. *The Intentional Stance*. Cambridge, MA: MIT Press.

Dennett, D. 1991. *Consciousness Explained*. Boston, MA: Little Brown.

Descartes, R. 1911. *Principles of Philosophy*. In *The Philosophical Writings of Descartes*, E. S. Haldane & G. R. T Ross (eds & trans.). Cambridge: Cambridge University Press.

Descartes, R. 1911. *Rules for the Direction of the Understanding*. In *The Philosophical Writings of Descartes*, E. S. Haldane & G. R. T Ross (eds & trans.). Cambridge: Cambridge University Press.

Descartes, R. 1984–91. *The Philosophical Writings of Descartes* [3 volumes], J. Cottingham, R. Stoothoff, D. Murdoch & [volume 3 only] A. Kenny (trans.). Cambridge: Cambridge University Press.

Devitt, M. & K. Sterelny 1987. *Language and Reality*. Oxford: Blackwell.

Dretske, F. 1995. *Naturalizing the Mind*. Cambridge, MA: MIT Press.

Dummett, M. 1977. *Elements of Intuitionism*. Oxford: Oxford University Press.

Dummett, M. 1991. *The Logical Basis of Metaphysics*. Cambridge, MA: Harvard University Press.

Feyerabend, P. 1975. *Against Method*. London: New Left Books.

Fichte, J. G. 1982. *The Science of Knowledge*, P. Heath & J. Lachs (trans.). Cambridge: Cambridge University Press.

Fodor, J. 1986. *Psychosemantics*. Cambridge, MA: MIT Press.

Gardner, S. 1999. *Kant and the Critique of Pure Reason*. London: Routledge.

Gibson, J. J. 1966. *The Senses Considered as Perceptual System*. Boston, MA: Houghton-Mifflin.

Gibson, J. J. 1979. *The Ecological Approach to Visual Perception*. Boston, MA: Houghton-Mifflin.

Goodman, N. 1954. *Fact, Fiction and Forecast*. London: Methuen.

Goodpaster, K. 1978. "On Being Morally Considerable", *Journal of Philosophy* 78: 308–25.

Gould, S. J. & E. S. Vrba 1982. "Exaptation: A Missing Term in the Science of Form", *Paleobiology* 8(1): 4–15.

Gurwitsch, A. 1965. "The Phenomenology of Perception: Perceptual Implications". In *An Invitation to Phenomenology*, J. M. Edie (ed.). Chicago, IL: Quadrangle Books.

Guyer, P. 1987. *Kant and the Claims of Knowledge*. Cambridge: Cambridge University Press.

Hawkes, T. 1977. *Structuralism and Semiotics*. London: Methuen.

Heil, J. 1988. "Privileged Access", *Mind* 97: 238–51.

Holmes, J. C. & W. M. Bethel 1972. "Modifications of Intermediate Host Behaviour by Parasites". In *Behavioural Aspects of Parasite Transmission*, E. U. Canning & C. A. Wright (eds), 123–49. London: Academic Press.

Horgan, T. (ed.) 1983, "The Spindel Conference 1983: Supervenience", *The Southern*

Journal of Philosophy **22** (supplement).

Hornsby, J. 1986. "Physicalist Thinking and Conceptions of Behaviour". In *Subject, Thought, and Context*, P. Pettit & J. McDowell (eds), 95–115. Oxford: Oxford University Press.

Hume, D. 1962. *Treatise of Human Nature*, P. S. Ardal (ed.). London: Fontana.

Hume, D. 1975. *An Enquiry Concerning the Principles of Morals*, P. H. Nidditch (ed.) Oxford: Oxford University Press.

Hurley, S. 1998. *Consciousness in Action*. Cambridge, MA: Harvard University Press.

Husserl, E. 1960. *Cartesian Meditations*, D. Cairns (trans.). The Hague: Martinus Nijhoff.

Husserl, E. 1983. *Ideas Pertaining to a Pure Phenomenology and to a Phenomenological Philosophy*, F. Kersten (trans.). The Hague: Martinus Nijhoff.

Jackson, F. 1982. "Epiphenomenal Qualia", *Philosophical Quarterly* **32**: 127–32.

Jackson, F. 1986. "What Mary Didn't Know", *Journal of Philosophy* **83**: 291–5.

Jameson, F. 1972. *The Prison-House of Language*. Princeton, NJ: Princeton University Press.

Kant, I. 1929. *The Critique of Pure Reason*, N. Kemp Smith (trans.). London: Macmillan. [Kant published two editions of the critique, and these are interwoven in the Kemp Smith translation. I follow tradition in referring to these by the letters "A" and "B".]

Kaplan, D. 1989. "Demonstratives". In *Themes from Kaplan*, I. Almog, J. Perry & H. Wettstein (eds), 1–31. Oxford: Oxford University Press.

Kim, J. 1984. "Concepts of Supervenience", *Philosophy and Phenomenological Research* **65**: 153–76.

Kim, J. 1993. *Supervenience and Mind*. Cambridge: Cambridge University Press.

Kirsh, D. & P. Maglio 1994. "On Distinguishing Epistemic from Pragmatic Action", *Cognitive Science* **18**: 513–49.

Kripke, S. 1980. *Naming and Necessity*. Cambridge, MA: Harvard University Press.

Kripke, S. 1982. *Wittgenstein on Rules and Private Language*. Oxford: Blackwell.

Kuhn, T. 1962. *The Structure of Scientific Revolutions*. Chicago, IL: University of Chicago Press.

Kuhn, T. 1977. *The Essential Tension*. Chicago, IL: University of Chicago Press.

Lenneberg, E. H. 1953. "Cognition in Ethnolinguistics", *Language* **29**: 463–71.

Levine, J. 1983. "Materialism and Qualia: The Explanatory Gap", *Pacific Philosophical Quarterly* **64**: 354–61.

Lewis, D. 1972. "Psychophysical and Theoretical Identifications", *Australasian Journal of Philosophy* **50**: 249–58.

Loar, B. 1981. *Mind and Meaning*. Cambridge: Cambridge University Press.

Ludlow, P. 1997. "On the Relevance of Slow-switching", *Analysis* **57**: 285–6.

Ludlow, P. & N. Martin (eds) 1998. *Externalism and Self-Knowledge*. Stanford, CA: CSLI Publications.

Luria, A. R. & L. S. Vygotsky 1992. *Ape, Primitive Man, and Child*. Cambridge, MA: MIT Press.

Lycan, W. 1996. *Consciousness and Experience*. Cambridge, MA: MIT Press.

Macdonald, C. 1990. "Weak Externalism and Mind–Body Identity", *Mind* **99**: 387–404.

Mackay, D. M. 1962. "Theoretical Models of Space Perception". In *Aspects of the Theory of Artificial Intelligence*, C. A. Muses (ed.), 83–104. New York: Plenum.

Mackay, D. M. 1967. "Ways of Looking at Perception". In *Models for the Perception of Speech and Visual Form*, W. Wathen-Dunn (ed.), 25–43. Cambridge, MA: MIT Press.

Mackay, D. M. 1973. "Visual Stability and Voluntary Eye Movements". In *Handbook of Sensory Physiology*, vol. 7, R. Jung (ed.), 307–31. Berlin: Springer.

Marr, D. 1979. *Vision*. San Francisco: W. H. Freeman.

McDowell, J. 1986. "Singular Thought and the Extent of Inner Space". In *Subject, Thought, and Context*, P. Pettit & J. McDowell (eds), 136–69. Oxford: Oxford University Press.

McGinn, C. 1981. *The Character of Mind*. Oxford: Oxford University Press.

McGinn, C. 1982. "The Structure of Content". In *Thought and Object*, A. Woodfield (ed.), 207–58. Oxford: Oxford University Press.

McGinn, C. 1984. *Wittgenstein on Meaning*. Oxford: Blackwell.

McGinn, C. 1989. "Can We Solve the Mind–Body Problem?", *Mind* 98: 349–66.

McGinn, C. 1989. *Mental Content*. Oxford: Blackwell.

McGinn, C. 1991. *The Problem of Consciousness*. Oxford: Basil Blackwell.

McKinsey, M. 1987. "Apriorism in the Philosophy of Language", *Philosophical Studies* 52: 1–52.

McKinsey, M. 1991. "Anti-individualism and Privileged Access", *Analysis* 51: 9–16.

Millikan, R. 1984. *Language, Thought, and other Biological Categories*. Cambridge, MA: MIT Press.

Millikan, R. 1993. *White Queen Psychology, and other Essays for Alice*, Cambridge, MA: MIT Press.

Moore, G. E. 1903. *Principia Ethica*. Cambridge: Cambridge University Press.

Nagel, T. 1974. "What is it Like to be a Bat?", *Philosophical Review* 83: 435–50. [Reprinted in his *Mortal Questions* (Cambridge: Cambridge University Press, 1979).]

Newton-Smith, W. 1981. *The Rationality of Science*. London: Routledge.

Nietzsche, F. 1968. *Twilight of the Idols*, R. J. Hollingdale (trans.). London: Penguin.

Noë, A. 2002. "On What We See", *Pacific Philosophical Quarterly* 83: 57–80.

O'Regan, K. 1992. "Solving the 'Real' Mysteries of Visual Perception: The World as an Outside Memory", *Canadian Journal of Psychology* 46(3): 461–88.

O'Regan, K. & A. Noë 2001. "A Sensorimotor Account of Vision and Visual Consciousness", *Behavioral and Brain Sciences* 23(5): 939–73.

O'Regan, K. & A. Noë 2001. "What is it Like to See: A Sensorimotor Theory of Perceptual Experience", *Synthese* 79: 79–103.

O'Regan, K., R. A. Rensink, J. J. Clark 1996. "'Mud Splashes' Render Picture Changes Invisible", *Investigative Ophthalmology and Visual Science* 37: S213.

O'Regan, K., R. A. Rensink, J. J. Clark 1999. "Change Blindness as a Result of Mudsplashes", *Nature* 398: 34.

O'Regan, K., H. Deubel, J. J. Clark, R. A. Rensink 2000. "Picture Changes During Blinks: Looking without Seeing and Seeing without Looking", *Visual Cognition* 7: 191–212.

Perry, J. 1993. *The Problem of the Essential Indexical*. Oxford: Oxford University Press.

Pippin, R. 1982. *Kant's Theory of Form*. New Haven, CT: Yale University Press.

Place, U. T. 1956. "Is Consciousness a Brain Process?", *British Journal of Psychology* 47: 29–36.

Popper, K. & J. Eccles 1977. *The Self and its Brain*. New York: Springer-Verlag.

Putnam, H. 1975. "The Meaning of 'Meaning'". In *Language, Mind and Knowledge: Minnesota Studies in the Philosophy of Science*, vol. 7, K. Gunderson (ed.). Minneapolis, MN: University of Minnesota Press. [Reprinted in Putnam, *Philosophical Papers*, vol. 2, *Mind, Language and Reality* (Cambridge: Cambridge University Press, 1975).]

Regan, T. 1981. "The Nature and Possibility of an Environmental Ethic", *Environmental Ethics* 3: 19–34.

Riehl, A. 1887. *Der Philosophie Kritizismus und seine Bedeutung für die positive Wissenschaft*. Leipzig: Engelmann.

Rowlands, M. 1995. *Supervenience and Materialism*. Aldershot: Avebury.

Rowlands, M. 1999. *The Body in Mind: Understanding Cognitive Processes*. Cambridge: Cambridge University Press.

Rowlands, M. 2000. *The Environmental Crisis: Understanding the Value of Nature*. Basingstoke: Macmillan.

Rowlands, M. 2001. *The Nature of Consciousness*. Cambridge: Cambridge University Press.

Rowlands, M. 2002. "Two Dogmas of Consciousness". In *Is the Visual World a Grand*

Illusion?, A. Noë (ed.), special edition of the *Journal of Consciousness Studies* 9(5–6): 158–80.

Rowlands, M. 2003. *The Philosopher at the End of the Universe*. London: Ebury.

Rumelhart, D. E., J. L. McClelland & the PDP Research Group 1986. *Parallel Distributed Processing: Explorations in the Microstructure of Cognition* 1, *Foundations*. Cambridge, MA: MIT Press.

Ryle, G. 1949. *The Concept of Mind*. London: Hutchinson.

Sapir, E. 1931. "Conceptual Categories in Primitive Languages", *Science* **74**: 578. [Reprinted in D. Hymes (ed.), *Language in Culture and Society: A Reader in Linguistics and Anthropology* (New York: Harper & Row, 1964). Page references are to this version.]

Sartre, J.-P. 1937. *The Transcendence of the Ego*, F. Williams & R. Kirkpatrick (trans.). Paris: Farrar, Strauss & Giroux.

Sartre, J.-P. 1940. *The Psychology of Imagination*, anon (trans.). [First published as *L'Imaginaire* (Paris: Gallimard, 1940).]

Sartre, J.-P. 1958. *Being and Nothingness*, H. Barnes (trans.). London: Methuen. [First published as *L'Etre et le Neant* (Paris: Gallimard, 1943).]

de Saussure, F. 1966. *Course in General Linguistic*, C. Bally & A. Sechehaye (eds), W. Baskin (trans.). New York: McGraw-Hill. [First French edition 1916.]

Searle, J. 1983. *Intentionality*. Cambridge: Cambridge University Press.

Smart, J. J. C. 1962. "Sensations and Brain Processes", *Philosophical Review* **68**: 141–56.

Sorrell, T. 1987. *Descartes*. Oxford: Oxford University Press.

Strawson, P. F. 1959. *Individuals: An Essay in Descriptive Metaphysics*. London: Methuen.

Strawson, P. F. 1966. *The Bounds of Sense*. London: Methuen.

Tye, M. 1995. *Ten Problems of Consciousness*. Cambridge, MA: MIT Press.

Tye, M. 1997. "A Representational Theory of Pains and their Phenomenal Character". In *The Nature of Consciousness*, N. Block, O. Flanagan & G. Guzeldere (eds), 329–40. Cambridge, MA: MIT Press.

Warfield, T. 1997. "Externalism, Self-knowledge, and the Irrelevance of Slow-switching", *Analysis* 57: 282–4.

Whorf, B. L. 1956. *Language, Thought, and Reality*. Cambridge, MA: MIT Press.

Williams, B. 1978. *Descartes: The Project of Pure Enquiry*. London: Penguin Books.

Wittgenstein, L. 1953. *Philosophical Investigations*, G. E. M. Anscombe (trans.), G. E. M Anscombe, R. Rhees, & G. H. von Wright (eds). Oxford: Blackwell.

Wittgenstein, L. 1960. *The Blue and Brown Books*. Oxford: Basil Blackwell.

Wittgenstein, L. 1983. *Remarks on the Foundations of Mathematics*, G. H. von Wright, R. Rhees, & G. E. M. Anscombe (eds). Cambridge, MA: MIT Press.

Index